Metaphor and Reconciliation

Routledge Studies in Linguistics

Metaphor and Reconciliation

The Discourse Dynamics of Empathy in Post-Conflict Conversations

Lynne J. Cameron

Routledge
Taylor & Francis Group
New York   London

First published 2011
by Routledge
711 Third Avenue, New York, NY 10017

Simultaneously published in the UK
by Routledge
2 Park Square, Milton Park, Abingdon, Oxon OX14 4RN

Routledge is an imprint of the Taylor & Francis Group, an informa business

First issued in paperback 2013
© 2011 Taylor & Francis

The right of Lynne J. Cameron to be identified as author of this work has been asserted by her in accordance with sections 77 and 78 of the Copyright, Designs and Patents Act 1988.

Typeset in Sabon by IBT Global.

Library of Congress Cataloging-in-Publication Data

Cameron, Lynne.
   Metaphor and reconciliation : the discourse dynamics of empathy in post-conflict conversations / Lynne J. Cameron.
      p. cm.
   Includes bibliographical references and index.
   1. Metaphor.   2. Discourse analysis.   I. Title.
   P301.5.M48C353 2010
   401'.41—dc22
   2010021545

ISBN13: 978-0-415-95675-8 (hbk)
ISBN13: 978-0-415-83903-7 (pbk)
ISBN13: 978-0-203-83777-1 (ebk)

remembering Ruth

Contents

Figures

Tables

Preface

Jo Berry and Pat Magee are not ordinary people, and their conversations together are extraordinary. Because of this, what may be learnt from researching how they talk together will not necessarily be easily transferred to other people and other situations. However, it is my hope that this applied linguistic study can contribute in some way to understanding responses to violence and conflict that avoid revenge and bitterness.

In this book, I have taken metaphor, familiar to me through years of empirical work, and put it to work to try to find out how Jo and Pat create and build empathy from their starting point as victim and perpetrator of violence. In the process, I have refined the methodology that I call 'metaphor analysis' for application to social science problems. The book aims to show the tools and methods that metaphor analysis provides for working with transcribed talk, and to illustrate its potential to arrive, through deep attention to the language and meaning of talk, at insightful interpretation. Inspired by Vygotsky and Bakhtin, I continue, somewhat unfashionably, to resist the separation of metaphor in thought from metaphor in language, and to insist on the inseparable nature of metaphor as discourse activity. It is to be hoped that sceptical readers will be persuaded of the necessity of this when they see metaphor analysis in action.

The book is the first publication from a three year project around empathy and metaphor called "Living with Uncertainty", part of the Global Uncertainties programme of the ESRC. The new dynamic model of empathy that emerges from analysis of Jo and Pat's conversations will, in time, be complemented by descriptive models of other types of empathy development as other parts of the project investigate responses to the Other in uncertain times. (Project website: http://www.open.ac.uk/researchprojects/livingwithuncertainty/)

Transcription Conventions

The following conventions are used in the transcriptions of talk:

Pauses:

. .	micro pause
. . .	longer pause, but less than one second
. . . (2.0)	two second pause

Overlapping talk is marked with square brackets: [ ]

The ends of intonation units are marked with the following symbols:

,	continuing intonation contour
.	final intonation contour
--	a truncated (incomplete) intonation unit
?	rising intonation contour

Other symbols:

<Q Q>	quoted or reported speech or thought
<X X>	indecipherable talk
<@ @>	laughter

Capital letters are used for *I* and for proper nouns but not at the beginning of intonation units.

Acknowledgments

First and above all, I must thank Jo Berry and Patrick Magee for their support for my research, for providing the recorded data and for giving permission to use it. I can only admire their commitment to the process described here. Although Jo and Pat have seen drafts of the book, the interpretation (and any mis-interpretation) of their words is my own.

The support of various funders is gratefully acknowledged: the UK Arts and Humanities Research Board (now Council) for an Innovation Award that supported the first analysis of the data; the UK Economic and Social Research Council for a Global Uncertainties Research Fellowship that supported the completion of the book manuscript as part of the Living with Uncertainty project; the University of Leeds and the Open University for small amounts of money and other support that kept the project going between grants.

Dr Juup Stelma, now at the University of Manchester, was the research assistant in the early days of the project. He did excellent work transcribing the data and contributed to the development of metaphor analysis. Ewa Biernacka transcribed the conversations at the seminar in 2009. Dr Robert Maslen, researcher on the Living with Uncertainty project, has valiantly taken on other tasks so that this book could be completed. Carol Johns-Mackenzie has provided secretarial and administrative support.

1 Coming Together
Background to the Conciliation Process

> and I saw very clearly.
> that the--
> the end of that journey,
> would be,
> sitting down and,
> talking to the people who did it.
>> —Jo Berry (second meeting with Pat Magee, 2000)

In this book you will read about two people who reach across pain and loss to make sense of one day in history and its consequences, a pivotal day when a bomb exploded and a family lost a father; when a paramilitary operation targeting a member of the British government was successfully carried out by a member of a politically motivated movement. His action— her father's killing. Fifteen years later, the two met and talked to share their stories, although when we look closely we find that these are more than stories, and that they can never actually be fully shared. Through a brave and difficult struggle towards understanding, Jo Berry and Pat Magee arrive at new perceptions of themselves and each other.

The histories of Jo Berry and Patrick Magee first intersected on the day that Jo's father was killed in the bombing of the Grand Hotel in Brighton, along with several other members of the British government. From this point, their paths diverged. Jo Berry began dealing with the grief of her loss, determined to learn more about the situation that had led to the bombing. Pat Magee was arrested and imprisoned, until a political settlement between the British government and Irish republicans in 1999 led to his release. Fifteen years after the bombing in Brighton, they met and sat down together across a table, each ready to talk and to listen.

As an applied linguist and metaphor scholar, I was privileged to be given access to recordings made at some of their meetings, to be funded to investigate how they used metaphor in their talk, and to meet Jo Berry and, later, Pat Magee. This book is a report of my study of their talk together, and the result of trying to resolve issues that arose in doing the research. Empirical research begins with a dataset; here the data came as recordings of conversations, a trace of the original human interaction. Combined with discourse analysis, metaphor analysis offers useful, although always partial, access to how participants are thinking about what they are saying, as they say it. Analysis pulls the talk to pieces in many different ways to try to understand it more deeply or more fully. But, knowing that the whole is more than can be ever revealed through analysis, what is gained from minute attention to detail must be balanced with thoughtful interpretation and synthesis. This book reports what I found out, about metaphor in talk, and about the need to push the limits of existing methodology, but, most importantly, about the effortful process of reaching an understanding of another human being who could well have been a bitter enemy. Pat Magee's act of violence created for Jo Berry the need to understand the people and politics of Ireland; she tried to bridge the gap between them and he came to meet her.

THE CONCILIATION PROCESS

How to label the process that Jo Berry and Pat Magee engage in is complicated. One of the goals of the research set out in this book is to understand more about the nature of this process. Jo often describes it metaphorically as *a journey,* as in the extract of data that opens the chapter. The title of the book uses the term 'reconciliation'; here, we need to adjust that slightly and select a label for the process that the book documents.

'Reconciliation' is not entirely suitable because it suggests an initial conciliated position, lost through conflict and then regained; this was not the case for Jo Berry and Pat Magee. Even to posit a single process that could be labelled may be inappropriate. Each participant engaged in multiple processes: Jo was dealing with the grief around her father's death, with knowing this was a politically motivated and violent death, and with the impact of meeting Pat face-to-face. Pat was also coping with the impact of meeting, while reflecting on his motivations as a younger man, and the implications of accepting responsibility for Jo's father's death. The separate processes were complemented by the shared process of engaging in discourse. The dynamics of the discourse changed with each meeting, including how words and phrases came to stand for ideas or events and the kinds of things that they felt comfortable introducing to the talk.

The term 'conciliation process' will be used as an overarching label for the evolving discourse between Jo Berry and Pat Magee as they try to understand more about each other across a divide caused by violence. The term is intended to encompass both the processes that each person separately engaged in and the shared processes in their meetings, recognising that people operate at the same time both as individuals and as a dyad (Poland, 2007).

When they met in the early years after Pat Magee's release from prison, the participants themselves were not sure where the conciliation process would take them, whether they could reach some understanding, whether each meeting would be the last one or there would be sufficient reason to meet again. After ten years, their conciliation process must be considered a success. Jo Berry and Pat Magee have continued to talk with each other, in public and in private, over the time since they first met. They work separately and together to encourage other people to engage in conciliation, to repair lives torn apart by violence. They have found ways to understand each other that enable empathy while not denying the horror and moral trespass of what happened. Throughout their conversations, Jo Berry and Pat Magee reflect on the conciliation process as it happens. Their own understandings of the process evolve alongside their evolving understanding of each other.

METAPHOR AND RECONCILIATION

Most of us do not, thank goodness, have such a weight of sorrow to deal with as the early death of a father in terrible circumstances. Nor do we have to face the man who made and put the bomb in the hotel with conscious intent to kill and injure other human beings. Jo Berry had to meet Pat Magee knowing that he had done this, knowing too that some relatives of other victims condemned what she was doing. She met Pat with her words, and, behind the words, with her thinking, and with her determination to be open to what he had to say to her. When Pat Magee agreed to meet Jo Berry, he expected to hear anger but instead found a willingness to listen to the words he had to say, about his move into the IRA and violence, about the dehumanising effects of conflict on those involved. Language is the most crucial tool we have when we encounter other people, and this book analyses how Jo and Pat spoke with each other, how they listened to what each other had to say and how language affected their thinking.

Extract 1.1   Jo reads a poem to Pat that she wrote before meeting him:

594 Jo   . . . (1.0) as a human being,
595   . . I listen to your suffering,
596   . . . (1.0) you <u>offer</u> me the <u>story</u>,
597   . . . <u>pain</u> of your war,
598   . . . (1.0) I learn,
599   . . . <u>bridges</u>,
600   . . can be <u>built</u>.

One particular way of using language turns out to be especially useful in this examination: metaphor. Metaphor can be loosely defined as "seeing one thing in terms of something else" (Burke, 1945, 503). A metaphor brings together two different ideas and, through some interaction of their meanings, produces a further sense. The words underlined in extract 1.1 have been identified as being used metaphorically.

Metaphor helps say the unsayable, whether that be thoughts too painful to speak directly or ideas that might threaten the person we are talking with. Metaphor can be a golden phrase, like Jo's *bridges can be built,* that illuminates the idea of reaching shared understanding with the people who killed her father, and that was used in the poem she read aloud to Pat, and from which extract 1.1 is taken. Such metaphors can capture thoughts in elegant or exciting words, lighting up ideas so that they suddenly mean much more than they could in a more literal form. Metaphor is also built into the very ordinary ways in which we use words to share our thinking with others. We *make* much more than physical objects like baskets or cakes; we metaphorically *make friends* or *enemies, make love* or *war, make do, make a noise, a deal, a fuss.* We make metaphor from the most ordinary words in the language, *coming up with ideas* or *going along with a plan.* Metaphor is everywhere once we look for it, or nearly everywhere; sometimes especially powerful and meaningful, but more often just mundane and ordinary. However, even when everyday and ordinary, metaphor does more than just saying; it connects into our thinking through the words used. By collecting the metaphors that people use, we can understand something of their thinking. We can catch glimpses of how their thinking has been shaped by the culture they grew up in, and by the people they live around; how thinking is shaped by participating in talk and by processing the ideas that others offer them in conversation. Plotting people's metaphors as they talk is rather like following the breadcrumb trail that led Hansel and Gretel out of the forest. Metaphors offer a path through the confusion of conversation, with its stops and starts, its deviations and back tracks. When people pick up a metaphor they used several years before and use it again to describe momentous events, we know that this way of talking and thinking matters to them. Metaphor will act as a guide through the conversations of Jo Berry and Pat Magee, helping track changes and constancies over a ten year period, and giving us insights into the process of reconciliation and the growth of empathy across the gap between them.

RECONCILIATION AND EMPATHY

The literature on reconciliation speaks of it as a 'rehumanisation' of people who were once enemies in conflict. In order for human beings to hurt each other, goes the argument, a process of dehumanisation must take place, in which the enemy becomes less than human, possessed with negative qualities that demand a violent response, or becomes simply a representative of a negatively evaluated group (Oberschall, 2000). Causing harm to individuals is recast into fighting or destroying the dehumanised group, state or institution. Dehumanisation may occur and spread as a result of violent incidents between individual members of opposing groups, gradually convincing individuals to perceive themselves as part of a group that must react or respond against the opposing group. Dehumanisation may begin or be encouraged at the level of the social group, as when war is officially declared or when propaganda shapes people's attitudes and values to other groups.

In the Irish situation, a long history of political decisions, conflict and violence contributed to the formation of social groups and negative attitudes to others. The provisional IRA, as one of the groups involved in violent conflict from the 1960s to the late 1990s, developed dehumanised views of the people they considered their enemies: the British establishment and Protestant organisations in Ireland. Pat Magee, as a young man, became a member of the provisional IRA (but is no longer), and, through that, was encouraged to dehumanise people like Jo Berry's father, Sir Anthony Berry, a British Member of Parliament and a member of the Mrs Thatcher's Cabinet in the British Conservative government in the 1980s. Pat explained this to Jo in their second meeting, extract 1.2, summarising with the metaphor *he was a legitimate target.*

Extract 1.2	He was a legitimate target:
369 Pat	. . . (2.0) Brighton,
370	. . . (1.0) from our perspective,
371	was a justified act.
372	. . . (1.0) your father,
373	and I don't--
374	. . I don't know if your father even spoke out about the war.
375	er I'm led to believe that he had*
376	. . . he--
377	he made no contributions to,
378	the sort of debate on it.
379 Jo	. . hmh
380 Pat	. . . but he was--
381	er,
382	. . . (2.0) he was a part of,
383	. . you know the,
384	. . . (1.0) you know,
385	. . . (1.0) the political elite.
386	the . . Tory government.
387	etcetera.
. . .	
401	. . he was a legitimate target.

When violent conflict comes to an end, through exhaustion with fighting or through interventions for peace, former enemies need to be rehumanised to avoid reigniting conflicts and for peace to become more permanent. The conciliation process requires Pat to see Sir Anthony Berry as *a human being,* no longer just as a dehumanised *target,* but as *father* and *grandfather* (extract 1.2 ctd).

Extract 1.2 (ctd):

```
402  Pat     . . . (2.0) meeting you though.
403          . . . (1.0) I'm reminded of the fact that he was also a human being.
404          . . . (1.0) and that he was your father.
405          . . . and that he was your--
406          . . . (1.0) your daughter's,
407          . . . grandfather.
408          . . and that's . . all lost.
```

Coming to see a former enemy as individualised human beings is a complex process much influenced by the nature of the particular conflict. It involves institutions and individuals if it is to be successful, and is often mediated these days by professional conflict resolution experts or official reconciliation processes, as happened in South Africa.

Looking more deeply into the process of rehumanising, Halpern and Weinstein (2004), who investigated the development of empathy in post-conflict reconciliation in the former Yugoslavia and in South Africa, make a connection between reconciliation and empathy. They suggest that empathy lies at the core of reconciliation, and is what must be developed by individuals towards members of the former conflicting group. Empathy, as they see it, is not just experiencing how another person feels, but something more subtle and powerful. Alongside sympathy or emotional attunement with others, empathy also works cognitively and morally. Cognitively, empathy requires that people seek to understand the other person's perspective on the world: their perspective on themselves and how they fit in their society; their perspective on history; their perspective on their future, and how conflict appeared necessary to improve that future. While empathy does not require a person to agree with the reasoning or rationalising that led to violence, at the same time, it does not let this ethical gap prevent perspective-taking and emotional attunement. Empathy becomes really powerful by separating out approval of a person's actions, choices or decisions from understanding why that person took those actions or made those choices and decisions.

> The work of empathy is precisely trying to imagine a view of the world that one does not share, and in fact may find it quite difficult to share. (Halpern and Weinstein, 2004, 581)

Such empathy requires finding ways to live with the 'emotional ambivalence', as Halpern and Weinstein describe it, of understanding the Other while retaining the right to disagree with them. It is not the easy option.

What is Known About Empathy

The initial idea of empathy was formulated within the discipline of aesthetic psychology, and concerned the interpretation of a work of art by

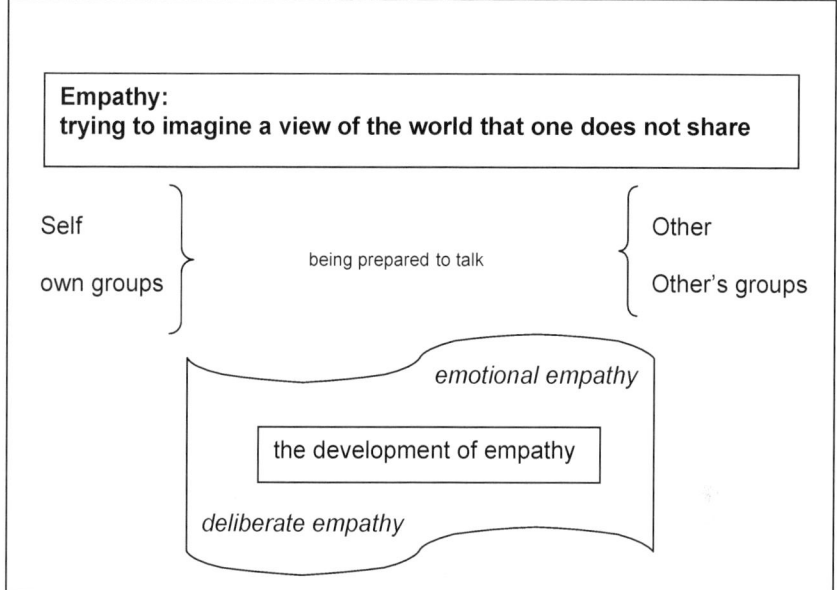

Figure 1.1 A basic model of empathy for the conciliation process.

projecting oneself 'into' the imagined perspective of it, experiencing the emotion of the artist and the art (Valentino, 2005). In the century that has passed since the idea of empathy was first introduced, as *Einfüh-lung* or 'feeling into' (Lipps, 1903), the construct has been developed and divided. In the last 20 years, advances in neuroscience have provided some clarity about the nature and mental basis of empathy, but much remains imprecise (Preston and de Waal, 2002). Empathy has been explored by philosophers, applied across the arts, is receiving increased attention in neuroscience through magnetic resonance imaging, and has received empirical attention leading to detailed development in the contexts of conflict resolution and post-conflict reconciliation. Figure 1.1 summarises current understandings of the nature of empathy that are described in this section.

Self and Other

Affective and cognitive processes of empathy take place within the mind of the individual, 'the Self' (also called 'the Subject' by some scholars). The object of empathising is 'the Other', with the capital signifying all that is encapsulated as the otherness of someone who is not oneself, sometimes incorporating their social as well as their personal identity. The philosophical notion of the Other who exists both in opposition to, and helps construct, the self can be traced from the work of Hegel, through Husserl and, later, Sartre. The notion was adapted for feminist philosophy by Simone de Beauvoir and for post-colonial studies by Edward Said. In identity theory, the idea of the Other underpins the construct of 'out-groups' and 'in-groups' through which the self builds a social identity through affiliation with the in-group and distancing from the Other as out-group (Tajfel, 1981).

Between Self and Other is a complex of distinctions and differences that comprise alterity, or 'otherness' (Bakhtin, 1981), and that makes the Other seem distinct and different from the Self. In most instances, people act on the basis of 'perceived alterity', i.e. their perception or understanding of the alterity between Self and Other, rather than any absolute, verifiable alterity. Alterity changes as people come to understand each other.

In order to understand the Other, Bakhtin suggests that the empathic process required is one of *vzhivanie* or "live entering", later developed as "creative understanding" (Morson and Emerson, 1990; Valentino, 2005). For Bakhtin, creative understanding is:

> to enter actively into another individuality, another perspective on the world—without losing sight even momentarily of one's own unique perspective, one's own "surplus" of life experience, one's own sense of self. (Valentino, 2005, 3)

The connection between Self and Other is not straightforward. Experimental findings confirm that a capacity for Self-Other differentiation is required for imagining how the Other feels in their situation (Lamm, Batson and Decety, 2007; Lamm, Meltzoff and Decety, 2009). On the other hand, the process of coming to understand the Other also affects the idea one has of oneself. We will see how the interaction of Self and Other plays out for Jo Berry and Pat Magee as they engage in the conciliation process.

The Possibility of Empathy

'Emotional empathy' is instantaneous and instinctive, in the sense that it occurs unless inhibited. 'Deliberate empathy', often described as 'perspective-taking' in the literature, is more conscious, takes time and involves more cognitive effort. The various affective and cognitive processes that facilitate empathy of both types are, in the basic model, labelled as 'the development of empathy'. It is one of the central aims of the book to describe the nature of the processes that contribute to the developing empathy between Jo Berry and Pat Magee across the wide and painful alterity created by the IRA killing of Sir Anthony Berry.

However, both types of empathy are subject to the prerequisite of being prepared to encounter the Other, described as *being open to the other story* in extract 1.3.

Extract 1.3   Being open to the other story:

1–521 Pat	. . . (1.0) well it's er--
522	. . . (1.0) there--
523	<u>there</u>'s the necessity,
524	. . . (1.0) to be er--
525	. . . (1.0) <u>open</u>,
526	. . . (1.0) <u>to</u> the--
527	er,
528	the other's <u>pain</u>,
529	. . . and [the]--
530 Jo	[hmh]
531 Pat	I suppose,
532	<u>the other story</u>,

Where people have closed their minds to the Other, through the dehumani-sation processes described earlier, there is no opportunity for empathy to occur. Something needs to prompt a shift from seeing the Other as dehu-manised to seeing him or her once again as an individual, to open up the possibility for empathy. Gobodo-Madikizela, cited by Halpern and Wein-stein (2004), described such a moment when the suffering of a perpetrator of violence facing the South African Truth and Reconciliation Commission moved the women whose husband he had killed; this temporary emotional connection opened up the possibility of developing empathy.

This kind of emotional resonance is not empathy in its fullest sense but may be important in enabling other kinds of empathic processes to take place. According to Halpern and Weinstein (2004), developing empathy between former (or potential) enemies can begin with emotional resonance, but then requires the finding of commonality with the Other. Emotional resonance and a sense of commonality can lead to sympathy; what takes empathy beyond sympathy is differentiation of Self and Other: "imagining and seeking to understand the perspective of another person" even when that perspective may be distasteful or lead to "emotional ambivalence" (Halpern and Weinstein 2004, 568).

Automatic and Deliberate Empathy

Empathy of some kind appears to derive from our biology; neuroscien-tists identify an automatic process of embodied simulation that enables an observer to make sense of the physical actions of others through mir-ror neuron activation (Gallese, 2003, 2005; Iacoboni, 2005). Simulation theory suggests that we understand others by simulating their actions, perceptions and emotions as if they were our own. The discovery of mir-ror neurons in the brain that are activated when we watch another per-son in action has suggested these provide the neural basis for simulation. These neurons have been shown to respond to the sound of an action, as well as to the sight of an action. The intimate relation of mirror neurons with language and gesture (Arbib, 2002) suggests that symbolic representations in language may also evoke mirror neuron activation, and thus directly influence people's ideas and attitudes about others through automatic empathy.

Automatic empathising, or 'emotional empathy', through neural activation or simulation is a process of *imagining the Self in the situation of the Other,* also called "affective empathy" (Wynn and Wynn, 2006, 1390), or "egocentric empathy" (Khalil, 2002). Empathy in post-conflict reconciliation emphasises going beyond this notion of 'walking in someone else's shoes', to the more cognitively demanding *imagining how the Other feels in that situation,* "cognitive empathy" (Wynn and Wynn, 2006, 1389) or 'perspective-taking'. Experimental psychological studies of empathy confirm this separation between "the ability to connect emotionally with another individual", and "the cognitive capacity to consider the world from another individual's viewpoint" (Galinsky et al., 2008, 378; Spreng, McKinnon and Mar, 2009). These competencies are held to be related and yet distinct.

Further support for the distinction between the automatic process of imagining Self in a situation and the slower, more conscious process of imagining the Other in the situation comes from studies using functional magnetic resonance imaging to investigate the affective states/processes of people empathising with people who respond to pain in similar and in different ways to themselves (Lamm, Meltzoff and Decety, 2009; Xu et al., 2009). Inferring the emotions of an individual who responds differently from oneself may need controlled cognitive mechanisms to be activated to overcome strong emotional responses.

CONNECTING ACROSS ALTERITY FROM SELF TO OTHER

The literature on empathy shows that, once the development of empathy is enabled, automatic feelings need to be complemented with conscious perspective-taking or deliberate empathy. Perspective-taking is an imaginative connecting to the Other, a process of coming to know about and understand the Other and their experience; this connecting further requires coping with one's own emotional responses while considering those of the Other. Empathy, seen in this way, is indeed a mature and demanding human response to violence.

Jo Berry exemplifies this kind of empathy. She wants to find out why Pat Magee joined the IRA and why he decided to place the bomb in the Brighton hotel knowing that people would be killed. She listens to his explanations and tries to understand his perspective on the Irish situation and his reasons for turning to violence. She comes to see some of the history between Britain and Ireland from his perspective. She sympathises with the horror of some of his experiences. She even states at one point that if she had been in his position she might have made the same choices. But at all times, she maintains her moral and ethical refusal to validate violence.

Pat Magee has a different, and also demanding, journey of empathy. He has to face the details of the personal consequences of his political action, and to deal with the emotions of accepting responsibility for those consequences. This side of post-conflict reconciliation features less in the literature.

Connecting, and empathy, for Jo Berry and Pat Magee happened through talking and listening, and through the thinking that was prompted by participating in the discourse:

Extract 1.4   Listening to the Other:

1–797	Jo	and <u>through listening</u>,
798		. . . (1.0) then we can <u>meet</u> the human being <u>behind</u>,
799	Pat	. . . (1.0) hmh
800	Jo	the <u>labels</u> and the prejudice.
801	Pat	hmh
802	Jo	. . . and then . . . (2.0) negotiation can happen,
803		and,
804		new kinds of conflict resolution can happen,
805		and,
806		. . you know,
807		wars can stop.

OUTLINE OF THE REST OF THE BOOK

In writing this book, I aim to reveal the dynamics of empathy made possible by talking together, to understand the various processes and the small 'gestures of empathy' that contribute to successful conciliation.

Metaphor is the research tool chosen to assist in understanding the discourse dynamics of empathy. We have already seen how the participants used metaphor to talk and think about:

- the conciliation process as a *journey*
- readiness to engage in empathy as being *open*
- a dehumanised human being as *a legitimate target*
- bereavement as having *lost* something.

Chapter 2 describes Jo and Pat as they started out on the conciliation process. It presents the dataset for the study and the theoretical framework that is assembled to investigate metaphor and the development of empathy through dialogue. Chapter 3 sets out the basics of metaphor analysis, showing how metaphors used in the conversations were found, grouped and labelled as systematic trajectories of connected metaphors. We then move to the study's findings and their interpretation. Chapter 4 shows how the conciliation process was seen metaphorically in terms of *journeys* and *listening to stories*. In chapter 5, I describe the method of distributional analysis of metaphor and the discovery that metaphors not only occur in clusters but are also sometimes hardly used at all, and that these metaphor absences mark a significant kind of talk in the context of post-conflict reconciliation. Chapter 6 presents the important metaphors that portray violence and conciliation in terms of *separation* and *connection*; these will become integral to the new model of empathy when it is assembled later in the book. Chapter 7 uses findings from metaphor analysis to present and discuss Pat Magee's description of how he came to join the provisional IRA, and chapter 8 considers the consequences of this decision, for himself and for Jo Berry. Chapter 9 brings together the various ways in which metaphors move between speakers and considers what this can reveal about the conciliation process and developing empathy. Chapter 10 is the summary chapter that brings together what has been discovered about metaphor in conciliation conversations. A new, multi-level model of the dynamics of empathy in dialogue is presented.

In the final chapter, I respond to the data I have been working with for six years, not just as an academic researcher, but as a creative human being, affected by the glimpses I have been given into the lives, traumas and determination of Jo Berry and Patrick Magee. Empathy is not just an object of study but an inevitable outcome, according to the empirical studies reported in this chapter, of encountering the talk of people affected by violence. Furthermore, deliberate empathy is, I believe, an essential characteristic to be cultivated by the hermeneutic researcher, and the impact of my own developing empathy insisted on being made visible—hence chapter 11's experiment with writing and images.

The appendix contains some implications of the project for mediators in similar situations; it suggests possible strategies for using metaphor to encourage conciliation and empathy.

2 The Discourse Dynamics Approach to Metaphor and Empathy

> I'm trying to--
> I'm trying to put words to feelings,
> as they are coming to me.
> if you understand
>
> —Pat Magee (second meeting with Jo Berry, 2000)

Jo Berry and Patrick Magee first met in late 2000, six months after Pat's release from prison. They met again shortly after, and then at intervals over the years that followed. The first meeting was private but at their second meetings they allowed a film crew to record them talking together, with a view to making a documentary. The filmed conversation took place after a private meeting and covered some of the same ground. Jo Berry sat next to Pat Magee on a sofa, and the two talked as they wished, wandering across any topics they wanted to cover. The only scripting for this conversation was a poem that Jo had written several months before to express her feelings and that she wanted to read aloud to Pat. The conversation is calm but at points clearly painful. Both Jo and Pat tell about difficult times and strong feelings; and each telling is acknowledged by the other.

The second recorded conversation used in the study took place three months later, after their fourth private meeting. Again, the conversation was not directed, and again Jo read her poem to Pat during the talk. This recording was about twice as long as the first, 110 minutes rather than 55 minutes. The video shows Jo and Pat sitting side by side, making eye contact but hardly moving, apart from some hand gestures from Jo. The talk is intense and sometimes difficult. There are two interjections from the camera operator which require them to re-start a topic. The television documentary, using parts of the filmed conversations, was broadcast in 2001. It won a prize for its quality, and my seeing it was in fact what initiated this project, but, because of the heavy editing that had been done on the conversations, it could be used only for background information, or secondary data.

In 2003, and now having met over twenty times, in private and also in public events, Jo Berry and Pat Magee participated in a radio interview at Easter to talk about their process of conciliation. The recording is the third component of the dataset.

The final recording in the dataset was made at a seminar in October 2009 when Jo and Pat shared the stage at the launch of the Living with Uncertainty project on empathy.[1] They described, to an audience of researchers and research users, the development of their understanding of each other over the years since they had first met. They spoke in turn and then responded to audience questions.

The dataset for the study in this book includes conversations from these four events spread over a time period of nearly 10 years. The timescale is important because it allows for changes and developments in metaphor and empathy to be investigated. Each conversation was analysed in detail and connections made across them.

In the flow of talk between Jo and Pat, metaphors appear and are adapted, adopted or abandoned. Compared to other types of talk, the conversations featured heavy use of metaphor, together with some rare but interesting episodes where metaphor was hardly used at all. Metaphor seemed to help Jo and Pat to explain their histories, their beliefs and feelings, and to find out more about each other. It assists talk about painful topics, and provides threads of continuity across long stretches of talk and across gaps between meetings.

This chapter introduces ideas from complexity and dynamic systems theory to construct a theoretical apparatus for researching the development of empathy through metaphor analysis. It begins with an illustration of key features of metaphor in spontaneous talk, as Jo and Pat describe how they felt at the start of the conciliation process. Extracts from the conversations show how Jo and Pat came to the conciliation process with differing ideas about their purposes and about the nature of their participation. The extracts also introduce many of the key features of metaphor that provide the basis for metaphor analysis, and a glimpse of what empathy looks like in action.

JO'S MOTIVATION FOR CONCILIATION

In the first episode (extract 2.1), from near the beginning of the first conversation in the dataset, Jo Berry speaks of how the Brighton bombing gave rise to her motivation for meeting Pat Magee. Each person comes to the conciliation process as an individual shaped by their history and memories. For Jo, the killing of her father in 1984 changed the course of her life, creating a purpose that directed much of what she did afterwards. Her response to the bombing was to find out about Northern Ireland, what had led to the violence and how people were affected by it. She visited Ireland several times and met other victims, as well as staying in contact with the families of other victims of the Brighton bombing. During that time, she had also married and had three daughters, creating an important new social group with herself as a key member. Importantly for the analysis of the talk, she had trained to work with parents developing their listening skills, and this training shows itself in how she often takes the lead in managing the talk in the one-to-one meetings with Pat.

This thumbnail sketch of a life can, of course, only indicate the richness of the social, cognitive and linguistic resources of an individual that are available to be called on or that may influence the moment of talk.

In extracts of talk, here and throughout the book, metaphors are underlined; short pauses are marked with two or three dots, and longer pauses approximated to the nearest second in round brackets. (Chapter 3 gives more detail on transcription method.) The first line of each extract indicates the conversation it is taken from: 1 = conversation at their second meeting, 2000; 2 = conversation at their fourth meeting, 2001; 3 = radio interview, 2003; 4 = seminar, 2009.

Extract 2.1   Jo's motivation for talking with Pat, as reported at their second meeting:

1–87 Jo	. . . (2.0) but as I said to you,
88	s- something I've wanted,
89	. . . almost since the moment the bomb went off.
90	. .I knew,
91	. . . (2.0) back in the moment,
92	wh- what I wanted to do,
93	. . . was bring as much--
94	. . . (2.0) something--
95	. . as much positive out of it as I could.
96	. . you know,
97 Pat	[hmh]
98 Jo	. . . (1.0) [and] I--
99	and I saw very clearly.
100	. . . (1.0) that the--
101	. . the end of that journey,
102	would be,
103	. . sitting down and,
104	. . . talking to the people who did it.
105 Pat	. . hmh
106 Jo	. . that just came in a moment,
107	and then went away,
108	and then--
109	. . there's been a long long . . sixteen years of [getting to this point].

The metaphors used by Jo in extract 2.1 to describe her motivation for meeting Pat and engaging in conciliation demonstrate how metaphor can offer the researcher insights into speakers' thinking, both what they are thinking—their ideas—and what they feel about it—their attitudes and values. For example, the metaphor that Jo uses to describe her motivation for meeting Pat is a desire to *bring something positive out of* the death of her father. In this metaphor we can find an image of Jo emerging out of some, possibly dark, place, carrying with her *something positive,* as yet unknown. The words *bring something . . . out of it* add a sense of movement, re-described as *that journey* in line 101. Because the meaning in the context is not concerned with literal, physical movement, we can say that the verb *bring . . . out of* is used metaphorically. Similarly, the *something* (lines 88, 94) that might come out of the death of her father is not a concrete object, but rather something abstract such as conciliation, empathy or understanding. In concretising this idea, *something* is said to be used metaphorically.

Making Metaphors from Everyday Reality

Jo envisaged her first meeting with Pat as *the end* of a metaphorical *journey,* and she follows this with a more precise and literal description of the meeting as *sitting down and talking to the people who did it* (lines 103–4). This last phrase moves the talk from the metaphorical to the physical world, but there is a resonance or semantic prosody (Louw, 1993) that spreads across from the metaphorical *the end of that journey,* so that the *sitting down* seems to carry with it some sense of relief and rest from the efforts of a journey. The spread of metaphoricity across the local context of talk can cause problems for identifying metaphor: should *sitting down* be classed as metaphorical? or is it metonymic, since literal, physical sitting down is involved but more seems to be implied? The fuzziness of metaphorical talk offers a powerful resource for speakers but, for researchers, presents a series of problems in need of solution.

Such connections, between the material, physical world (where people sit down together to talk) and the metaphorical world (where people go on *journeys* of conciliation), occur throughout the data and remind us that metaphors are no less effective for being constructed out of the everyday business of a life, that the prosaic is not so far from the poetic.

Metaphor Systematicity

Even in this short extract we can notice the systematicity or patterning of metaphor. The metaphors between lines 93 and 104 together create a metaphorical scenario or story (Cameron, Maslen, and Low, 2010) of the journey out of the negative place created by the bombing to a place where Jo can sit down and talk with the bombers, with Jo carrying the positive rewards of the journey. The final line of the extract also fits with this journey or quest scenario, with *long* used metaphorically for a period of time and *getting to this point* metaphorically for achieving the goal. The emphasis on the length of the journey, with the repeated *long,* tells us something about Jo's feelings about it—the length of Jo's metaphorical journey highlights the effort it has entailed for her—the affective impact of the metaphor.[2]

The fitting together of metaphors into a coherent story or scenario, along with attached attitudes and values, is one type of systematicity, and may be found locally, as here, in just a few lines of talk, or more globally, extending across stretches of talk.

Other metaphors in the extract also fit together. When Jo says *I saw very clearly* in line 99, she means that she understood very well. Here she is using conventionalised metaphors that connect the quite different ideas of 'understanding' and 'seeing', in which *seeing clearly* implies unproblematic understanding. This type of metaphor systematicity lies in the structural analogy made between the two ideas, rather than in its creation of a coherent scenario or story, and the metaphorical connection between 'understanding' and 'seeing' is systematic not just locally, but at a cultural level or even more universally (Sweetser, 1990).

In 106 and 107, metaphors of journeys or movement are again used, but this time to refer to processes of thinking, as an idea *came* and then *went away*. The opposition or contrast of *coming* and *going* in the domain of movement is transferred when it is used metaphorically in the quite different domain of thinking processes. Once again there is analogical systematicity at a cultural level in connecting 'thinking' with 'movement', and 'ideas' or 'thoughts' with some kind of entity that can move. The uses of these metaphors in this moment of talk are, most probably, conventionalised ways of talking and are unlikely activate any live metaphorical processing. In the approach to metaphor used here, such conventionalised metaphorical uses are included as (a type of) metaphor.

Enacting Two Levels of Conciliation in Talk

We can also see in this extract how two levels of conciliation are enacted in the talk: at one level, Jo *does* conciliation by sharing her ideas and feelings with Pat; at a more 'meta' level, she also reflects on the conciliation process. Metaphor helps at both levels. Through the metaphors that a speaker uses in conversation, the other person can come to know their thinking and emotions, an important component of empathy. At the same time, the speaker can come to understand his or her own experience by thinking and reflecting through metaphor.

PAT'S MOTIVATION FOR CONCILIATION

A sketch of what Pat Magee brought to the conciliation process would include influences from growing up in a Catholic family in England, returning to Belfast at the age of 19 and growing awareness of the political 'oppression' he found there; his joining the provisional Irish

Republican Army (IRA), which would have had a profound impact as a social group membership, and moving towards active participation in violence through experiencing arrest and imprisonment (more in chapter 7). Not long after the Brighton bombing, he was arrested and imprisoned for life, but released when a political settlement was reached in 1999. During the years in jail, he studied literature and wrote a novel. On leaving prison, he did not rejoin the IRA. It took several months for Pat to find out that Jo wanted to meet him and for the first meeting finally to be organised.

Extract 2.2 is Pat's presentation of his motivation and goal for meeting Jo from the first conversation. 'Positioning' (Van Langenhove and Harré, 1999) occurs when a speaker situates him or herself in respect of what is said, as Pat does when he explicitly states that he is talking *as a republican* (535). Pat positions himself with this phrase in terms of his beliefs and group membership, giving himself a 'collective identity' *as a republican*. He explains elsewhere in the talk that, although he did not rejoin the IRA on leaving prison, he still believes in the republican cause.

Extract 2.2   Pat's motivation for talking with Jo, as reported at their second meeting:

1–535 Pat	. . . (2.0) as a republican,
536	you know,
537	. . . (1.0) I'm--
538	I--
539	I feel,
540	there's a need,
541	like a sort of a human need,
542	there's a er--
543	and a political need,
544	. . and a cross over,
545	. . . (2.0) to . . be open,
546	. . . (1.0) [to you],
547 Jo	[hmh]
548 Pat	. . and er--
549	. . . (2.0) in any way I can.
550 Jo	. . hmh
551 Pat	. . . (1.0) and,
552	. . . (1.0) also,
553	. . you know,
554	. . . (1.0) to explain,
555	you know ,
556	like er--
557	like er the reasoning behind it.
558	[I think] that you need to know that,

The Theme of the Personal and the Political

Comparing the language and metaphors used here with those used by Jo, in extract 2.1, we find Pat using the impersonal *there's a necessity* (523) and *there's a need* (540, 541 543, 558), where Jo spoke more personally, using *I wanted*. The idea of a general *need* in line 540 is broken down in the following lines to two types of *need: human* and *political*. This is an early mention of what becomes a theme in the conciliation talk: the contrast between personal, or human, concerns and politically motivated concerns. In deciding to use violence, political motivations led Pat to disregard the personal; in meeting Jo, he is confronted with the personal consequences of his actions.

Differences in their language and their metaphors indicate how Jo and Pat come to the conciliation process from different starting points and with different motivations. Jo, as we have seen in extract 2.1, wanted to bring something positive from her loss and to understand why Pat planted the bomb that killed her father, while Pat, as in extract 2.2, wanted *to explain . . . the reasoning behind* the bombing (554–57). These starting points affect all that happens once they meet and engage in talking together.

Enacting Empathy in Talk

In the final line of the extract, we see an explicit instance of empathy in action when Pat says *I think you need to know that*. In saying these words, Pat is making what will be called 'a gesture of empathy'. He is 'entering into' Jo's perspective, trying to imagine how it is to be her and what she might need to know.

THEORETICAL FRAMEWORK FOR EMPATHY AND METAPHOR IN DISCOURSE ACTIVITY

The discussion of extracts 2.1 and 2.2 provide some idea of what metaphor-led discourse analysis (hereafter, metaphor analysis) can produce. Metaphors are identified and considered in terms of what the speaker was saying and doing—their discourse activity and discourse function.[3] Understanding discourse activity requires the researcher to examine the minute details of language use, such as choices of pronoun, tense and lexis, as well as the topic of the talk, and to consider how these change as times goes by. The theoretical framework[4] that underpins this kind of method is called the 'discourse dynamics' approach, and this section sets out its main principles and commitments.

Applying Ideas from Complexity Dynamics Systems Theory to Discourse, Metaphor and Empathy

At the heart of the discourse dynamics framework lies an understanding of talking and thinking as processes, flows or movement, rather than in terms of objects (words, ideas etc). Complexity theory and dynamic systems theory, which originate in biological science and mathematics, offer ways of thinking about change and evolving systems that can be helpful in illuminating and analysing applied linguistic concerns too (Cameron, 2003, 2007a; Cameron and Deignan, 2006; Cameron et al., 2009; Gibbs and Cameron, 2008; Larsen-Freeman and Cameron, 2008).

What does it mean to think about reconciliation conversations in terms of complexity and dynamic systems? It means that we see the conversations between Jo and Pat as the activity of complex dynamic systems in interaction, influenced by their starting points, as seen earlier, and by the history of their talk together up to this point. The complex dynamic system of their discourse develops, adapts and flows as their contributions to the conversation build on each other, and as they develop their own meanings or explore each other's ideas. Within the flow of discourse, metaphors appear, and can be used to track discourse activity and to guide the researcher's understanding of changes in thinking and attitudes. Empathy is understood as emerging from the flow of talk, a complex dynamic system in its own right and integral to the discourse system. This perspective on empathy leads to the dynamic model that will be developed as the book proceeds.

A complex dynamic system is an evolving collection of heterogeneous elements or agents (people, language resources, ideas etc). These elements of the system are dynamic (always changing), and change also occurs in the connections, or relations, among components. As a result of these dynamics, the system develops as a whole that is more than, and cannot be reduced to, the combination of its component elements. A conversation is more than the sum of the words spoken. When two people come together to try to understand each other through talk, a complexity perspective sees a process of multiple interacting complex dynamic systems, where the component elements (which may themselves be systems) are the individuals and their linguistic and cognitive resources. Each moment in the talk changes the participants' understanding of the other and affects what is said next. A 'conversation' is a discourse event[5] that results from the interaction of these complex dynamic systems, involving language, understanding, emotions, attitudes and values in the activity that will be called 'talking-and-thinking'. The hyphenated label emphasises the inseparability of thought and speech (Slobin, 1996; Vygotsky, 1962).

People in conversation are not independent of wider networks of environmental, social and cultural systems; the complex systems are 'open', not closed and bounded. When Jo Berry and Pat Magee come together to talk and to try to understand each other, two complex dynamic systems of talking-and-thinking interact to produce the system that is their conversation: two brains or minds engage in dynamically constructing understandings of the Other; two patterns of thinking and speaking built up over lifetimes are brought into use; two sets of memories and histories are called upon. Figure 2.1 tries to capture this idea, although, of course,

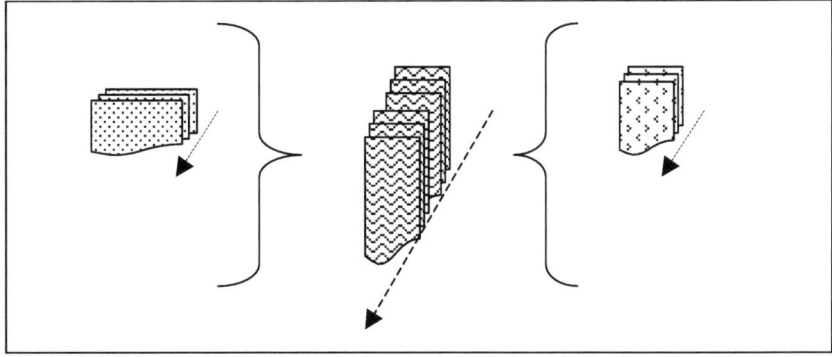

Figure 2.1   Two people talking-and-thinking together produce a conversation, metaphors, and empathy.

it is difficult to show multi-dimensional dynamics in a two dimensional graphic. The brackets represent two people talking face-to-face. Their central, unfolding, conversation is to be imagined as coming towards the viewer out of the diagram, and represents the discourse activity or talking-and-thinking, flowing as an outcome of the interaction of the unfolding activity in the embodied minds of the two individuals. Metaphors occur as an integral aspect of this discourse activity, and empathy occurs within it and develops from it.

The Timescales of Talk

Any moment of talking-and-thinking links into various interconnected dimensions and timescales. It is also impossible graphically to show unfinalisable interconnectedness; each discrete shape used to represent talking-and-thinking in figure 2.1 should be understood as unbounded or fuzzy, and as multiply connected.

On the micro timescale of the interactional dynamics, meaning is negotiated utterance by utterance between the speakers as they contribute dialogically, trying to ensure that what is said makes sense to the other person. They monitor what they say as they say it, and may notice that it could be clearer, leading to repetition or adjusting of words and phrases. The other person may ask for clarification or may challenge what is said. The talk proceeds through these bouts of negotiation, adjustment and clarification. Eventually, one topic is replaced by another, through questions or through interventions. Sometimes a speaker talks at length, narrating an event or explaining an idea. Occasionally, the talk reaches a difficult or critical point where something particularly painful or difficult must be said or something is understood in a new way. Sometimes the emotional equilibrium of one or both speakers is disrupted in a way that threatens the conversation, and work is done to restore balance. In later conversations, reference is made back to talk in earlier meetings, and the discourse itself becomes the discourse topic. When Jo and Pat meet for the radio interview and the seminar, they take a longer perspective on their understandings of the Other, and reflect back over three years on what was said, of expectations and of changes that resulted from talking together.

Driving the Dynamics of Conciliation

A key driving force in the dynamics of the conciliation process is alterity, or 'otherness'. As they try to explain their feelings and experiences to each other, Jo and Pat need to find ways to reduce or cross the gaps between them by presenting and explaining their different histories, beliefs and actions. This desire to reduce or connect across alterity produces the shape of the flow of the talk. Alterity may, for example, motivate the questions that they ask each other or the effort they put into understanding the Other.

There will be other forces at work too, as when Pat takes special care in how he formulates his utterances so as not to upset Jo,[6] which sometimes produces talk at a slower rate and with more hedges. A further driving force in the interaction arises from the fact that people talking together generally strive to maintain their own (and the other's) 'face', their dignity and self-respect. Conciliation talk, where a perpetrator of violence comes face-to-face with a person affected by that violence, presents a particular problem with the maintenance of face. If the perpetrator is to accept the human consequences of his action, he has to admit to himself and to the other what he caused to happen. To accept this and to still maintain self-respect and dignity is massively demanding of the perpetrator, and Pat Magee has to handle this dilemma.

The complex dynamic systems of the two speakers co-adapt to each other, under the pressures of needing the Other to understand ideas and information accurately, of expressing appropriate affect, and of maintaining self-respect and emotional equilibrium. Their talking-and-thinking evolves and changes, little by little, but also in bigger leaps, as we will see later in this chapter. Through both gradual and sudden changes, Pat and Jo arrive at understandings different from those they brought to their first meeting.

The Emergence of Empathy

Emergence is the development of something new through the interaction and self-organisation of systems. Dynamic systems can change gradually, remaining within a fairly stable phase, or they can undergo a sudden 'phase shift', in which the system moves dramatically from one stable phase to another that is different in nature as a result of the shift. A system may pass through a period of variability or fluctuation, as it wobbles between possible futures and prior to emergence. Emergence occurs at all levels and scales in complex dynamic systems.

Understanding the emergence of empathy from the conciliation conversations is the central goal of the book, and is accessed through metaphor analysis. To understand change occurring through talking-and-thinking, complex dynamics systems theory tells us to examine the trajectory of the discourse, to look in detail at the micro and macro timescales, and to find connections across scales. New understandings emerge as new information is combined with existing understandings (Cameron, 2003). Changes in understanding, that may contribute to empathy at the macro timescale over several years of conversations, will not, in a complex system, necessarily be reducible into smaller and smaller components at micro timescale, but may emerge from the local dynamics and gestures of empathy, through gradual self-organisation or through sudden perturbation and re-organisation.

Figure 2.2 tries to capture this idea of local action combining with sudden perturbations or changes in the discourse activity.

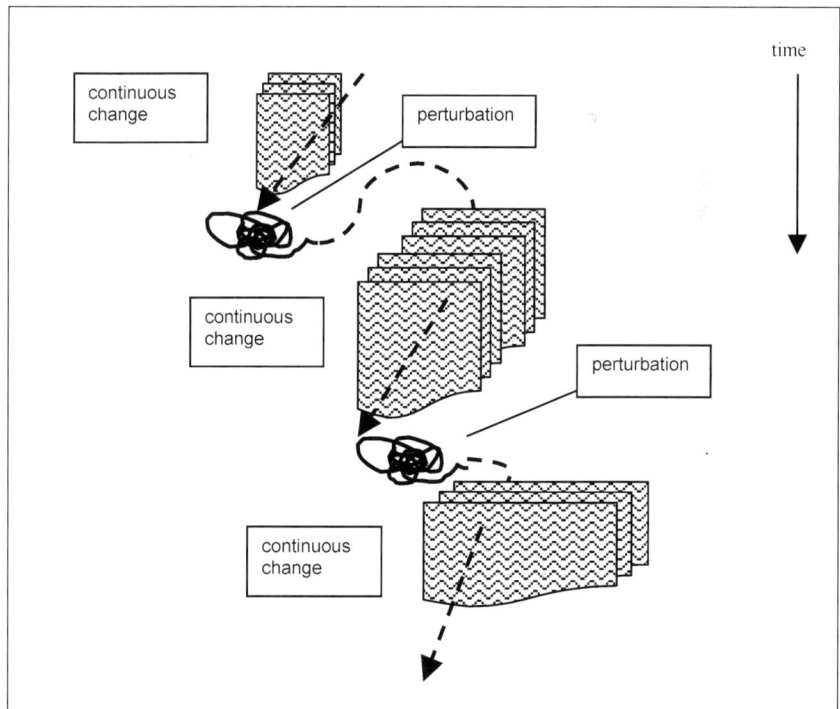

Figure 2.2   Types of change in dynamic systems of discourse activity and empathy.

The path of the system (the flow of discourse) is represented by the dashed line, to be imagined as moving down the page as time passes. In some phases of discourse activity, the system changes in a stable and continuous manner, shown with the icon for unfolding talking-and-thinking used in figure 2.1. A continuous phase may come to a sudden end with a period of perturbation, shown in the diagram as a scrambled mess of line. This perturbation causes sudden change, shifting the system to a different type of activity, graphically shown as a different area of the diagram, where more stable activity resumes in the changed system. An example of a perturbation causing a phase shift was described in the previous chapter, when seeing the suffering of a perpetrator of violence moved the victim's wife to open up to the possibility of empathy. The first meeting between Jo Berry and Pat Magee acted as a perturbation, to each in different ways, as we see later in this chapter.

Gestures of Empathy

Gestures of empathy, such as the one made by Pat in extract 2.2, are local instances of the processes that link Self and Other in the development of empathy (figure 1.1). Labelling these discourse actions 'gestures' is a deliberate metaphorical choice; expressive physical gestures made with the hands, head or torso during talk are holistic, are formulated in advance of the linguistic utterance, and convey much of the affect (McNeill, 1992; McGilchrist, 2009). Likewise, gestures of empathy are holistic and dialogic, related to what is said but not necessarily identical to it, and, by reflecting attitudes and emotions, carry crucial affective force. In the everyday metaphorical sense of 'gesture', a non-physical gesture is made by one person towards another, often for the other person's benefit. So it is with gestures of empathy: one of the speakers offers the other something in the discourse, perhaps an opportunity to understand better or to explain more deeply, perhaps a readiness to listen or refusal to judge. Gestures may be more or less comfortable for recipients; sometimes a gesture may be positive for the other participant, but gestures can also result in awkward or painful moments.

Long term developments in empathy, such as coming to understand the other's perspective and feelings, can be seen as the emergent outcome of multiple such gestures of empathy. Some gestures of empathy are highly charged and make a major impact to the conciliation process; most are not so strong, but smaller and more local, but still, I argue here, contribute powerfully to the dynamics of empathy.

THE DISCOURSE DYNAMICS OF METAPHOR

Metaphors are produced in the flow of talk, as an integral aspect of talking-and-thinking. Because they often contain information about the speakers' thinking and emotions, and because they often stand out against the flow of talk, metaphors offer the researcher an interesting way to track the development of ideas, attitudes and values over the timescales of the discourse system. As the discussions of extracts earlier in the chapter illustrated, metaphor analysis works with metaphors as discourse activity, unpicking the connections between the metaphors and the discourse actions of participants. It works from the micro timescale through segments and episodes of talk up to the scale of the discourse event as a whole, and beyond that to a series of connected discourse events, as Jo and Pat continue to meet over the years.

Our concern with metaphor as a discourse phenomenon and as multi-dimensional socio-cognitive activity distinguishes the discourse dynamics approach to metaphor from other approaches that understand metaphor only in terms of cognitive activity or that focus on metaphor as an object in the language system of a speech community. While the cognitive and the language system influence, and are influenced by, what happens in discourse, and are thus of concern in the discourse dynamics approach, it is discourse activity that is the focus of the researcher's attention, providing data and evidence. The term 'discourse activity' is used to highlight the dynamic understanding that we want to bring to metaphor data. When metaphors are analysed, they are to be understood through their role in the flow and activity of discourse.

Discourse Dynamics as an Alternative to Cognitive Metaphor Theory

Cognitive metaphor theory, born with *Metaphors We Live By* (Lakoff and Johnson, 1980) and developed since then inside the broader field of cognitive linguistics (e.g. Lakoff, 1993, 2008), holds that metaphor is a matter of mind, not of language, and works with metaphor as general human phenomenon, not as context-specific (Gibbs, 1994). 'Conceptual metaphors' are generalised large-scale mappings between concepts, established across speakers of a language and brought ready made to a discourse event. What is seen in transcripts or texts is assumed to be linguistic manifestations of conceptual metaphor. From a cognitive theoretic standpoint, Jo's use of *bring out of, journey* are linguistic expressions of a conceptual metaphor that might be formulated as SELF-INITIATED CHANGE OF STATE IS SELF-PROPELLED MOTION (Lakoff, Evenson and Schwarz, 1991).

The goals of cognitive metaphor theory are to provide universalist accounts of metaphor, not to explain what is happening when metaphor is used in discourse, and so it is perhaps unfair to critique it for not providing this. However, since cognitive metaphor theory sometimes tries to account for what people do in specific instances of discourse (e.g. Ponterotto, 2003) despite not being set up to do so, such a critique becomes necessary. Because of its use of complexity and dynamic systems theory, the discourse dynamics approach seems to be able to account for metaphor across speech communities as well as for metaphor in specific discourse events (Cameron and Deignan, 2006; Gibbs and Cameron, 2008). Computer modelling of agent-based systems show that conventionalised metaphors can emerge from the dyadic interactions of agents (Barr, 2004), and thus there seems to be no need to require conceptual metaphors to be innate mental structures (Lakoff and Johnson, 1999). We can, however, allow the possibility of metaphor operating at a conceptual level, although it would not be possible to know whether individual discourse participants are making use of this level as they speak, or whether metaphors come to be spoken via other mechanisms.

Work in conceptual metaphor theory has served to uncover the breadth and depth of systematicity of metaphor across the language of a speech community. Corpus exploration of metaphors in discourse undermines some of the claims of cognitive metaphor theory by showing that the systematicity is both less predictable and more specific than claimed (Deignan, 2005). However, whether systematic patterns originate from conceptual metaphors or emerge through discourse dynamics probably matters less than the fact that such patterns can be described in data and that they can help in understanding metaphor use.

The position adopted here is that cognitive metaphor theory can inspire and inform the discourse dynamics approach, particularly at the level of the language of a speech community, but remains essentially incompatible with it. Conceptual metaphors are not required for a valid theoretical account of metaphors in discourse, and, further, using them to account for the discourse activity of participants may be misleading and direct attention away from important metaphor phenomena that occur in the moment of talk. Consequently, the term 'metaphor' in this book always refers to metaphor as discourse activity unless otherwise stated. This is reflected by using italics in formatting words and phrases taken from discourse data, and for larger patterns of metaphor based on this data.

Metaphor as Multi-dimensional

In the discourse dynamics approach, a metaphor in discourse activity may involve any of the interconnected and multiple resources of participants: dimensions that can be described as linguistic, social, psychological or cognitive, affective, cultural, physical (Gibbs and Cameron, 2008). Resisting artificial theoretical separations between connected aspects of human behaviour requires the discourse dynamics approach to find ways to maintain connections between these dimensions of discourse. An initial step is the use of the label 'talking-and-thinking' (Cameron, 2003) to describe discourse dynamics in the moment, keeping the cognitive and linguistic connected, in contrast to their deliberate separation in cognitive metaphor theory. However, both 'metaphor' and 'talking-and-thinking' are to be understood as including all dimensions of discourse activity.

Work on embodiment in psychology (Gibbs, 2006a) and work on gesture and metaphor in the expression of ideas (Cienki, 2010; Cienki and Müller, 2008) have emphasised the interconnectedness of the physical with discourse activity. Connections between metaphor and people's physical interaction with the material world have also been made by cognitive metaphor theory, but with universalist claims made at a general level rather than more locally in terms of the effect in, and of, discourse activity (Gibbs, 2006a; Grady, 1999; Lakoff and Johnson, 1999). The ways in which our bodies are shaped and can move influence how humans relate to and affect the material world, and impact on the kinds of metaphors used, as we saw in extract 2.1.

Physical and material realities also contribute to discourse and metaphor, via emotional states. Neuroscience is increasingly uncovering such connections, in particular through work on simulations (Barsalou, 2008; Damasio, 1994, 1999, 2003). Simulations are 'as-if' activations in the brain that mimic or mirror the emotions and actions that have come to be connected with particular experiences. Damasio's somatic marker hypothesis explains how emotions come to be connected with experiences (Damasio, 1994). Through experiencing situations and related emotions, the brain builds memories with 'somatic markers' that then work to simulate emotions in response to subsequent experiences of similar situations. Because simulations occur in the brain, they provide a much quicker response than would come from physically experiencing emotions. In actual experiences that involve the body as well as the brain, responses are much slower because physiological activity, such as the production of hormones, is involved and that works at a slower pace than neurological activity. Neuroscience has also discovered mirror neurons (Arbib, 2002), neurons in the brain responsible for producing simulations of bodily actions and perceptions, in a similar way to simulations of emotional states. When bodily actions are observed, mirror neurons create simulations of those actions, while the brain also inhibits actual performance of the action in situations where that is not required (Barsalou, 2008; Gibbs, 2006a, 2006b).

The importance of simulations for researchers concerned with metaphor in discourse dynamics lies in the fact that simulations may be generated, not just in response to a physical situation, perceptions or emotions, but also in response to mention of these in discourse. As Gibbs (2006b) suggests, "[L]anguage use is closely tied to embodied imagination" (p. 444), and automatic simulation processes are likely to contribute to understanding metaphors encountered in discourse. Many metaphors involve mention of physical action, such as the movement metaphors in extract 2.1, often with an affective force as well, and so may activate simulations of physical action and emotions. The specific discourse context serves to inhibit physical response and support interpretation (Gibbs, 2006b; Ritchie, 2006, 2010). Metaphors and their relation to the physical, material world will turn out to be very significant in the conciliation conversations.

The Emergence of Metaphorical Meaning

Metaphor may be actively processed by bringing together two ideas or domains to produce a new understanding, emergent on this micro timescale between discourse participants. Metaphorical scenarios or stories, such as those seen in extract 2.1, may also emerge locally as coherent understandings. Conventionalised metaphors have meanings that have emerged and become entrenched at a higher level of social organisation and over a longer timescale (Cameron, 1999b). In between the local and the global, coherent patterns of metaphors may emerge across discourse events. A discourse event level pattern of this type should be understood as a trajectory of connected metaphors, that I have elsewhere called a 'systematic metaphor'.[7]

Systematic metaphors will be described in more detail in following chapters but an example of one type may be useful here. 'Framing metaphors' emerge at this level between the macro and micro as speakers converge on shared[8] metaphorical ways of talking-and-thinking about key themes. Brennan and Clark (1996) showed how speakers carrying out a discourse task quite quickly home in on shared ways of referring to what they are talking about, which they called 'conceptual pacts'. Framing metaphors are one kind of what Cameron (2007b) relabelled lexico-conceptual pacts. Seeing conciliation as *a journey*, for example, emerged over time as a systematic framing metaphor in Jo and Pat's talk, entering the discourse in Jo's contributions, but soon used by Pat as well. (The evidence for this is presented in chapter 4.)

In later chapters, we will also see stretches of talk that resemble systems in fluctuation, where several metaphors cluster together in rapid succession, used to talk about the same idea, or where a metaphor, originating with one speaker, is passed back and forth between them, changing form or content as it goes, until it settles down into an emergent 'shared' metaphor that is accepted and used by both. Tracking the emergence and trajectories of systematic metaphors will be of importance in researching the development of understanding of the Other's perspective as part of growing empathy.

A PHASE SHIFT IN THE DISCOURSE

We return now to the data, with the discourse dynamics framework outlined and equipped with terms and ideas from complexity and dynamic systems theory. In 2009, Jo Berry and Pat Magee reflected on their early meetings and recounted a moment when their way of talking together suddenly changed. In complexity terms, their discourse underwent a phase shift in which the system moved to another region of its phase space landscape[9] as the result of a perturbation in the system (figure 2.2). This phase shift is described by Jo and Pat with a metaphor of *changing hats*. In this section, the accounts of this shift given by each of them are examined, demonstrating the process and outcomes of metaphor analysis before, in the following chapter, the process is described in detail.

The phase shift in the discourse was very powerfully revealed as Jo and Pat described how Pat suddenly changed from talking from his political identity to talking as one human being to another. In the seminar, Jo spoke before Pat, and her narrative of the sudden shift that took place in the first meeting begins by setting the scene (extract 2.3). At first, Pat, *wearing his political hat,* was responding to Jo's questions *as a republican* (extract 2.2):

Extract 2.3   Jo sees Pat as wearing a political hat:

458	Jo	. . and the first half,
459		or the first hour,
460		. . erm.
461		I was asking Pat questions,
462		and . . erm.
463		. . wanting to <u>find out</u>,
464		. . what <u>led</u> him to <u>join</u> the IRA,
465		and wh--
466		. . what'd been his motivation an--
467		an--
468		Pat was,
469		. . erm.
470		telling me <u>things</u> like,
471		<Q X this was for X
472		political reasons Q>,
473		which I was familiar with,
474		and I,
475		sort of,
476		say,
477		<X that X>
478		Pat was,
479		like,
480		sort of,
481		<u>wearing this political hat</u> an--
482		which is,
483		what I expected.
484		and . . erm.
485		justifying and,
486		and <u>giving</u> v--
487		<X you know X>
488		very good reasons I--
489		I was familiar with the reasons.

The many continuous *-ing* verb forms, *asking, wearing, giving,* create the scene-setting focus of this section of talk, where what was being said was adding to Jo's understanding but not changing it dramatically. In extract 2.4 a change in grammar to the simple past marks the moment of change, as Pat *took off this hat and just opened up:*

Extract 2.4   The hat is taken off:

512	Jo	. . but after about an hour and a half,
513		<u>something</u> happened an--
514		and . . erm.
515	Pat	w--
516		sort of,
517		tell you about this,
518		<u>in</u> his own words I'm sure,
519		but i--
520		. . erm.
521		to me it was like.
522		he sort of,
523		<u>took off,</u>
524		<u>this hat.</u>
525		an--
526		and just <u>opened up.</u>
527		and said,
528		<Q I--
529		I never met
530		anyone like you before.
531		I want to <u>hear</u>
532		your <u>pain</u>
534		and your anger an--Q>
535		you know
536		<Q how can I help Q>

We can know this was a sudden shift because Jo narrows down the time it happened to *after about an hour and a half* (512) and describes it in terms of a discrete *something* (513) that *happened*. The word *just* in line 526 reinforces this sense of a sudden dramatic shift. Pat's question in the last line represents an explicit gesture of empathy.

The metaphors of *took off this hat* and *opened up* describe the action and its consequence. They do not make a coherent scenario but draw on quite different ideas. The *political hat* that Pat *took off* represents a particular allegiance that the metaphorical wearer adopts and speaks from; to take it off is to change point of view and voice. Pat can now speak more as himself, person to person—he can *open up* to Jo and let her see him as a person and not just as a representative of the political view. By incorporating Pat's words as if he spoke them, Jo reinforces the idea of him as a person suddenly more visible and present in the talk.

In complexity theory terms, the moment at which the hat came off marks a phase shift in the dynamic system of their talking-and-thinking together. By this act or gesture of empathy, Pat causes a perturbation that shifts the talking-and-thinking into a new area of its phase space landscape; the system enters a new phase of stability where continuous change can move it in new directions that were not available up to this point.

Jo's continuing narrative (extract 2.5) provides more support for seeing this moment as a phase shift, caused by Pat's perturbation of the discourse system. She describes the effect on herself of the phase shift, using a dense cluster of metaphors:

Extract 2.5　The beginning of another journey:

538 Jo	. . and <u>at</u> that moment,
539	<X sort of X>
540	<u>part</u> of me wanted to,
541	<X kind of r--X>
542	. . run fast,
543	because I kind of knew,
544	this was,
545	. . kind of <u>the beginning of another journey</u> in which,
546	we were going to,
547	<u>open</u> the,
548	. . dialogue as two human beings without <u>wearing these--</u>
549	<u>these hats</u> when--
550	and . . erm.
551	I was going to be,
552	. . <u>taken out from</u> my <u>comfort zone,</u>
553	and it'll be scary.
554	. . <u>another part</u> of me,
555	really wanted this.
556	because this was real and this was,
557	more than I'd,
558	hoped for.
559	<u>dreamt</u> for.

The cluster of metaphors includes another *hat* metaphor: *two human beings without wearing these hats* (548); and two *journey* metaphors: *the beginning of another journey* (545) and *taken out from my comfort zone* (552). There is also the metaphor that lets her talk about herself as having two different *parts,* one that wants to run away and is scared, and the other that is pleased with the new opportunity.

What we have here, then, is a shift in talking-and-thinking, caused by a perturbation and marked by a cluster of metaphors. When Pat comes to retell this story himself (extract 2.6), he uses some of the same metaphors: *the political hat came off, opened up.* We also see how this was not just a shift in Jo and Pat's dialogue but, perhaps even more significantly, a shift in Pat's own thinking and in empathy.

Extract 2.6   Pat's account of the hat coming off:

4–747 Pat	<u>something</u> else occurred,
748	during the encounter.
749	. . and.
750	. . and some <u>point</u> I--
751	I f--
752	I <u>felt</u> I couldn't <u>go on</u> with this.
753	. . I <u>felt</u>,
754	I <u>felt</u> this is wrong.
755	and I--
756	I think <u>at that point</u>.
757	<u>the political hat did come off</u>.
758	. . and for the first time,
759	the very first time,
760	I really did <u>open up</u>,
761	to what I had done <u>in</u> human <u>terms</u>.
762	while it was a political action,
763	with . . erm.
764	a rationale <u>behind</u> it.
765	with a--
766	you know,
767	intent <u>behind</u> it.
768	. . suddenly I'd <u>see</u> it <u>in terms of</u> the harm that--
769	. . . the harm done.
770	. . and that--
771	. . that had never happened before.

Understanding his action, i.e. the bombing that killed Jo's father, *in terms of the harm done* is a shift for Pat, that reverses the dehumanising and closing down that had been necessary for him to engage in violence all those years ago, and thereby opens up the possibility of empathy with Jo as another human being. The shift changes how Pat participates in the talking-and-thinking; it changes his identity in the discourse. The conversations that followed this meeting are affected by this perturbation in discourse identity, metaphorically described as the removal of *hats,* and the discourse system can now enter a new phase where *opening up* to the Other, and the development of empathy, become more possible.

CONCLUSION

In this chapter, the idea of metaphor analysis has been introduced to demonstrate how the examination of metaphors as discourse activity, and the tracking of changes in metaphor use over time, can illuminate our understanding of how people engage in conciliation and move towards greater empathy. We have seen how Jo Berry and Pat Magee came to the conciliation process with different motivations, and how an early shift occurred for Pat when he accepted the need to talk about the personal as well as the political.

The theoretical framework of discourse dynamics that underpins the study has been explained, and the constructs offered by complex dynamic systems theory have been assembled for use in understanding the development of empathy: looking for stabilities and perturbations in talking-and-thinking, tracking trajectories of metaphors across scales, looking for the emergence of metaphor sharing and of new understandings of, and attitudes towards, the Other. From metaphor trajectories and metaphor systematicity, the researcher can uncover insights into participants' changing ideas, attitudes and values. Metaphor becomes the thread that can help connect the immediacy of face-to-face talk with the conciliation process and with emerging empathy. The following chapter presents the methodology for employing metaphor as a research tool in more detail.

3 Metaphor Analysis

By following the threads of metaphor through the transcribed discourse events, metaphor analysis can help to understand the outcomes of discourse activity and to answer the question:

- How does metaphor contribute to the conciliation process and the development of empathy?

Metaphor analysis works by examining metaphors in discourse activity as they occur, and then looking for patterns and changes in metaphors across the discourse events. The patterns and changes in metaphors help us to understand patterns and changes in the talking-and-thinking of Jo Berry and Patrick Magee, how they come to understand each other through the conciliation process and how this changes the empathy each has towards the other.

Having received the raw data on video film and audio CD, the first step was to convert it into a form suitable for the fine-grained analysis of metaphor in discourse activity. When a transcription had been prepared as text that could be printed for reading or manipulated electronically, the next task was to find metaphors.

TRANSCRIPTION OF DISCOURSE DATA

The original video film of the two conversations was converted to digital audio files and then transcribed into intonation units (Chafe, 1994; Du Bois et al., 1993). In comparison with other units of transcription and analysis, the intonation unit can be more reliably identified than the utterance, and is both more consistent and usually shorter than the turn, which can vary enormously in length. It also has a psycholinguistic rationale which makes it an appropriate unit for the analysis of metaphor in talking-and-thinking. According to Chafe, "an intonation unit verbalizes the speaker's focus of consciousness at that moment" (1994, p. 63). As ideas move in and out of consciousness, the varying focus of the speaker's attention is reflected in the talk. As the transcribed talk is divided into intonation units, it is also split into the speakers' foci of attention.

A prototypical intonation unit is spoken under a single intonation contour, with boundaries marked by prosodic changes such as changes in tempo or pitch, the use of creaky voice, and pausing. In the transcription, the ending of an intonation unit is marked in terms of its completeness, with a comma indicating lowered but not final pitch, a question mark indicating raised pitch, and a full stop or period indicating a finalising pitch movement. In practice, it is often easier to hear the start of a new unit than a unit closing. Many intonation units are not prototypical in their closing but are left hanging in the air, as it were, as the speaker moves on to a new unit. These incomplete intonation units are marked with two dashes, as in lines 93 and 94 of extract 2.1. The multi-dimensional nature of intonation units means that, unlike pauses for example, they cannot always be identified objectively or mechanically. However, with training, high levels of intra-rater reliability, and reasonable levels of inter-rater reliability are possible to attain (Stelma and Cameron, 2007).

As can be seen in the extracts, intonation units tend to be quite short, with a length between one and two seconds. The intonation unit (IU) offers an approximation to a temporal measure—extracts of transcriptions include intonation unit numbers and multiplying the number of an intonation unit multiplied by 1.5 gives a fairly reliable indication of the time in seconds since the beginning of the conversation.[1]

Transcriptions of the two filmed conversations include accurately measured pausing, differentiating very short pauses (shown as dots in the transcriptions) from longer pauses, which were timed to the nearest second. The radio interview and seminar were transcribed more 'lightly', into 'approximated intonation units', less accurate, in that pauses are not measured, but sufficiently accurate for the type of analysis to be carried out on the data.

The first conversation was transcribed into 2769 IUs and the second into 4043 IUs. The radio interview was transcribed into 1207 (approximated) IUs, and the seminar into 1302 (approximated) IUs.

IDENTIFYING METAPHOR

Identification of metaphor in the first two conversations was carried out by a research assistant after a process of rater training, and inter-rater comparison of samples. A further round of identification was carried out by the author, who also identified metaphors in the other discourse events.

In metaphor analysis, the primary data and evidence are linguistic metaphors, identified in their discourse context. So far, metaphor has been described, rather than defined, with Burke's view of metaphor as "seeing one thing in terms of something else" (1945, 503). For identification, this was operationalised, i.e. turned into a procedure to validly and reliably identify all metaphors, and only metaphors. Given the inherently fuzzy nature of metaphor in discourse, metaphor identification is never entirely straightforward (Cameron, 1999a, 2003; pragglejaz group, 2007).

Two Requirements for Metaphor

The first identifying feature of linguistic metaphor is the "something else", the use of a lexical item from a semantic field that is distinct from that of the "one thing", which is called the topic of the metaphor. The lexical item, which may be a word, phrase or clause, is called the 'vehicle' term of the metaphor.[2] The underlined lexical items in extracts are the vehicle terms of metaphors; some are single words (*saw, in, open, behind*); others are longer phrases (*end of the journey, bring . . . out of; a cross over*). The second requirement for identifying an instance of metaphor is that the vehicle term can contribute to the meaning in context: for example, Jo meeting Pat as the bomber can be understood in terms of the *end of the journey;* Jo's desire to find something positive in her loss can be understood in terms of *bring . . . out of*. It is important to note that there is no requirement for participants to process metaphors by consciously mapping ideas from the vehicle on to the topic, actively and in the moment;[3] the requirement is only that the researcher is able to make a convincing case of a contrast between the vehicle term as it might be understood in some other context, usually more basic and physical (such as a real *journey*), and its contextual meaning.

Solving Problems in Finding Metaphor

Experience with metaphor identification shows that around 70% or so of vehicle terms will be uncontroversially identified and accepted by several raters working on a text; agreement can be reached through discussion on a further 15–20% but around 10% are likely to remain disputed because of the inherent fuzziness of human meaning-making (Cameron, 2003; pragglejaz group, 2007).

Metaphors were identified by working through the transcripts line by line and underlining vehicle terms. Because the same word used in different contexts can be metaphorical, non-metaphorical, or both at the same time, each instance has to be considered as contextualised discourse activity. Some uses of *journey,* for example, involved non-metaphorical, physical movement, while others seemed to carry both metaphorical and literal senses. In taking a complex dynamic systems approach to metaphor in talk, the profile of these difficult boundary and hybrid cases is raised from inconvenient 'noise' in the system, to potentially interesting evidence of the system in flux. Later chapters show how paying particular attention to these cases can inform investigation.

The identification of metaphors is most straightforward with nouns and verbs that have strong lexical content (like *journey, open* or *saw*), giving the term a clear 'basic' sense, usually more concrete or physical, that clearly contrasts with the contextual meaning (pragglejaz, 2007). It is much more difficult with less 'content-ful' words and for these, explicit decisions must be made as to what is included as metaphor. Most problems occur with prepositions, phrasal and prepositional verbs, and delexicalised verbs like *make, do*

(Cameron, 1999a, 2003). Prepositions *in, out (of), into, between, behind* were included in metaphor identification here but not *before, after, to, from, by, of* (unless part of a phrasal verb, which would be considered as a single lexical unit); the verbs *takes, make, put* were included but not *do, have. Thing, something, anything* were included when referring to non-concrete entities, but *nothing* was excluded.[4] The pronouns *here* and *there* sometimes act metaphorically by bringing a sense of a location to non-physical entities, as when Pat says, *there's a question comes to my mind* (extract 3.1, 111–12).

Another type of problem arises because the boundaries of the vehicle term are not always clear in the dynamics of talk, particularly in the case of verb phrases that can spread across several prepositions or particles, as with *bring . . . out of.* The solution is to underline outwards from the most obviously metaphorical word, stopping when a new lexical unit begins or when the vehicle semantic field changes. If quantitative measures work with the number of vehicles, rather than the number of metaphorically used words (and in contrast to pragglejaz group, 2007), there are no knock-on effects from this decision.

772 metaphors were identified in the conversation after Jo and Pat's second meeting, 1383 in the conversation after their fourth meeting and 435 in the radio interview. Metaphors were identified only in key episodes of the talk in 2009, so an overall number is not available.

Metaphor densities, calculated as the number of metaphors per 1000 words of transcribed talk, were found to be 98 and 107 in the two one-to-one conversations and 68 in the interview. As suspected, metaphor densities are much higher in the conciliation talk than in classroom discourse activity analysed in an earlier study (Cameron, 2003).

METAPHOR VEHICLES AND DISCOURSE TOPICS

A metaphor topic is what a metaphor is used to talk about; this equates to the meaning in context of the metaphor vehicle. However, explicit metaphor topics connected to metaphor vehicles are not often found in spontaneous talk where vehicle terms tend to be used on their own in the flow of talk. To decide on the topic of a metaphor, the researcher must therefore make inferences from the discourse activity around the vehicle, combined with knowledge of contemporary meanings and uses of the lexical items.[5]

In carrying out this study we started by trying to infer metaphor topics quite precisely for each vehicle term, but soon realised that approximation was unavoidable and might lead to inferences that drifted too far from evidenced discourse activity. The solution was to identify, not specific metaphor topics, but what the speaker was talking about at the time the metaphor was used. These 'discourse topics' were refined into a small set of 'key discourse topics'. Having a key discourse topic assigned to each vehicle term helped to understand how metaphor was used in the main themes of the discourse events.

To illustrate how key discourse topics provided a solution to the problem of identifying metaphor topics, consider extract 3.1. This talk is a continuation of extract 2.1, where Jo had described her motivation for meeting Pat and closed her turn with *there's been a long long . . . 16 years*. In extract 3.1, Pat moves the talk by asking Jo a direct question, gradually formulated over six intonation units.

Extract 3.1   The metaphor of *the big political picture:*

1–110	Pat	[hmh hmh]
111		. . . (2.0) I suppose <u>there</u>'s a question,
112		that er <u>comes to</u> my mind from that.
113		. . er I don't . . . (1.0) think we've . . <u>covered</u> before.
114		. . . (1.0) um er--
115		. . . did you <u>see</u> it as like individuals,
116		or did you <u>see</u> it as a sort of a--
117		. . . (1.0) the <u>big</u> . . political <u>picture</u>,
118		the IRA,
119		or,
120		. . the war.
121		. . . (1.0) um you know what I mean,
122		er,

In line 117 the metaphor *the big political picture* is produced. To identify the topic of this metaphor, we work backwards and forwards in the local discourse activity looking for topic-related talk. First of all, the topic-related word *political* occurs inside the metaphor phrase, and shows that the metaphor concerns politics in some, unspecified, way. The premodifier *political* is developed with more precise examples of political entities: *the IRA* (118), *the war* (120). Working backwards, we find two uses of the pronoun *it* in lines 115 and 116 that seem to connect to the metaphor topic. There is no explicit noun phrase in the preceding talk that this pronoun overtly refers to; rather, it seems as if *it* is being used as a general pronoun to cover Jo's ideas around meeting Pat. A further clue comes from the either-or question in lines 115 and 116, where a contrast is made between *individuals* and *the big political picture,* suggesting that the *big picture* is not about *individuals* but about social groups. We can find no single lexical item that can be said to be the metaphor topic relating to the vehicle *the big . . . picture;* instead we have a collection of topic-related references [*it / (not) individuals / political / the IRA / the war*]. When these references are put together, the researcher can infer a discourse topic that is something like 'an understanding of the Irish political situation'.

Jo, as addressee of this talk, must interpret the metaphorical expression *the big political picture* on the basis of these clues and how they fit into her ongoing understanding of the discourse activity. The interpretive steps made by participants come from 'inside' the talking-and-thinking, as they make sense of the talk through their embodied minds (as in figure 2.1). Because each person and their experience are unique, what is interpreted can never completely match what was intended. The best that two humans in communication can achieve is a workable approximation of intersubjectivity. Differences in linguistic and other resources available for interpretation may sometimes lead to problematic differences in understandings. The implicit nature of metaphor topics can contribute to misunderstanding or confusion for speakers (Cameron, 2003).

For researchers, identifying key discourse or metaphor topics is usually an interpretive move. Interpretation by the researcher is unavoidable in the study of metaphor, and, rather than avoiding it, we need to take precautions to guide and control it. The precautions that are appropriate in taking this particular interpretive step, and others, are to stay close to the actual data, and to have support from the data for each part of the interpretation.[6]

To identify key discourse topics, we asked, for each vehicle, 'What topic is the metaphor used to talk about?' Across the data, this produced the set of topics displayed in figure 3.1. 'Understanding the Other' is placed centrally and at the top to indicate its importance in the study of empathy. Both speakers spoke about all of these topics. There were also topics that pertained mainly to one or other of the speakers. Pat was the

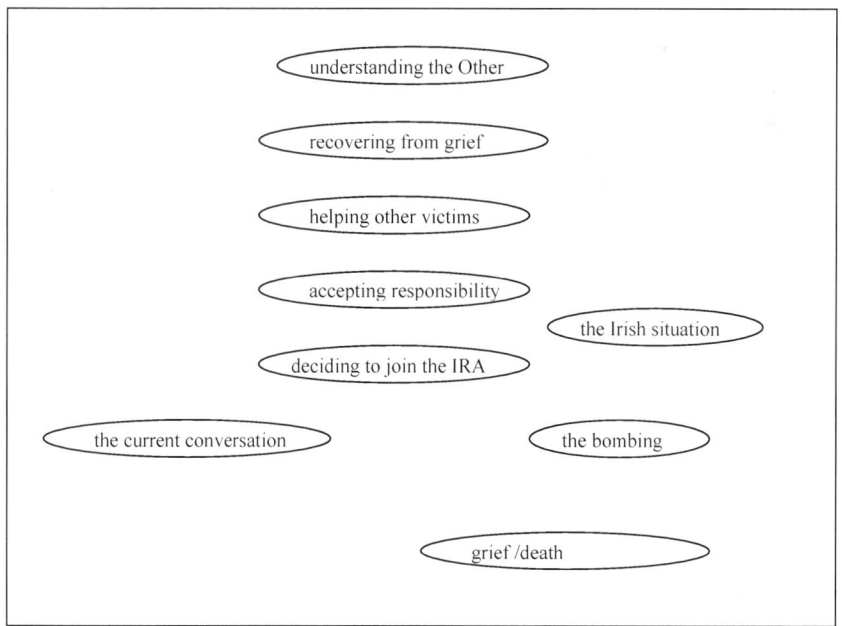

Figure 3.1   Key discourse topics in the conciliation conversations.

main speaker on the topic of his decision to join the IRA, for example, while Jo spoke of the impact of her father's death on various members of her family.

The same set of topics appeared in all the discourse events, but with somewhat different emphases. The topics broadened out as time passed, and attention shifted somewhat from Jo's and Pat's own experiences to those of other victims of violence and to wider conflict resolution issues.

TRACKING METAPHORS IN THE DISCOURSE DYNAMICS OF TALKING-AND-THINKING

The discourse dynamics approach seeks for patterns in metaphor use over time, holding that these can provide insights into people's ideas, attitudes and values, here into Pat's and Jo's changing understandings of each other. In chapter 2 we met three different types of change that occur in the complex dynamic system of talking-and-thinking:

- gradual change;
- sudden perturbation followed by new types of discourse activity;
- self-organising change over the longer timescales of discourse events.

The first two types of discourse activity occur on the 'local' or micro timescale, while the third emerges over a longer timescale.

Metaphor analysis contributes to understanding the discourse activity of each of these:

- analysis of how metaphors connect to each other in episodes of gradual change and what is developed through the talking-and-thinking in these periods;
- analysis of how metaphor contributes to sudden perturbations in the discourse and what emerges from these perturbations;
- analysis of self-organising systems of metaphor that emerge over multiple phases of stable, gradually changing talking-and-thinking.

The various strands of metaphor analysis work together in practice but will be outlined separately in the following sections. What happens on the local level, at the timescale of 'the moment of talk', is where metaphor analysis begins.

Discourse Activity Metaphor in Periods of Gradual Change

In a stable phase of activity, the discourse system of talking-and-thinking changes gradually. Talk produced in this mode comes in what we can call 'continuity episodes'. Analysis of such episodes shows that they feature discourse activity such as explaining, reflecting and questioning. In continuity episodes, Jo and Pat ask about and tell each other:

- this is how it seemed to be at the time / how it seems to be now
- this is how I was then / how I am now
- this is how I see you / the situation / myself.

Continuity episodes of discourse activity occupy a timescale of seconds, sometimes up to a couple of minutes. To use a metaphor to describe continuity episodes, this mode of talking-and-thinking offers the Other contributions towards conciliation, putting them on the table, and hoping they will be accepted. These contributions are generally presented sensitively and cautiously, taking account of the Other's feelings, and so in themselves are gestures of empathy.

Metaphor analysis uncovers the many functions that metaphor offers in these continuity episodes. Metaphor helps a speaker finds ways to describe themselves, their experiences and their feelings. More than that, metaphors can show how these descriptions are designed with the other person in mind, i.e. dialogically: for example, using a metaphor that was previously used by the other can create some temporary solidarity prior to asking a confrontational question. Metaphor is often used in the coda of an explanation or narrative, to summarise the main point while also summarising the speaker's attitudes and values in respect of the content. The movement of metaphors across speakers in continuity episodes is particularly interesting in the study of developing empathy.

Metaphor analysis of continuity episodes makes use of a typology of metaphor shifting (Cameron, 2008) to help understand how changes in ideas, attitudes and values are gradually taking place. Metaphor shifting concerns the small range of possible changes that can follow the first mention of a metaphor in an episode. To see examples of 'metaphor shifting' in local discourse dynamics, we can look back at extract 3.1, where the metaphor of *see the big political picture* to mean an understanding of the Irish political situation was gradually 'soft assembled'[7] by Pat across several intonation units. In talking-and-thinking, a speaker continuously selects from and adapts resources, which include metaphor, to meet the local and immediate demands of the conversation. Sometimes this involves repeating or reformulating metaphor vehicles, as when Pat repeats the metaphor vehicle *see* and then develops it into *the big political picture*. Jo uses a different form of the verb *see* in her response to Pat's question, saying: *I saw it as both*.

Repetition and reformulation of metaphors are examples of 'vehicle development', which can also feature explication of the vehicle or introduction of a contrasting vehicle. Two other kinds of metaphor shifting are identified in local discourse dynamics: 'vehicle redeployment' and 'vehicle literalisation' (Cameron, 2008). An example of vehicle redeployment occurred in extract 2.1, when *journey* metaphors were first used to talk about conciliation, as in *the end of that journey,* and then about the idea of meeting Pat that *just came in a moment and then went away.*

Vehicle development is the process in which, after a vehicle has been introduced into the discourse, it is extended or modified through repetition, reformulation, explication or contrast (Cameron, 2003, 2008; Goatly, 1997; Steen, 1992). Even though it may look as if an identical metaphorical phrase is repeated, as with *did you see . . . did you see* (extract 3.1, 115–16), from a complexity perspective, each assembling of words and ideas is unique because it occurs at a different point in time.[8]

A further example of vehicle repetition can be seen in extract 3.2, from the later conversation. The *whole picture* metaphor has here been redeployed to a different topic: the understanding of the Other in conflict.

Extract 3.2   Redeployment of the *picture* metaphor vehicle:

2–732 Pat	it's never <u>the whole picture</u>.
733	. . . it's never <u>the whole picture</u>.
734	. . . that's why,
735	you know,
736	<u>on reflection</u> you--
737	. . sometimes you <u>get</u> a--
738	like a <u>glimpse</u>.
739	even <u>in the midst of</u>--
740	er,
741	a lot of <u>struggle</u>.
742	. . of the other person's humanity.

Extract 3.2 contains a nice example of metaphor shifting by contrast, where one metaphor is followed by another that expresses an antonymic or contrasting meaning: *never the whole picture* is followed by *sometimes a glimpse* (737), with a contrast in both the adverb (*never/sometimes*) and the metaphor (*the whole picture/a glimpse*). The meaning of the talking-and-thinking in lines 732 and 733 is gradually shaped by the first mention and the contrast. Metaphor contrasts are found to be an important type of vehicle development in the conciliation talk, and will be shown to enable several significant types of discourse activity.

The third type of metaphor shifting, described as vehicle literalisation, may be better understood as the interplay between the metaphorical and the literal, usually physical, world (Cameron, in press; Goatly, 1997). In vehicle literalisation, a metaphor vehicle may be used in a non-figurative sense, in a shift from metaphorical to literal. An example was noted in extract 2.1, where *the end of the journey* was literalised to *sitting down and talking*. In the other direction, a shift to the metaphorical can take place, in a process of 'metaphorising' or 'symbolising'. Sometimes, it is difficult to separate literalising and symbolising, and it is more accurately described as an interplay between the metaphorical and the literal. In Jo's description of how she saw *the end of the journey*, the literalising shift to *sitting down and talking* seems, at the same time, to create a symbolic resonance around the physical act of *sitting down*. The physical world, in particular, is tightly connected into the metaphorical in the conciliation talk, particularly in Pat's talk. The conflict in Ireland was about national allegiances and thus about territory; in the 1970s, it was manifested on the streets of cities, where different sides held power over different areas, erected barriers to keep the other out, and where the British army was sent to take control. The interplay of metaphor and physical place—or what we might call 'the poetics of place'[9]—will be an important feature in the analysis of metaphor as discourse activity.

Identifying the nature of metaphor shifting in continuity episodes can help understand the local discourse dynamics of the system of talking-and-thinking in its stable phases. As we saw in chapter 2, the metaphors in episodes of talk sometimes connect together into coherent local scenarios. The dialogics of metaphor in these episodes is also telling—how metaphors of the Other are used, or not used, or adapted, can shed light on the development of empathy.

Metaphor analysis examines episodes of continuity talking-and-thinking from all these aspects to see how metaphor contributes to explanations, questioning and reflections, and how the talking-and-thinking cumulatively builds conciliation and empathy.

Metaphor in Perturbation Events

Stable phases of continuity talking-and-thinking do not continue indefinitely. They are interrupted by mundane events like running out of time, or by more interesting events such as the perturbation described at the end of chapter 2, when Pat suddenly *changed hats* to acknowledge the personal as well as the political, and the talk moved abruptly into a different phase.

Other 'perturbation events' in the discourse activity, and that are discussed in later chapters, include:

- Jo reading aloud a poem she had written to Pat;
- a narrative told by Jo about her daughter's reaction to her meeting Pat;
- direct questions asked by Jo about Pat's use of violence;
- Pat accepting responsibility for the human consequences of the bombing;

- Jo accepting a degree of responsibility for the political causes of the Irish conflict;
- narratives told by Pat about being detained by the British army as a young man.

Perturbation events are not the gentle offerings of continuity episodes but something more violent and confrontational. Responding to them requires some strength, and they characterise different kinds of acts of empathy. Responding, rather than avoiding response, often takes the discourse in new directions, back into more stable phases of continuity talking-and-thinking but changed by the perturbation. A perturbation event may be remembered and recalled in later conversations, as happens with Jo's narrative about her daughter (chapter 8).

Perturbation events are not hard to identify in talk, as alongside their content and response, they are marked by prosodic features, pausing and hesitations, and often by intensive use of metaphor, or by almost complete absence of metaphor (chapter 6).

Analysis of the distribution of metaphors across the talk reveals where metaphors are particularly heavily used. These episodes are 'metaphor clusters' (Cameron and Stelma, 2004). Metaphor clusters quite often signal critical moments in the talk, and so can sometimes take the researcher straight to incidents that disrupted the discourse in some way. As we see in chapters 7 and 8, narratives in which metaphor is scarcely used at all can also bring about perturbations in the talking-and-thinking.

Systems of Metaphor over Longer Timescales

When we analyse metaphor use across discourse events, in both continuity talk and perturbation events, we find multiple uses of connected metaphors. For example, more than 170 instances of metaphors relating to *journey* were identified in the first conversation, including metaphorical uses of the verbs *come* and *go* and metaphorically used nouns such as *situation, position* and *way*.

Metaphor analysis brings connected metaphors together and considers them across the longer timescale of months and years to reveal emergent patterns in talking-and-thinking. This technique is inspired by the central idea underpinning conceptual metaphor theory, that metaphors in language and thought are systematically patterned, but is adjusted for the discourse dynamics approach by being combined with ideas of interaction and emergence across timescales. Semantically connected metaphors, each a unique instance of discourse activity used at a specific time, are grouped together, forming both a grouping and a trajectory. The grouping of connected metaphors is called a 'systematic metaphor trajectory'.[10]

The systematic metaphor trajectories produced as an outcome of this strand of metaphor analysis are long term evolving patterns that, together with analyses of metaphor in continuity episodes and perturbation events, will help show how Jo's and Pat's ideas, attitudes and values change through the conciliation process. The remainder of the chapter explains the method of grouping metaphors into a systematic metaphor trajectory.

SYSTEMATIC METAPHOR TRAJECTORIES

The first step in grouping metaphors across time is to code vehicles by their semantic content, their more basic or physical meaning. After that, within each collected grouping of vehicles, a further sub-grouping is carried out, this time by key discourse topic. The outcome of this process of grouping and sub-grouping is the set of metaphor trajectories or systematic metaphors (see also Cameron et al., 2009; Cameron, Maslen and Low, 2010).

Collecting Metaphor Vehicles Together into Groupings

When we first met Jo's use of *journey* metaphors in extract 2.1, we noted that her metaphors: *the end of the journey, bringing something out of, long . . . long, getting to that point* could be connected as relating to a broader semantic field of travelling over a physical landscape. These metaphor vehicles, and others from across the transcribed discourse event, were put into a larger grouping that was labelled JOURNEY.[11] Table 3.1 shows twenty of the over 300 JOURNEY metaphor vehicles extracted from the first conversation, with their intonation unit number showing the time at which they were produced.[12]

Collecting vehicles into groupings is done inductively, working up from the data, rather as in grounded theory approaches (e.g. Charmaz, 2001). Because the concern here is with specific and contextualised discourse activity and not, as in cognitive approaches, with making generalised hypotheses about human thinking, metaphor patterns are not generalised upwards away from the data more than is justified, and labels for groupings are, as far as possible, taken from the actual words that participants use. Thus, JOURNEY is preferred as a label for the metaphors in table 3.1, rather than a more generalised label, such as EVENT STRUCTURE, as might be used in cognitive metaphor theory. The additional formatting of the small capitals in italics represents the link back to the discourse data. More specific sub-trajectories will also be important (e.g. types of JOURNEYS are examined in the next chapter).

Grouping of vehicles is interpretive and flexible; there is no one 'right answer' waiting to be found and judgements must be made about how

Table 3.1   Example JOURNEY Metaphor Vehicles Used in the First Conversation

37	Pat	. . <u>saw</u> this as a journey etcetera.
93	Jo	was bring as much . . positive <u>out of</u> it as I could
202	Jo	. . <Q <u>walking</u> the <u>footsteps</u> of the bombers Q>,
264	Jo	. . and then .. that's the sort of a <u>journey</u> I have <u>been on.</u>
260	Jo	what is <u>going</u> on here,
275	Pat	. . . (1.0) <u>brought</u> us together,
410	Pat	. . . (1.0) <u>as far</u> that's --
493	Jo	and together we are <u>looking at ways</u> in which,
544	Pat	. . and a <u>cross over,</u>
549	Pat	. . . (2.0) <u>in any way</u> I can.
561	Pat	as <u>part of the journey.</u>
625	Jo	. . I <u>move</u> <u>from</u> us,
271	Pat	. . . (2.0) what was <u>my journey.</u>
319	Pat	. . . that was <u>the start of</u> . . <u>my journey.</u>
444	Pat	. . . (1.0) explain <u>my journey</u> to you,
1061	Pat	explanations of why I <u>got here.</u>
1087	Pat	I have to <u>stand over</u> them,
1097	Pat	there was <u>no other way.</u>
1184	Jo	. . . (1.0) very much <u>where you are coming from,</u>
1195	Jo	that's what <u>led to</u> Brighton.

best to group the metaphors on the basis of available evidence. The set of groupings evolves as the researcher works through the list of vehicles; each new addition may lead to adapting and adjusting the existing groups, and initial decisions remain open to revision until the latest stage of analysis. Initial groupings may be split into two separate trajectories: for example, HEARING/SAYING vehicles were initially grouped with SEEING/LOOKING vehicles as PERCEPTION but then separated out as it became clear that their differences were more important in the discourse activity than their similarities. Groupings may be sub-divided on a more temporary basis: for example, for some parts of the analysis, the JOURNEY grouping was split into MOVEMENT, SOURCE, GOAL, STAGES. A degree of overlap in vehicle groupings is unavoidable; for example, *coming face-to-face (with* consequences of violence*)* is a JOURNEY metaphor, but it is also a BODY metaphor where the phrase *face-to-face* has an important sense of embodied immediacy, possibly implying threat or danger. There is no reason why a metaphor cannot be placed in more than one grouping, but if quantitative comparisons are to be made then overlaps need to be clearly marked. Difficult grouping decisions were recorded in notes so that similar decisions were made for similar cases.

The purpose of grouping metaphor vehicles is to help the researcher make sense of the data by condensing it into meaningful metaphor trajectories. It is not claimed, unless there is evidence to back such claims, that the speakers themselves are aware of the metaphor trajectories. The process of deciding on groupings contributes importantly to the researcher's familiarity with the metaphor data. Although being rigorous is always a guiding principle, the grouping process is unavoidably hermeneutic, and its success depends upon combining imagination and creativity with as much methodological rigour or 'trustworthiness' (Lincoln and Guba, 2001) as possible.

Nineteen vehicle groupings proved sufficient to cover the metaphors used in the conversations, and these are listed in table 3.2.

Table 3.2   Metaphor Vehicle Groupings Used in the Analysis

JOURNEY (including SOURCE, PATH, GOAL, LOCATION, OBSTACLES)

WATER (including SEA)

LARGE SCALE

SEEING (including LOOKING)

HEARING / SAYING

SEPARATION / CONNECTION (including OPEN, LOSS)

PHYSICAL ACTION (excluding VIOLENT OR NEGATIVE PHYSICAL ACTION)

VIOLENT OR NEGATIVE ACTION (including PAIN, MILITARY)

CULTURAL (including FICTION, PLAY, RELIGION)

VALUE (including MONEY, ACCOUNTING)

WORKING

TEXTILES

SCIENCE (including MACHINE, NATURE)

PARTS OF THE BODY

LIVING WITH (including KEEPING)

COMPONENT PARTS

THING

PREPOSITIONS

Other

These vehicle groupings will become familiar as the book proceeds, but comments are needed here on the final three. Although words like *something* and *anything* were marked as metaphor if they were used to refer to non-concrete entities such as ideas, they were left in the grouping THING and did not contribute further to the analysis here. Some prepositions, for example *behind,* were straightforward to put into a grouping (JOURNEY); the rest were left in their own grouping PREPOSITIONS. The final category of 'other' was for those that did not fit the rest of the groupings, with the usual principle applied of minimising this 'dustbin' category.

Bringing Vehicles Together by Topic

Once a vehicle grouping was formed and labelled, the metaphors inside were grouped according to their discourse topics into a metaphor trajectory. The metaphors in table 3.1 relate to two different key discourse topics: THE CONCILIATION PROCESS and DECIDING TO JOIN THE IRA.

Both Jo and Pat use some JOURNEY metaphors to speak of CONCILIATION:

37	Pat	. . <u>saw</u> this as a <u>journey</u> etcetera.
93	Jo	was <u>bring</u> as much . . positive <u>out of</u> it as I could
202	Jo	. . <Q <u>walking</u> the <u>footsteps</u> of the bombers Q>,
264	Jo	. . and then . . that's the sort of a <u>journey</u> I have <u>been on</u>.
260	Jo	what is <u>going on</u> here,
275	Pat	. . . (1.0) <u>brought</u> us together,
410	Pat	. . . (1.0) <u>as far</u> that's—
493	Jo	and together we are <u>looking at ways</u> in which,
544	Pat	. . and a <u>cross over</u>,
549	Pat	. . . (2.0) <u>in any way</u> I can.
561	Pat	as <u>part of the journey</u>.
625	Jo	. . I <u>move</u> <u>from</u> us,

Pat uses JOURNEY metaphors to talk about HIS DECISION TO JOIN THE IRA, and Jo adopts the same kind of metaphor when she refers to this part of Pat's life:

271	Pat	. . . (2.0) what was <u>my journey</u>.
319	Pat	. . . that was <u>the start of</u> . . <u>my journey</u>.
444	Pat	. . . (1.0) explain <u>my journey</u> to you,
1061	Pat	explanations of why I <u>got here.</u>
1087	Pat	I have to <u>stand over</u> them,
1097	Pat	there was <u>no other way</u>.
1184	Jo	. . . (1.0) very much <u>where you are coming from,</u>
1195	Jo	that's what <u>led to</u> Brighton.

Metaphor topics and vehicle groupings are brought together into a trajectory of systematically connected metaphors. The data from table 3.1 thus belong to two systematic metaphor trajectories: CONCILIATION AS A JOURNEY; DECIDING TO JOIN THE IRA AS A JOURNEY.

Choosing an Appropriate Label for a Metaphor Trajectory

Choosing an appropriate descriptor for a metaphor trajectory or systematic metaphor is a delicate process that can be illustrated with SEEING metaphors. Extracts 3.1 and 3.2 yielded a grouping of vehicles that were used with two discourse topics:

UNDERSTANDING THE IRISH SITUATION

1–115	did you <u>see</u> it as like individuals
1–116	or did you <u>see</u> it as a sort of a
1–117	. . . (1.0) <u>the big</u> political <u>picture</u>

UNDERSTANDING THE OTHER IN CONFLICT

2–732	it's never <u>the whole picture</u>
2–733	. . . it's never <u>the whole picture</u>
2–736	on <u>reflection</u> you
2–738	like a <u>glimpse</u>

Conceptual metaphor theory posits the generalised metaphor UNDERSTANDING IS SEEING and, at first sight, it might seem that this will fit both cases here. Certainly, the first set of metaphors seems to fit the label UNDERSTANDING THE IRISH SITUATION IS SEEING IT. The second set, however, has a more restricted sense of SEEING, contrasting *the whole picture* which is *never* seen with *a glimpse,* and it is this restricted or partial sense of SEEING that understanding of the Other may be based on. The significance of this restricted or partial sense to Jo and Pat's talking-and-thinking is reinforced by other metaphors in the set:

1–1358	Pat	would only <u>see</u> . . . the stereotypes.
1–1756	Pat	. . . (1.0) got a <u>distorted picture</u> of me.
1–2172	Pat	. . . failing to <u>see</u> their humanity.
1–2449	Pat	who I would've <u>seen clearly</u> as enemies
1–2729	Pat	it's a <u>reflection</u> of—
1–2739	Pat	to . . <u>reflect on</u> the past.
2–497	Pat	don't just <u>see</u> me as a perpetrator
2–848	Pat	. . to <u>lose sight of</u> the other person's humanity.
2–907	Pat	if you're not <u>seeing</u> a human being in front of you.
2–908	Pat	. . . if all you're <u>seeing</u> is an enemy
2–1487	Jo	. . . (1.0) our differences <u>disappear,</u>

An extract of talk in the radio interview, shown in extract 3.3, further confirms the importance of this restricted or partial sense of SEEING to conciliation and empathy:

Extract 3.3   PARTIAL SEEING of the Other as enemy (2003):

3–1137 Pat	until we do <u>see</u>
1138	each other
1139	<u>in our true light</u>
1140	or er in the sense our humanity
1141	you know
1142	we're always going to be <u>dealing with</u> some <u>reduction</u>
1143	or <u>a caricature</u>

An appropriate label for this metaphor trajectory is chosen to be: UNDERSTANDING THE OTHER IS CORRECTING A DISTORTED OR PARTIAL IMAGE OF THE OTHER. This label keeps the power of the metaphors active in the condensing of the set into a systematic metaphor, in a way that a more generalised label cannot.

Nine years after first meeting, Pat makes even stronger use of this systematic metaphor, as shown in extract 3.4. The dehumanising of the Other in times of conflict is explicitly spoken of as metaphorical VIOLENT ACTION that reduces vision, as *being forced to wear these blinkers* (791) reduces what can be seen of the Other to a *form* (802) or devoid of colour *in black and white* (792–93).

Extract 3.4   PARTIAL SEEING of the Other as enemy (2009):

4–791	you are <u>forced</u> to <u>wear these blinkers</u>.
792	and <u>see</u> the world <u>in very black an--</u>
793	<u>and white</u> terms.
794	<X I mean X>
795	that's totally,
796	the <u>opposite</u> of empathy.
797	I mean,
798	that is <u>closing</u> of aspects of,
799	the humanity of others.
800	<u>seeing</u> them,
801	<u>purely</u> in . . erm.
802	. . a dehumanised <u>form</u>.

In choosing and labelling systematic metaphors, the researcher has to decide on how to collect together connected metaphors to best reflect the discourse activity. It is not just a matter of putting together metaphors, but of assessing how the metaphors contribute to the discourse activity, keeping the collected set small enough to capture this but at the same time large enough to usefully condense the data. Thus in some instances, a single metaphor may be so important for the discourse activity that it should not be collected together with others.

Table 3.3   Most Frequent Systematic Metaphor Trajectories Across the Two
Conversations

UNDERSTANDING THE OTHER	AS	CONNECTING
		A JOURNEY
		CHANGING A PARTIAL OR DISTORTED IMAGE
		PHYSICAL ACTION
		VIOLENT OR NEGATIVE ACTION
UNDERSTANDING THE IRISH SITUATION	AS	A JOURNEY
		VIOLENT OR NEGATIVE ACTION
THE EMOTIONAL EFFECT OF THE BOMBING	AS	VIOLENT OR NEGATIVE ACTION
JOINING THE IRA	AS	A JOURNEY
ACCEPTING RESPONSIBILITY	AS	A JOURNEY
RECOVERING FROM GRIEF	AS	VIOLENT OR NEGATIVE ACTION
		A JOURNEY
HELPING OTHER VICTIMS OF VIOLENCE	AS	A JOURNEY

Metaphor Trajectories Across the Data

How then do metaphor trajectories, or systematic metaphors, once assembled, contribute understanding conciliation and the development of empathy?

Firstly, systematic metaphors give an overview of metaphorical ways of talking-and-thinking. The systematic metaphors in table 3.3 include the most frequently used metaphors in the conversations:

By looking across systematic metaphors, we can find out the range of metaphors used with any given discourse topic, and the scope of a particular vehicle type for being used as metaphor. The discourse topics with the widest range of metaphors relate to UNDERSTANDING THE OTHER, the central activity of the conciliation process and the core of empathy. The most fruitful semantic fields in terms of offering metaphor vehicles are JOURNEYS and VIOLENT OR NEGATIVE ACTION (e.g. *breaking down barriers*).

Figure 3.2 displays the systematic metaphors as links between the vehicle groupings and the key discourse topics.

More information is available from examining the detail of the individual metaphors that comprise the systematic metaphors. We can look inside to find out who uses the metaphors: who uses them first in the talk; how metaphors are picked up and used, or not, by the other speaker. Because metaphors remain attached to their discourse activity throughout the analysis, via their intonation unit and back into the transcript, we can also see change in the content, form and use of metaphors over time.

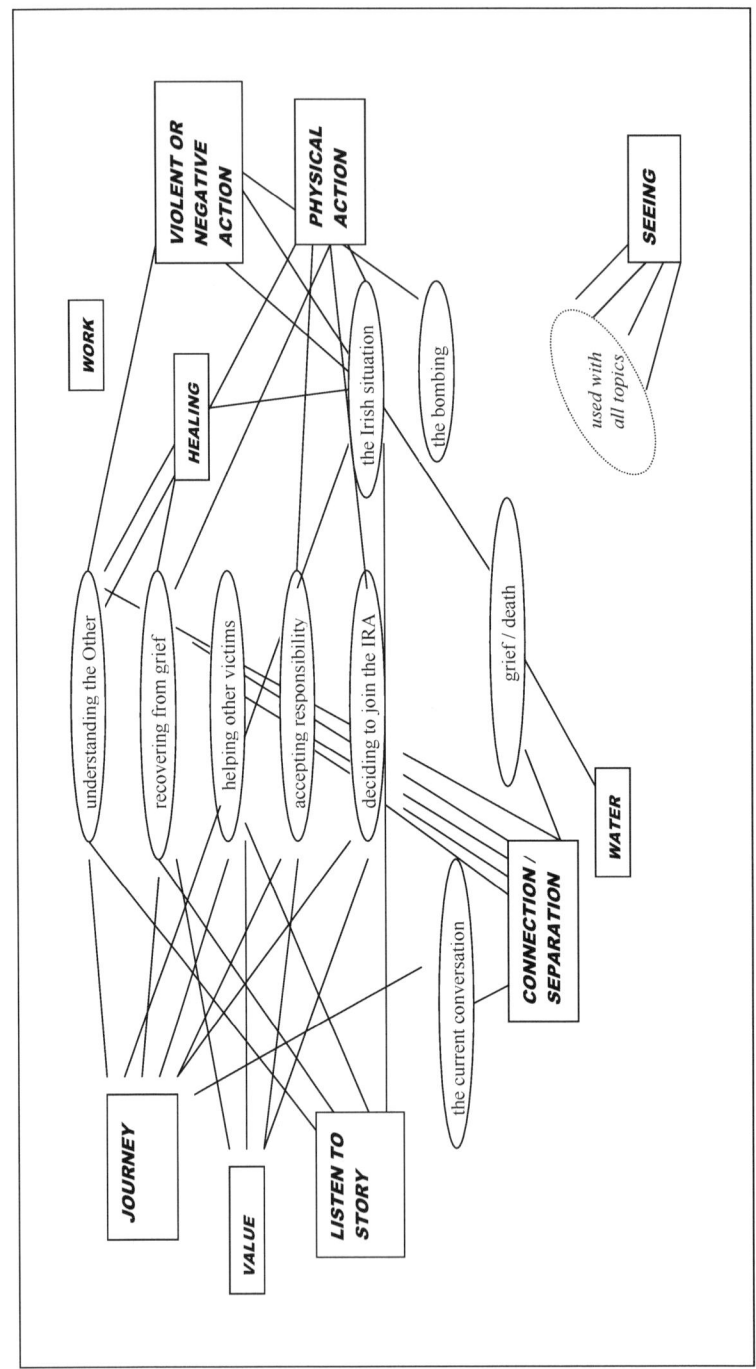

Figure 3.2   Systematic metaphors in the conversations.

USING SYSTEMATIC METAPHOR TRAJECTORIES TO EXPLORE THE DYNAMICS OF JO'S AND PAT'S MOTIVATIONS FOR MEETING

To close this chapter, we return to Jo's and Pat's motivations for meeting together, as seen in chapter 2, to examine the dynamics of the metaphors over the timescale from their first meeting to the radio interview, a period of two and a half years. Extracts 2.1 and 2.2 illustrated Jo's and Pat's initial descriptions of their motivations for participating in the conciliation process. At this point, Jo described the conciliation process in terms of JOURNEY metaphors, whereas Pat used metaphors of being *open* and explaining the *reasoning behind*. Examining how they spoke of motivations in later conversations, we find both stability and fluctuation in metaphor use.

Extract 3.5, from the conversation that took place on the occasion of Jo and Pat's fourth meeting, three months after extract 2.1, illustrates stability in Jo's metaphorical talking-and-thinking about why she wanted to meet Pat. She again describes her aim as *bringing something positive out of* the *tragedy* and *trauma* of her father's death:

Extract 3.5	Jo's motivation as reported in the second conversation, 2001:
2–294	. . . (1.0) that's a tragedy.
295	. . that's a <u>trauma</u>.
296	. . . and now,
297	. . how can I <u>bring something</u> positive <u>out of</u> this.
298	and that's been my--
299	. . . (2.0) whole intent,
300	. . . (1.0) literally,
301	since the day it happened.
302	. . . (1.0) only,
303	I didn't know what that meant then.
304	. . . (2.0) ehm,
305	it's been <u>a very long journey</u>,
306	. . <u>one step at a time</u>.

The specific systematic metaphor CONCILIATION IS A JOURNEY TO FIND SOMETHING POSITIVE continues to be developed, with a further use of *bring something positive out of* and *(a very long) journey*, along with an additional metaphor *one step at a time* (306), which describes the mode of the JOURNEY. There is no explicit reference here to the *end of the journey*, but later in the same conversation, Jo states her goal explicitly with the phrase *sit here with you* (extract 3.6, 1575). The phrase in extract 2.1 *sitting down and talking with the people who did it* has developed and been personalised in a further interplay of the physical and metaphorical.

Extract 3.6   Jo's goal as reported in the second conversation, 2001:

2–1570	. . . (3.0) that is <u>where</u> I wanted to g--
1571	. . <u>get to</u>.
1572	. . . (1.0) <u>at</u> the beginning.
1573	. . . (1.0) after the Brighton bomb.
1574	. . . (1.0) that's . . like . . . (1.0) been my goal.
1575	. . . (1.0) to be able to sit here with you.
1576	. . and it's <u>something</u> I want--
1577	I wanted this.
1578	. . . for [so] <u>long</u>.

Two years later, in the radio interview (extract 3.7), the first phrase is again used:

Extract 3.7   Jo's goal as reported in the radio interview, 2003:

3–89 Jo	I remember
90	<u>in</u> er,
91	the first few days after the bomb
92	just thinking
93	if only I could <u>bring something</u> positive <u>out of</u> this

and later in the interview she uses a *journey* metaphor to refer to coming to meet Pat:

424	this is just a very personal <u>journey</u>
425	I have <u>made</u>

The metaphor trajectory of CONCILIATION IS A JOURNEY TO FIND SOMETHING POS-ITIVE is thus added to and expanded in each discourse event. Later metaphors are very similar to earlier ones (*bring something positive out of it*), with some variations (*a very long/ personal journey*). By considering both the degree of variation and the trajectory over time within the systematic metaphor, a high level of stability is found in Jo's ideas, attitudes and values around her goal and motivation for participating in the conciliation process.

Alongside these JOURNEY metaphors, however, there was a change in the way Jo talks of her reasons for meeting Pat over the time frame of the study. Another systematic metaphor[13] gradually became more prominent: CON-CILIATION IS LISTENING TO THE OTHER'S STORY.

Extract 3.8   Jo's goal as <u>hearing a story</u>, 2003:

3–328	and I realised
329	I wanted to <u>hear</u> Pat's <u>story</u>
330	because I believe that
331	if anyone <u>opens up</u> and <u>shares</u> their <u>story</u>
332	ehm
333	it's very hard to hate

334	and my idea of Pat
335	was of someone
336	without much humanity
337	and I wanted to meet him
338	and <u>hear</u> his <u>story</u>
339	and <u>discover</u> his humanity
340	later on also <u>came</u> the idea that I wanted him
341	to <u>hear</u> my <u>story</u>

We will see later (in chapter 4) how the systematic metaphor CONCILIA-TION IS LISTENING TO THE OTHER'S STORY evolved over the course of the talk, and how it became an important way for both speakers of framing, not just conciliation, but other political processes too. Here, we note that it entered the conversations as an alternative metaphorical way of talking-and-thinking about conciliation and understanding the Other, and that the two metaphor trajectories overlap in the use of *discover* (339), which is here the outcome of *hearing his story* but might also be one candidate for the *something positive* that Jo seeks to find through conciliation.

Pat's talk in the radio interview (extract 3.9) develops his motivation for participating in the conciliation process from his republican identity, with the addition of a theatrical metaphor, and a glimpse of how his stance shifted when he met Jo, probably referring to the *changing* hats moment reported at the end of chapter 2.

Extract 3.9   Pat's report of his motivations, 2003:

3–381	I <u>felt</u> obliged
382	as a republican
383	to sit down and talk about that
384	and <u>against the backdrop</u> of the political reasons
385	<u>given a platform</u>
386	for a republican <u>message</u>
387	that had been censored for decades
388	so
389	when <u>offered</u> an opportunity
390	to sit down
391	and talk about
392	what motivated you
393	then you should
394	avail of that
395	so that's the <u>way</u> I <u>walked into</u> it
396	but as I said
397	when you meet somebody
398	who's so <u>open</u>
399	to understanding your <u>perspective</u>
400	then you're obliged to somehow reciprocate

The explanation of extract 2.2 has here become *a message* (386) to be delivered from *a platform* (385) *against a backdrop* (384). The THEATRE metaphor fits with, and helps to construct, Pat's sometimes impersonal, indirect style. Pat's early adjustment in his discourse identity, described at the end of chapter 2, is spoken of in the last five lines as *reciprocating* Jo's *open* approach.

We can note an intensive interplay of the metaphorical and physical in lines 390–97. The metonymy of *sit down and talk* is used for the conciliation process in 390; in a coda in 395, metaphors of *way* and *walked into* summarise his position as he prepared to meet Jo; the literal *meet* reverts back to the physical world but seems to have a meaning that is more than literal, is somewhat figurative or symbolic, in which the meeting of two people represents a meeting of all that those people have experienced and carry with them.

This section has followed the trajectory of metaphors used to reported Jo's and Pat's feelings and motivations as the conciliation process began. They arrived at their first meeting with differing intentions as to what might happen; in the first meeting, Pat changed his stance and subsequent discourse identity. Their metaphors from this point are remarkably stable, changing very little in form and reference over the timescale of the data. The content of the talk in the dataset will be seen to result, at least in part, from these differing starting points. Change is seen in the use of two key words that appear in the talk from the start and frequently throughout: *story* and *open*. (These are examined in more depth in chapters 4 and 6.) In each case, the scope of the term broadens over time as the words are used in more situations or to refer to a wider range of people. While the words and phrases that express individual identity offer stability, these seem to offer a kind of bounded variability and flexibility.

CONCLUSION: METAPHOR ANALYSIS, CONCILIATION AND EMPATHY

To understand how metaphor contributes to the process of conciliation, we have to connect what happens minute by minute with longer term changes in the understandings of the speakers. In a complex system, small moves and changes can lead to large effects because of the multiple non-linear connections between elements of the system. It is not always clear which changes will have such an impact, but with data covering a significant period of time, we can look back and trace the origins of major shifts that have become apparent over time.

Metaphor analysis has been developed as a discourse dynamics methodology which moves across various scales of talk, from the intonation unit through episodes inside a single conversation to the series of conversations over the years. A thorough understanding of local dynamics is needed: what happens to metaphors as they enter the flow of talk; gestures of empathy made towards the Other; the stance of participants towards the discourse activity. By understanding how metaphor is used at the detailed micro level, patterns of change in the system of talking-and-thinking can be identified from a higher level. If major shifts occur, explanations can be constructed by tracing the change back through the system to the local level.

This chapter has introduced the basic tools and techniques of metaphor analysis, used to investigate how metaphors shift and change in the course of talking-and-thinking. Metaphors at the micro level are identified through the appearance of vehicle terms in the topic flow. The local discourse dynamics produce shifts in metaphors that can be collected together into systematic metaphors through processes of vehicle grouping and grouping by topic. Systematic metaphors, as sets and trajectories of connected metaphors, offer both a summary of metaphor use and a resource for further interrogation of the data.

The next two chapters delve more deeply into the systematic metaphor trajectories of talking-and-thinking about the conciliation process.

4 Conciliation as *JOURNEYS OF UNDERSTANDING* and *LISTENING TO STORIES*

> and in a way
> we're still looking,
> to try to understand it.
> because it is--
> does feel like
> something new.
> it's almost like an experiment
> —Jo Berry (speaking about the conciliation process, 2009)

In chapter 2, we saw that two levels of conciliation are enacted in the talking-and-thinking of Jo Berry and Pat Magee when they come face-to-face. In their talk about the conciliation process, the process itself becomes the discourse topic, as in the opening extract. They also 'do' conciliation in the sense that their discourse activity works towards increasing understandings of each other. And of course both of these levels can be enacted in a single utterance. This chapter focuses on two systematic metaphors that came to frame the conciliation process.

Systematic patterns of metaphors, found through metaphor analysis, let us see Jo's and Pat's emerging understandings of the conciliation process that they are engaging in. In their early conversations they talk about the impact of meeting each other; in later discourse events, they often reflect on the initial meeting three years and nine years later. What we are calling 'the conciliation process' was, as Jo says, "something new"; there was no tried and tested pattern or formula for them to follow. The Glencree Centre for Peace and Reconciliation[1] had held events for victims of violence in Ireland, that Jo had attended before she met Pat, but one-to-one meetings were much more unusual. Metaphor was probably helpful in finding ways to talk about a process that was unknowable in advance. The conciliation process, and the metaphors used to talk about it, evolved through engaging in the conciliation process, in a cycle of interaction across timescales. Metaphors that they found useful to talk and think about what they were doing are likely, in turn, to have influenced that activity. The conciliation process continues still to evolve as Jo and Pat continue to meet and explore the alterity between them.

Four systematic metaphors were found to be significant in framing talking-and-thinking about the evolving conciliation process (Cameron, 2007b):

- *JOURNEYS*
- *LISTENING TO THE OTHER'S STORY*
- *CHANGING A PARTIAL OR DISTORTED IMAGE OF THE OTHER*
- *CONNECTING WITH THE OTHER.*

In chapter 3, metaphors that contributed to the systematic metaphor trajectory of *UNDERSTANDING THE OTHER AS CHANGING A PARTIAL OR DISTORTED IMAGE* were shown. This chapter takes the most frequent, *THE CONCILIATION PROCESS AS A JOURNEY*, and examines how *JOURNEY* metaphors contribute to the processes of developing empathy. It then describes how the metaphor of *LISTENING TO THE OTHER'S STORY* entered the discourse alongside *JOURNEY* metaphors. The *CONNECTION* framing metaphor will be discussed in chapter 6.

THE CONCILIATION PROCESS AS MULTIPLE JOURNEYS

When identified metaphors were grouped by their vehicle meaning, it was quickly obvious that *JOURNEY* metaphors proliferated, and that they were important to the talking-and-thinking about what was happening in the meetings and beyond:

Extract 4.1	The conciliation process described as a journey:
1–35 Pat	I was aware from speaking to certain people,
36	. . . (1.0) how . . . y- you--
37	. . <u>saw</u> this as a <u>journey</u> etcetera.
1573 Jo	. . and your commitment to . . <u>go on this journey with me</u>.

As can be seen in extract 4.1, Jo and Pat did not just talk about the conciliation process 'in terms of' a journey but also used the actual word *journey* to describe the process and parts of it. Consequently, *JOURNEY* was selected as a label for the systematic metaphor trajectory that collects together related metaphors used in talk.

JOURNEY metaphors are highly conventionalised and frequently used in English to talk about all kinds of processes. They feature strongly in the poetics of place that haunts everyday discourse. Talking in terms of metaphorical *JOURNEYS* has become part of our socio-cultural heritage but is also closely connected to embodied experience, in which moving from place to place is how we survive and live our lives. When journeys are used to talk metaphorically about careers, relationships or other parts of a life, the rich experiences and vocabulary relating to movement from one place to another are available for talking-and-thinking about the topic. These include the idea that a traveller begins a journey in one place and moves to another place along a path or a road, experiencing difficulties or delights en route. Cognitive metaphor theory describes this as the SOURCE-PATH-GOAL structure of the EVENT STRUCTURE metaphor (Gibbs, 1994; Lakoff, 1993). JOURNEY metaphors also bring affective content to the discourse. Attitudes and values associated with JOURNEYS include the bravery required to overcome obstacles on the way, and the achievement or relief felt on arriving at one's goal. More subtly but significantly, the emotional correlates of physical activity often come to be associated with the metaphor topic through the embodied experience that the language of JOURNEY metaphors may simulate. When walking for example, tension is decreased and people find it easier to talk with companions, perhaps because gaze is directed ahead rather than directly at the other and because the rhythm of walking encourages speech. As described in Chapter 1, neuroscience is beginning to explain how, through mental simulations, one person's talk of actions and physicality can have an effect on the listening Other. Close examination of the JOURNEY metaphors therefore includes checking which aspects of journeys are used metaphorically and what kinds of affect may be evoked.

The following box contains a synthesis or summary of how Jo and Pat use systematic JOURNEY metaphors to talk about the conciliation process and about other aspects of their lives (adapted from Cameron, 2007b).

After the Brighton bombing, Jo and Pat complete separate journeys, long and on foot, until they meet face-to-face and try to understand each other. Jo's journey has the aim of understanding the roots of violence and is a long, uphill journey on foot, sometimes following the path of journeys made by the bombers, sometimes stopping to meet other victims. The journey out of grief becomes a healing process.

Pat does not talk much about his life between the bombing and the meeting, but speaks of an earlier journey when, as a young man, he joined the IRA and agreed to use violence.

When Jo and Pat meet and sit down to talk to each other, it is, for both and in different ways, a momentous point in their journeys. It is not, however, where the journeys end; rather it is a new starting point. For Pat, meeting Jo is a confrontation with an unavoidable obstacle, the consequences of his actions. He will have to face this and cannot walk away from it.

JOURNEYS TO THE FIRST MEETING

This section explores the separate journeys that Pat and Jo describe as taking place before or leading to their first meeting.

Jo's *JOURNEY OF UNDERSTANDING*

Jo applied *JOURNEY* metaphors to two interconnected discourse topics. She is engaged in an *inner journey* of coping with the grief caused by her father's death. She chooses to deal with her grief by undertaking a second *JOURNEY* that she calls *walking the footsteps of the bombers* (1–202) in which she tries to understand the roots of violence and what motivated Pat's actions.

Out of the many aspects of *JOURNEYS* available for metaphorical use, including the SOURCE-PATH-GOAL structure, Jo's and Pat's metaphors for the conciliation process are concentrated into certain corners of the semantic and lexical fields. Jo uses *JOURNEY* metaphors to focus in particular on the *PATH*, both on the manner of moving, and on the various staging or stopping *PLACES* along the *PATH*. Both of her key *JOURNEYS* are spoken of as long and difficult, e.g.:

1–1912   there's another <u>mountain to climb</u> now

with frequent uses of *steps* and *footsteps* suggesting a *JOURNEY ON FOOT*, that by implication requires effort and can be exhausting:

2–306   <u>one step</u> at a time

The metaphorical *JOURNEY* to try to understand Pat's perspective involved non-metaphorical, physical journeys from England to Northern Ireland to meet other victims and, eventually, members of the political organisation, the provisional IRA. Both physical and metaphorical *JOURNEYS* include a range of staging places and encounters with people on the way to the first meeting with Pat Magee.

Extract 4.2 shows Jo talking about a non-metaphorical journey she made to Ireland in 1985, and reflecting, as she does several times in the data, on how she was helped by talking to the people she met. Line 1347 makes reference to her metaphorical *JOURNEY* of coming to understand the Irish situation, and in line 1355 she speaks of how it felt to meet other victims of violence as *I've come home*. The emotional journey and the physical journey seem to overlap in the poetics of place, both taking her to a place, spoken of as *here* in 1359, where she feels understood and, from the positive attitudes and values attached to the idea of *home*, safe and welcomed.

Extract 4.2   Meeting other people involved in conflict as *coming home:*

1–1346 Jo	. . . (1.0) I've been fortunate,
1347	to meet so many people <u>on the way</u>,
1348	to--
1349	. . . to help me.
1350	. . . (1.0) I . . . first . . came to Northern Ireland <u>in</u> '85.
1351	. . . beginning of '85.
1352	. . . (1.0) and,
1353	. . . (2.0) when I arrived,
1354	I'd such a <u>feeling</u> of,
1355	. . . (2.0) I've <u>come home</u>.
1356	. . which might seem an odd <u>feeling</u>.
1357	. . . but I <u>felt</u>,
1358	. . . (1.0) [I'm]--
1359	[[I'm understood here]].

Jo's JOURNEYS out of grief and towards understanding of the violence are difficult, and the meetings and places along the route offer insights, comfort and reassurance, which in turn give strength for the ongoing journey towards empathy. Being understood by people who share something of her experience helps her in coming to understand the world of the Other that she cannot ever share, reducing alterity while maintaining the distance of history. Extract 4.3 describes how the physical places that she visits may help develop empathy with the Other, coming to understand his *very different reality* (extract 4.3, 146), in which her father became a *target* (149) rather than a real person.

Extract 4.3   A journey of understanding:

4–133 Jo	. . places I went to,
134	was like a war zone.
135	and it was--
136	it was--
137	. . the army was stopping me all the time,
138	. . erm.
139	I was going to places where I was--
140	. . erm.
141	I was <u>at</u> risk if I--
142	if I spoke.
143	<X you know X>
144	it was,
145	a very different reality.
146	. . but I began to meet people who,
147	. . could,
148	help me understand,
149	. . why my father'd been a <u>target</u>.

150	<X you know X>
151	and . . erm.
152	. . and it was the beginning of--
153	<X sort of X>
154	a <u>journey</u> of understanding.

PAT'S JOURNEYS BEFORE MEETING JO

Places, their role in his life choices and their affective load, make forceful appearances in Pat's talk too. As the perpetrator of the violence that led to Jo's father's death, the conciliation process requires Pat to explain the background to the conflict and to his decisions. Jo asks him explicitly to tell her about why he joined the IRA and how he came to decide the violence was the only solution to political problems. His discourse task is to make his account accessible, appropriate and convincing. Metaphor is one of the tools he has available to help in this task.

Some of Pat's *JOURNEY* metaphors are used in speaking about Jo's experiences or thinking (as in extract 4.1), but many are also used in talk about his own experience, particularly his decision as a young man, returned from England to Belfast, to join the IRA (extract 4.4). Physical places intersect with the metaphorical *journey* in which Pat moves across the social landscape to *join* the organisation that he describes as *the republican movement* (2–2984).

In the introduction to this chapter, I mentioned how *JOURNEY* metaphors key into our real embodied experience. Sometimes this 'keying in' is so tight as to blur the boundary between the literal physical world and the metaphorical world. Extract 4.4 describes something of Pat's physical world at the time of his decision to join the IRA where British soldiers stood *on your corner* (316) with guns, and armoured cars patrolled the roads and flats (307) of the area of Belfast.

Extract 4.4	Place and the Irish conflict:
1–296 Pat	. . . (1.0) and it seemed to me <u>at</u> the time,
297	and I am talking about the early '70s.
298	that er,
299	. . . (1.0) there--
300	there were <u>no avenues open</u>.
301	. . certainly <u>no avenues open</u> to people living in areas like,
302	the--
303	er,
304	. . . (1.0) New Lodge Road.
305	. . . er,
306	. . Ardoyne.
307	. . Unity Flats as it was then.

308	. . . (2.0) I mean,
309	if you were there . . then,
310	. . . (1.0) it would have been the most--
311	er,
312	. . . natural <u>thing in</u> the world,
313	. . . (1.0) to <u>come to</u> the realisation,
314	that you had to,
315	. . . (1.0) fight the British state.
316	. . . (1.0) because it was on your corner.
317	. . it was the oppression <u>around</u> you.
318	. . . (1.0) and er--
319	. . . that was <u>the start of . . my journey.</u>
320	<u>coming to</u> that realisation.

In the poetic dynamics of place, the topic domain of the streets of Belfast seems to provide or prime the metaphor vehicle *no avenues open,* used in line 300 to refer to the perceived lack of a political voice for republicans at the time, but resonating with the literal idea of street barricades built by both republicans and loyalists to keep out the army and the other side.

Pat's metaphorical *journey* towards the IRA and violence (319) was supported by the physical situation he found in Belfast. Pat's description of the physical situation uses metonymy: soldiers are referred to as *the British state* and their unwelcome presence on neighbourhood streets as *on your corner* (31516). The use of the phrase *on your corner* recreates the sense of threat that people felt by contrasting the humble location, with its conventional expectations of peaceful neighbourly encounters, with what they found there instead, the faceless, enormous and powerful presence evoked by the phrase *the British state.* Metaphor is used to speak of *oppression* as physically present *around you* (317). He explains to Jo how these physical effects made fighting seem like *the most natural thing in the world* (310–12).

Part of what Jo needs to understand about Pat's world is how the physical realities of 1970s Belfast contributed to his decision to join the IRA. Engaging in talking-and-thinking with this poetics of place (the interplay between the physical, literal and the metaphorical), particularly around the topic of troubled city streets, may connect with her own experiences in Ireland and to both aspects of empathy: the emotional attunement and the more deliberate understanding of his perspective. This is a theme that will recur.

THE FIRST MEETING

The individual JOURNEYS of Jo and Pat intersected when they eventually managed to meet in 2000. Setting up their meeting had taken some time because of various communication problems but when they did at last meet, it was an overwhelming experience. Coming face-to-face with a living human being forces an acknowledgement of shared humanity; the physical presence of the Other denies earlier reductions to a *figure* or dehumanised *target*. The quality of their talking-and-thinking determined how deep that acknowledgement would go and how effective the outcomes would be towards empathy.

The first meeting and their talk together has an impact on all that happens afterwards. In complexity terms, their meeting is a major 'perturbation' in the dynamic systems of Jo and Pat's discourse and thinking, shifting the systems radically to different areas of their phase space landscapes. From these new places arise the possibilities of new phases of empathy and conciliation, described in terms of new JOURNEYS and with quite different metaphors.

The first meeting is a site of multiple intersections. Jo's and Pat's individual and separate metaphorical JOURNEYS intersect at this point. Non-metaphorical physical journeys intersect with metaphorical JOURNEYS, and once again the physical space intersects with the affective, as the simple kitchen table at which they first meet contrasts fiercely for Pat with the complicated emotions underlying their presence there. In extract 4.5 Pat explains in the radio interview what it felt like to meet Jo. Very few metaphors are used here. The simplicity of the physical place of the meeting is emphasised as a *wee kitchen* and, just as Jo had envisioned as the end of her journey in extract 2.1, there is mention of the fact that they were *sitting* together. As Pat speaks, he seems to focus the impact of the meeting into the contrast between the simplicity of the scene in the kitchen and the emotional depth and drama internal to each of them.

Extract 4.5   Sitting in the kitchen:

3–547	Pat	but
548		beforehand
549		I thought I'd be there
550		I wouldn't say simple <XX>
551		I'd be there
552		explaining my motivations
553		to somebody I--
554		I was told
555		wanted to hear them.
556		I didn't really <u>see beyond</u> that.
557		but as I said,
558		suddenly <X you're X> <u>in</u> the presence of somebody
559		who you've <u>hurt</u>,
560		you know
561		er,
562		I'm sitting there beside the woman
563		whose father I have killed
564		and at that time I was sitting

565	in this wee kitchen
566	talking to this woman for the first time
567	whose father's dead.
568	I was aware of
569	I have responsibility for that
570	and the other victims of that IRA operation,
571	but you're there,
572	meeting this person.
573	that does change <u>things</u>

Between lines 558 and 572, Pat speaks four times about meeting Jo as a person. He had not anticipated the impact of meeting someone he had caused harm to (556). When it happens, it gives him a huge jolt, reflected in his reformulation of the idea in recounting it in the interview. The first time, in lines 558–59, he uses the pronoun *you* and the vague *somebody*. The second time, 562–63, *you* becomes *I*, *somebody* becomes *the woman*, and *you've hurt* becomes the much more direct *whose father I have killed*. The third time, 564–67, he expands *sitting beside* to *sitting in this wee kitchen talking to*, focusing here on the simple place in which they met. The bluntness of *whose father I have killed* is retained in *whose father's dead*, but with a switch into Jo's perspective. The simplicity of the physical setting seems to evoke simple and direct acceptance of responsibility.

The sense of his responsibility for the killing, spoken in 563, returns in 569–70 with a clear statement *I have responsibility for that*. The phrase *IRA operation* (570) is technical and political, and is contrasted with the effect on real *person* (572) who he is meeting. The final line of the extract, *that does change things*, is a coda, reformulating and condensing the idea of the impact of meeting Jo.

The impact on Jo is best exemplified in an extract from their conversation in Dublin which took place at their second meeting, just two weeks after the first (extract 4.6). The significance of the meeting is evidenced by the metaphors of *enormity* (54), from Pat, and, from Jo, a VIOLENT OR NEGATIVE ACTION metaphor, *I have just been struck* (66).

Extract 4.6	The impact of their first meeting:
1–54 Pat	. . . (1.0) or the . . <u>enormity</u> of it.
55 Jo	[hmh]
56 Pat	. . [perhaps],
57	you know,
58	. . . the- there's nothing prepares you for it.
59 Jo	. . [no].
60 Pat	. . [of course] that's er--
61 Jo	. . . (1.0) no.
62	well I <u>felt</u> [. . .] com- completely the same.

```
63 Pat      [hmh]
64 Jo       . . . (1.0) and that--
65          . . in the last two weeks I have walked down the street,
66          and I have just been struck,
67          . . . (1.0) by what's happened.
68 Pat      . . hmh
69 Jo       and I just looked at people,
70          and,
71          . . . and just thought,
72          . . . (1.0) I haven't--
73          . . . (1.0) it's like--
74          . . I can't . . . (1.0) integrate,
75          what what happened between us.
76 Pat      [hmh]
77 Jo       . . . and just [normal] life [going] on around me.
```

The impact of the meeting on Jo makes her feel excluded from other people whose lives continue on their everyday JOURNEYS in a way hers cannot. The physical act of *walking down the street* contrasts with the metaphorical *life going on around me,* emphasising the impact of their meeting through the reaction of feeling separated from other people and everyday life.

Meeting the Other in person for the first time is a critical point in the conciliation process. Coming face-to-face with the Other makes things happen that are impossible from a distance. The process of rehumanising the Other is accelerated by the first encounter and sitting down together. The JOURNEYS leading up to the first meeting have contributed to what happens there and what will happen afterwards.

CONFRONTING CONSEQUENCES IN THE CONCILIATION PROCESS

As we saw in extract 4.5, the impact of meeting the Other for Pat, as perpetrator of violence, came from being forced to see Jo as a person who had suffered as a consequence of his actions and from no longer being able to dehumanise the victims of the violence. As a perpetrator of violence comes to new understandings of how the Other has been affected by his actions, he must find ways to accommodate this new sense of responsibility into his view of himself. This is far from straightforward, and examining how it is talked about may help us to understand more about it. In the conversations between Jo and Pat, this idea and its emotional effects was expressed through a particular subset of JOURNEY metaphors: CONFRONTING AN OBSTACLE ON THE PATH (extract 4.7). In addition, other systematic metaphors come into play.

Extract 4.7   Confronting consequences:

1–1131 Pat	. . . be--
1132	be <u>confronted</u>,
1133	. . with your <u>pain</u>.
1134	. . . that's a consequence that--
1135	er,
1136	. . . (3.0) you know,
1137	I suppose I deserve.

The metaphor of *confronting* is sometimes phrased as *coming face-to-face,* and in the following extract the poetics of place is again active as this phrase is used both literally and metaphorically.

Extract 4.8   Coming face-to-face with the Other:

2–697 Pat	. . . (1.0) <u>coming</u> face-to-face,
698	with somebody who suffered because,
699	of a conseque--
700	as a consequence,
701	is another <u>thing</u>.
702	. . . and,
703	. . . (2.0) I suppose,
704	you only <u>come face-to-face</u> with it <u>in</u> a <u>situation</u> like that.
705	there is--
706	. . . (1.0) it's so easy to <u>lose</u>,
707	. . . <u>sight</u>,
708	. . . (1.0) <u>of</u>,
709	. . you know,
710	the enemy's humanity.

The first use in 697 is non-metaphorical, because Pat does see Jo's face when they meet. The *coming* here can be a JOURNEY metaphor as well as being literal and physical. By the time the phrase is used a second time, in line 704, the topic has shifted to *it* as the consequences of violence, and so the whole phrase is now metaphorical. We can note here how the metaphors of JOURNEYS work with the PARTIAL SEEING metaphor *lose sight of the other person's humanity.* In the metaphor scenario (Musolff, 2004) created by *coming face-to-face* in a *situation,* the idea of seeing something that was previously lost to sight makes sense, since the face contains the eyes and face-to-face normally entails seeing. The interplay continues at a more micro level. *Lose* can be seen as a JOURNEY metaphor embedded within the PARTIAL SEEING metaphor *lose sight of,* since it carries the physical sense of displacing an object which is metaphorically applied to the view or *sight of* something.

A local scenario, or metaphor story, also emerges from the interplay of JOURNEY and SEEING metaphors in extract 4.9. Here too the unavoidability of the confrontation with responsibility is emphasised, through use of the metaphor *can't walk away from* in line 1429.

Extract 4.9   Confronting responsibility:

1–1420	Pat	bottom line is,
1421		that is true.
1422		. . I am the person who caused your pain.
1423		. . even though it was a--
1424		. . . it was the Irish Republican Army,
1425		it was the Republican movement,
1426		it was the Republican struggle.
1427	Jo	. . hmh
1428	Pat	that caused your pain.
1429		but I can't walk away from the fact that it was--
1430		. . . (1.0) I was directly,
1431	Jo	[hmh]
1432	Pat	[responsible] too for that.
1433	Jo	. . [hmh]
1434	Pat	[I can't] hide behind the--
1435		you know the--
1436		. . . sort of,
1437		the bigger picture.

As in the previous extract, Pat speaks of Jo's *pain* (1428) as a way of encapsulating her grief and other consequences of her father's death. If physical pain is taken as the basic meaning of the word, then its use here to mean emotional pain, is metaphorical, although recent advances in neuroscience are blurring this boundary (Eisenberger, 2004). The key part of this extract through is Pat's acknowledgement of his individual responsibility. The JOURNEY metaphors, *walk away from* and *hide behind,* describe the alternative—to let the organisation take the responsibility—that Pat rejects here. The last line includes a PARTIAL SEEING metaphor that we met earlier, where *bigger picture* refers to the political situation in Northern Ireland.

In the first line of this episode is an instance of a systematic metaphor that played an interesting role in the talk, *the bottom line,* from the semantic field of ACCOUNTING, meaning a final summing up. This is explored further in chapter 8.

The JOURNEY metaphors of *confronting* and *coming face-to-face* vividly describe how it felt to Pat to have to acknowledge his responsibility for Jo's father's death and its consequences. They carry the affective force of meeting some unavoidable and possibly threatening or frightening obstacle, and so capture something of Pat's emotions and attitudes about the perturbation event.

BEYOND THE FIRST MEETING

The first meeting created a phase shift for the dynamic systems of Jo and Pat's talking-and-thinking, leading to new phases of empathy marked by further types of JOURNEY metaphors, and by different metaphors altogether.

A Shared Journey?

While Jo and Pat can continue on separate journeys, their meetings also opened up the possibility of a *shared journey*. However, any kind of sharing would be a huge move across the history that separates them, and the idea of a *shared journey* does not feature much in the talk, apart from a mention by Jo in the first conversation, where the conciliation process is seen as a *journey* made together:

> 1–1573 Jo   . . and your commitment to . . go on this journey with me.

She reflects on this in the later conversation (extract 4.10):

> Extract 4.10   The beginning of another journey:
> 2–1867 Jo   . . . (1.0) rather than,
> 1868   . . meeting you . . being the end of the journey,
> 1869   which I had thought,
> 1870   . . this is actually,
> 1871   . . . the beginning of the journey.
> 1872   and that,
> 1873   . . . there was a whole other journey to go on.
> 1874   . . . (1.0) and that journey is about us.

Helping Other Victims of Violence

Helping other victims of violence becomes a GOAL for future JOURNEYS, in which both parties can collaborate to help others, firstly through making a documentary film (extract 4.11).

> Extract 4.11   Helping other victims:
> 2–1744 Pat   . . . (2.0) the way that er--
> 1745   to take this experience forward?
> 1746 Jo   . . hmh
> 1747   . . . (4.0) well.
> 1748   . . . (2.0) I think in--
> 1749   . . . (1.0) in making this documentary,
> 1750   . . . (1.0) we are taking this to a--
> 1751   . . a wider audience.

The use of the pronoun *we* in this extract is far from insignificant. It brings Jo and Pat together in the JOURNEY metaphor of *taking* the idea of conciliation *to a wider audience.*

Jo speaks more about helping other victims as a result of their own conciliation process in the radio interview, extract 4.12. She first generalises from her own experience, describing the conciliation process as *to go on a journey.*

Extract 4.12   Creating safe places:

3–1068 Jo	all I can say that
1069	if anyone makes a commitment to <u>go on a journey</u>
1070	then I believe that life will <u>bring</u> the opportunities
1071	and the <u>support</u> that is needed
1072	and the other thing is that
1073	I am <u>seeing</u> more and more a need for
1074	<u>creating</u> safe places
1075	for people to <u>share their stories</u>
1076	and in a non-judgemental <u>space</u>
1077	<u>where</u> they can <u>share</u> their <u>pain</u>
1078	without <u>feeling</u> judged

Physical *safe places* for meetings between perpetrator and victim become a metaphorical, non-judgemental *space where* they can *share stories* and *their pain.*

Understanding Oneself as a JOURNEY

Yet another type of metaphorical JOURNEY that appears in the talk is the journey to understand oneself, which appears to be a side-effect of increasing empathy, most likely as a result of explaining one's experiences and choices to the Other, and which affects both Jo and Pat.

Pat, talking about other combatants in the Irish conflict accepting their feelings of loss, reflects back on his own self-knowledge using a JOURNEY metaphor:

2–3339 Pat   . . . (2.0) I probably myself have still <u>a long way to go.</u>

Just minutes later, Jo speaks of her own *inner journey* (extract 4.13):

Extract 4.13

2–4017 Jo	I know the <u>part of</u> me that can be very destructive.
4018	. . could want to <u>hurt.</u>
4019	and,
4020	. . . (1.0) and I'm . . . <u>coming to terms</u> with that.
4021	that's like my--
4022	. . my <u>inner journey.</u>

The literature of empathy shows that differentiation between self and Other is a pre-requisite for empathy to develop (Lamm, Batson and Desety, 2007; Lamm, Meltzoff and Decety 2009; Pedersen, 2008). Engaging in empathy changes the self and seems to sharpen knowledge and awareness of the self through increasing understanding of the Other.

AN ONGOING JOURNEY

To finish this section, we return to Jo's journey. We saw in chapters 2 and 3 that Jo used *JOURNEY* metaphors to speak of her motivation for engaging in conciliation as *bringing something positive out of* her father's death. As her meetings with Pat continue and empathy between them grows, a new metaphor turns the rather vague *something positive* into the more precise *transformation* of grief into *compassion and empathy*. This shift is a result of her *inner journey* (extract 4.14).

> Extract 4.14   The inner journey:
>
> | 2–1302 Jo | . . . (2.0) well that's the journey that I've-- |
> |---|---|
> | 1303 | I've been on, |
> | 1304 | understanding that. |
> | 1305 | . . . (3.0) I wo-- |
> | 1306 | . . . (1.0) and the journey's . . . been an inner journey. |
> | 1307 | . . . (1.0) of transforming the-- |
> | 1308 | . . the feelings that were there at the beginning. |
> | 1309 | . . the pain. |
> | 1310 | and the loss. |
> | 1311 | and the anger. |
> | 1312 | . . . (1.0) and the grief. |
> | 1313 | . . . (1.0) and, |
> | 1314 | . . discovering that they can be transformed. |
> | 1315 | . . . (1.0) ehm, |
> | 1316 | . . . through the heart. |
> | 1317 | . . . (1.0) into, |
> | 1318 | compassion and empathy. |
> | 1319 | . . . (1.0) and, |
> | 1320 | . . . (1.0) it's a journey that, |
> | 1321 | . . goes on and on. |

This transformation will be discussed further in chapter 9.

CONCILIATION AS LISTENING TO THE OTHER'S STORY

The systematic metaphor LISTENING TO THE OTHER'S STORY,[2] used to frame the idea of the conciliation process, appeared 21 times in the first conversation and became more important throughout the second, with 67 uses.

In the radio interview (13 uses), it was Jo's preferred way of describing what she and Pat have done, and hope to do, for other victims. The power of this metaphor does not come from the flexibility and productivity that characterised JOURNEY metaphors, but instead from its adaptability in use: it was used in talk about several, slightly different ideas, and it was redeployed in a shift from one topic to another in a particularly significant gesture of empathy.

Since to have a story is to be human, in a post-conflict conciliation context merely allowing that the Other **has** a story is in itself an act of rehumanisation (extract 4.15). Being prepared to listen to that story initiates connecting processes that can build empathy. LISTENING TO THE OTHER'S STORY assists in developing and answering curiosity about the Other and in finding commonality with the Other, both of which contribute to sympathy and may help the listener move beyond sympathy to empathy by enabling them to imagine themselves in the Other's position.

Extract 4.15   Open to the Other's story:

1–90 Pat	and I <u>find</u> you very <u>open</u>.
91	. . . to my <u>story</u>.
92	<u>where</u> I--
93	. . er,
94	. . . I *feel* there is more to me than just a perpetrator.
95	. . . (1.0) and er,
96	. . . (1.0) I suppose,
97	. . . (1.0) what we're doing here.
98	. . . is,
99	. . <u>exchanging</u> our <u>stories</u>.

THE ADAPTABILITY OF *LISTENING TO THE OTHER'S STORY*

Examining the language used in these metaphors and how they are employed in the discourse activity reveals their particular adaptability.

Collocation

The LISTENING TO THE OTHER'S STORY metaphor created richness and potential partly through its adaptability for use with a range of collocates[3] and forms. The word *story* is collocated in metaphors with several different verbs: *listen, hear, tell, offer, exchange, share*. The last two of these emphasise the two-way nature of LISTENING TO THE STORY. The frequent collocation with *open*, such as that in extract 4.15, further suggests that successful conciliation demands more than simply *listening* or *hearing*—attentive, empathic listening in which the hearer is *open* to what is heard and really tries to understand the perspective of the story teller. (The metaphor of *open* is discussed in chapter 6.)

Listen and *hear* are themselves used with collocates other than *story*, including *pain, anger, struggles, inner voices*. The collocating and re-collocating of elements of the metaphor contribute to a spreading affective 'climate' across the talking-and-thinking, in which attentive, effortful LISTENING describes what both participants aspire to in the conciliation process.

Redeployment and Topic Shift

While positive aspects of the LISTENING TO THE OTHER'S STORY metaphor are used to frame the conciliation process, negative contrasts are used to explain the roots of violence in a vehicle redeployment, or shift of topic, that marks an important moment in the talk. This perturbation event occurred early in the first conversation, suggesting that it was an idea Jo had thought about in advance of meeting Pat.

Extract 4.16 shows Jo introducing the idea that *not being heard* (760) can lead to frustration and violence.

Extract 4.16   Listening and the causes of violence:

1–758 Jo	. . . (1.0) <u>feels</u> like violence happens,	
759	. . . (1.0) when,	
760	. . . (1.0) the <u>feeling of not being heard</u> gets so <u>strong</u>,	
761 Pat	certainly.	
762 Jo	. . . and er,	
763	. . . you know as--	
764	. . as a daughter of a conservative MP,	
765	I . . can sort of <u>take</u> responsibility for the--	
766	. . . (1.0) what the government . . didn't do.	
767	and,	
768	. . the <u>not listening</u>,	
769	<u>not hearing</u> [their story].	
770 Pat	[hmh]	
771	hmh	
772 Jo	. . and--	
773	. . . I can <u>see</u> it <u>in</u> my children,	
774	when they are <u>not heard</u>,	
775	. . . then anger and violence,	
776	. . . (1.0) is one <u>way</u> of really making sure they get <u>heard</u>.	

The significance of this moment comes from Jo, as the 'victim' in the conciliation process, taking responsibility for the violence, attributing it to *not listening/hearing their story* by the British government at the time. Jo suggests that the consequent lack of understanding contributed to the conflict in Ireland. The word *story* had been used three times up to this point, twice by Pat and once by Jo. Jo had also used the word *responsibility* once, but there had been no talk thus far of *taking respon-sibility*. By taking responsibility in this way, Jo makes a gesture of empathy that re-positions her relative to Pat. She 'enters into' his perspective by trying to understand what might have caused the conflict, and at the same time she steps down from her 'victim' position and positions herself as responsible for violence, albeit at one remove. Her status is not permanently shifted though, as in the last four lines, extending her argument about *not listening* leading to anger, Jo also reminds Pat of her identity as a mother with children

The negative metaphor, *not being heard*, which implies lack of *listening*, is proposed as the cause of violence (760). In lines 766–69, *the* (UK) *government* is described as *not listening . . . not hearing their story*, where *their* refers to people in Ireland. Jo gives another example from closer to home in the last few lines of extract 4.16 when she describes her children as responding with *anger and violence* to not being *heard*. The physical acts of *listening* and *hearing* are loaded here with meaning beyond the basic, physical sense; *listening* and *hearing* become deliberate, intentional and effortful actions in which the listener pays careful attention to what the other person says in order to try to understand their meaning and their perspective.

The detail of the language tells us more. The use of the verbs of *listening* and *hearing* in the passive voice or as agentless participles gives a sense of absence of people to do the listening and hearing; the continuous *-ing* tenses emphasise the process, or its absence, and its long duration; the negated forms (*not being heard* rather than *being ignored*) suggest a deliberate avoidance of attention to what is being said.

Listening and *hearing* as used here imply a dialogic and two-way interaction of trying to establish shared understanding, rather than a solitary one-way process of interpretation. When Jo says: *we need to do a lot of listening,* or describes her reaction to meeting Pat as: *I felt heard,* she suggests deliberate actions that acknowledge the other person as a human being with something to say, with a story that is worthy of close attention.

The Metaphorical Use of STORY

The words *story* or *stories* occur 8 times in the first conversation in the dataset, 25 times in the second conversation, 12 times in the interview, and just twice when Jo and Pat reflect back on their meetings nine years later. The second conversation has the most uses, and is also where there is the most equal distribution across the two speakers; after this, *story/ies* is used only by Jo. Since Jo also used it first in her poem, we might conclude that she brought it to the conversations, that Pat temporarily adopted it and used it, particularly in the second conversation, without it becoming, over the long term, his normal or preferred way of talking about this idea.

Story/ies was used across the talk to refer to the personal stories of Jo or Pat, but also more broadly to refer collectively, as earlier, to the stories of other victims or perpetrators, or, by Pat, to the *republican story*.

People's choices and uses of words and metaphors can be interesting in what they tell us about how individuals are thinking, although making these connections can be problematic. The importance of choice comes from the fact that there are always alternative ways of saying something; a pattern of choices over a period of time then becomes interesting for what it can reveal about biases or tendencies in a person's talking-and-thinking. Such bias or tendency may merely be a reflection of conventional usage or individual experience, but it may also reflect some deliberate action on the part of the speaker. In the case of *story*, an alternative word would be *account*, while a still more figurative and emotive choice would be *testimony*, as used in the South African Truth and Reconciliation Commission. Without evidence from the data, we can only surmise as to the choice of the particular word *story*. The situation of meeting a stranger and having to recount the events of several years is likely to produce a discourse event very like a storytelling; the teller will have to include details of people, places and events, just as in a prototype story, and temporal distance from the events may encourage a tidying up of the messiness of what actually happened into a neater and more condensed 'story'. The pragmatics of recounting past events while face-to-face with someone who may have caused or suffered from those very past events also seems likely to produce codas of the sort found in stories to emphasise the emotional impact (Chafe, 1994). Repeated thinking about traumatic events may also result in emphasising or highlighting certain episodes in memory, that then appear in tellings in more finished or complete forms than could be expected in spontaneous talk about seldom revisited events.

The use of the word *story* in connection with post-conflict reconciliation is, furthermore, strongly conventionalised, particularly in the discourse of Christianity-connected mediation. It has become a familiar way to describe what perpetrators and victims tell each other when they meet in post-conflict reconciliation situations. When Jo speaks of the time she spent at the Glencree Centre for Peace and Reconciliation in Ireland, where the second conversation in the dataset also took place, she talks of people there *sharing stories* and *experiencing each other's stories*.

We have seen how LISTENING TO THE OTHER'S STORY is used adaptively through collocation and topic shift. It also operates with a further kind of adaptability, in which it varies in how metaphorical it is, its 'metaphoricity'. Sometimes the *listening* and the *stories* are not metaphorical at all, but refer to physical listening to anecdotes or narratives with characters, plot and other dimensions of stories. For example, in extract 4.17, Pat seems to be using the word *stories* with a meaning close to the basic sense, a narrative of a particular event, rather than as a metaphorical way-of-telling that has come to represent a life history through reflection and in conversations with former enemies.

Extract 4.17   Literal stories:

2–1272 Pat	six killed—
1273	people killed <u>in</u> one night.
1274 Jo	. . . hmh
1275 Pat	. . I mean,
1276	and there are so many other **stories** like that.
1277	. . in other areas all over,

Since metaphor offers a way of "seeing one thing in terms of something else" (Burke, 1945, 503), the case for *story* as metaphor relies on being able to separate a more basic sense of *story,* described as a narrative telling of an event as a sequence of actions, from its use as in extract 4.16 to mean a particular 'way-of-telling', or formulation, of a life history, or part of it, between perpetrator and victim. That more basic sense, of the narrative telling of an event as a sequence of actions, is what we find in folktales, fictional stories and anecdotes, formulated and told for information, entertainment and possibly education. A conventionalised narrative pattern would begin with presentation of characters and setting, some problem or challenge faced by characters, leading to a series of actions in an unfolding plot, and culminating in a resolution and possibly a moral coda (Chafe, 1994; Labov and Waletzky, 1967). Categorising a specific use of the word *story* as metaphorical then hinges on their being (a) sufficient difference between the two senses and (b) a comparison or transfer of meaning between the two that adds extra meaning to the use in this context. If we can justify claiming that Jo's recount of everything that happened to her since and including the Brighton bombing, all her responses, reactions and feelings, is different from the telling of it as a narrative, then we may claim something metaphorical is being done.

It is not possible to make one single decision across all instances; instead, each use requires its own decision. However, without being present when such *stories* are told, it is not always clear whether metaphor or metonymy is involved. When Jo in her poem says *I listen to your suffering,* there is something figurative or non-literal about the phrase, since *suffering* does not speak or make a noise. What is *listened to* is either a description of *suffering* or, although less likely here, might be the results of *suffering,* such as screaming or crying. Both of these interpretations can be activated by *I listen to your suffering* because the contextual meaning is related to, or contiguous with, the basic, physical meaning, thus giving a case of metonymy, rather than metaphor.

While metaphor involves "seeing something in terms of something else", metonymy is "seeing something in terms of something related to it". This broad sense of metonymy, as seeing something in terms of something connected to it, includes constructs from literary theory or rhetoric such as synecdoche (or *pars pro toto*), in which some part or aspect of an entity is used to refer to the whole, and traditional metonymy (or *toto pro pars*), in which the whole of an entity is used to refer to just part of it. *Story* works as metonymy if it is used to refer to an account that includes stories (e.g. this is now how the word *narrative* is used, as in *the narrative of colonialism*). So, for example, if speaking of everything that has happened to Jo since and including the Brighton bombing, all her responses, reactions and feelings, is described as her *story* (extract 4.18), then this might be classified as metonymy on the basis that several narratives are included in this *story*, but it also amounts to much more than that, justifying its identification as metaphor.

Extract 4.18   Metonymical stories:

2–1365 Jo	. . . (1.0) I <u>found</u> that people wanted to <u>hear</u> my <u>story</u>.
1366	they really really wanted to <u>hear</u> it.
1367	. . . and that <u>through</u> me <u>telling</u>,
1368	. . <u>where</u> I was <u>at</u>,
1369	. . . (1.0) it was also helping them.
1370	. . . (1.0) and when I realised,
1371	. . . for the first time,
1372	. . that I could,
1373	. . . help others,
1374	. . by <u>sharing</u>,

The shifting between metaphor and metonymy found with *story* causes methodological problems but what is important is that something 'metaphor-like' happening: one thing is being seen in terms of something else, and the 'seeing in terms of' contributes something important in the discourse activity. Some key aspects of the basic sense of *story* are transferred to the quite different situation of the retelling of traumatic memories, in particular transferring a sense of wholeness and finalisability to what is more likely to be messy and in flux.

Story versus Truth

The claim that LISTENING TO THE OTHER'S STORY works as an emergent framing metaphor for Jo and Pat is based on its increasing, and increasingly shared, use in the second conversation. When the talk is analysed for the use of the related words and phrases, a pattern emerges of consistent use of the word *story,* accompanied by variation in use of *listening, hearing* and *open to.* Over the timescale of the data, the variation settles down: *listening* and *hearing* come to work in similar ways as metaphors for reaching a shared understanding, while also contributing to an explanation for violence and a possible way to avoid conflict. It comes to be used by both of them, and is used between them. The metaphor has been shown to be adaptable in use, and to offer a range of degrees of metaphoricity from literal through metonymy to metaphor.

The systematic metaphor contributes to the conciliation process by offering a further framing of the process as LISTENING TO THE OTHER'S STORY. In this scenario, the other person, once, but no longer, an enemy, has a story to tell, and taking the time and effort to listen to what he or she has to say is a gesture of empathy. However, allowing the Other to tell their story remains distinct from giving validity to that story as 'truth', and it seems likely that participants in post-conflict conciliation need to retain this distinction. Victims in particular may need to be able to listen and hear, and thereby better understand the Other's perspective, without needing to accept the justification for violence. CONCILIATION AS LISTENING TO THE OTHER'S STORY offers a discourse space in which to deal with the "emotional ambivalence" that can be produced by understanding the Other more deeply (Halpern and Weinstein, 2004, 568). While making an effort to understand their perspective of the Other, one can, at the same time, maintain disagreement with or disapproval of the moral or ethical decisions.

CONCLUSION

Metaphors from Jo's and Pat's lived experience of the conciliation process reveal systematic patterns of talking-and-thinking about the process as it evolved over the years. The data are the metaphors that Jo and Pat use to help conceptualise the process of conciliation that they are engaged in. Talking-and-thinking about conciliation as a JOURNEY or as LISTENING TO THE OTHER'S STORY emphasises particular aspects of the process and helps us as outsiders to understand the process more deeply.

The poetics of place is particularly active in uses of JOURNEY metaphors. The flexibility and richness of JOURNEY metaphors allows each participant to select aspects that best convey their ideas, emotions and feelings. JOURNEY metaphors contributed to describing the impact of the first meeting between Pat Magee and Jo Berry, as meeting in person brought with it the necessity of confronting personal responsibility for violence. Places on journeys were important, for explaining the roots of violence or for conveying affect. Talk about places featured much blurring and shifting between the metaphorical and the physical world. JOURNEY metaphors mixed easily with other groups of metaphors in developing detailed metaphor stories or scenarios in local discourse dynamics.

Examination of JOURNEY metaphors has shown how engaging in conciliation as a victim can be effortful and difficult, and how meeting other victims, metaphorised as a place to be welcomed, feel safe and to rest in, can offer support to continue. For the perpetrator, the meeting face-to-face is necessarily highly significant and difficult since human consequences can no longer be denied or hidden behind political justifications. The relationship of the two participants outside of the conciliation process is both individual and shared; there is a need to remain separate despite engaging in some shared activity, such as helping other victims. Engaging in understanding the Other has knock-on effects on understanding oneself.

Metaphors, and metonymies, that speak of the conciliation process as LISTENING TO THE OTHER'S STORY offered adaptability through use with a range of collocations and topics. A negative formulation, NOT LISTENING, enabled Jo to make a 'gesture of empathy' in taking some responsibility for what led to the conflict, perhaps thereby encouraging Pat to reciprocate by taking responsibility too.

The metaphor emphasises LISTENING in conciliation as necessarily effortful and attentive. STORY demonstrates an important affordance of metaphor in offering discourse space for disagreement and emotional ambivalence to be accommodated alongside increased understanding. For the development of empathy, the 'breathing space' between story and truth may support participants in the effort of understanding the Other's perspective by relieving them of any pressure to have to accept the moral stance of that perspective.

Two gestures of empathy have been noted:

- Jo, as 'victim' in the conciliation process explores the causes of the conflict and takes some responsibility for it through her social group affiliation.
- Both Pat and Jo re-position the Other from 'enemy' to someone with a story to tell, and time and effort is taken to listen to and understand what the Other has to say.

5   Metaphor Clusters and Absences

The previous chapter showed how systematic patterns of metaphor about the conciliation process emerged over a timescale of months and years from multiple instances of discourse activity in the moment. Before moving on to consider the framing metaphors of CONNECTION and SEPARATION, and their important contribution to the development of empathy, we need a further piece of methodology: the distributional analysis of metaphors.

This chapter explains how metaphor clusters were located in the data, and how this distributional analysis also revealed 'metaphor absences'. We also discover some more of the small discourse actions made by participants that we are calling 'gestures of empathy' occurring inside both clusters and absences.

METAPHOR CLUSTERS AND ABSENCES

As we saw in chapter 3, metaphor analysis offers several tools for investigating gestures of empathy, one of which is to consider the distribution or spread of metaphors across the discourse events. As with other types of talk and text, metaphors in the conversations are not evenly spread but cluster together in certain places, very often at what seem to be difficult moments for participants and sometimes around perturbation events. In addition, metaphors may be virtually absent from other stretches of talk, and some metaphor absences signal significant perturbation events in the process of coming to understand the Other.

Fine-grained analysis inside metaphor clusters considers the shifting of metaphors, and the interaction of metaphors with non-metaphorical language, including lexical and syntactic choices. Analysis also takes account of who is speaking and how this changes. These details are understood in terms of the discourse action inside a cluster, and because our goal is to understand conciliation, we look for action that takes participants towards conciliation, often through what are called 'gestures of empathy'.

After an example of a metaphor cluster analysed for metaphor and discourse action, the chapter describes the method for finding and analysing clusters and absences, and summarises what was found in the distributional analysis of the conversations between Jo and Pat.

EXAMPLE OF A METAPHOR CLUSTER

The high density of metaphors in extract 5.1 marked it out as a 'metaphor cluster' when compared with nearby talk. Here Jo is talking about her father, about her differences with him and what she shared with him. She feels that he would approve of what she is doing in conciliation, unlike some other victims' families, who disapprove of her meeting with Pat.

Extract 5.1	Not betraying my father:	
2488 Jo	his <u>way</u> was as a conservative MP.	
2489	. . . (1.0) and,	
2490	yet we could <u>share</u>.	
2491	. . . that our goals were the same.	
2492	. . . and now,	
2493	. . . (1.0) I'm . . doing this for--	
2494	. . for peace.	
2495	. . . (2.0) as . . . my l--	
2496	. . <u>little contribution</u> to . . . the <u>bigger picture</u>.	
2497	and,	
2498	I can feel him <u>supporting</u> me.	
2499	. . . and that's--	
2500	. . . (1.0) this--	
2501	. . I can <u>draw strength from</u> that.	
2502	. . . those . . who say I <u>betray</u> his memory.	
2503	. . . (2.0) many will say that,	
2504	I'm <u>betraying</u> him.	
2505	. . . (1.0) the <u>deeper</u> truth is,	
2506	. . . (1.0) that he is <u>with</u> me.	
2507	. . . (1.0) and <u>betrayal</u>,	
2508	. . . (1.0) is actually more about,	
2509	. . . me <u>betraying</u> myself,	
2510 Pat	hmh	
2511 Jo	. . by not . . doing this <u>work</u>.	
2512 Pat	. . . you <u>feel</u> that er--	
2513	he would understand,	
2514	. . . why you're going to Derry,	
2515	why you're sitting here?	

Within this metaphor cluster there is an even denser, shorter cluster from 2501 to 2509. As happens quite often, clusters develop from repeated use of a metaphor—here *betrayal*—in several different forms. Very conventionalised metaphors like *way* and *feel* occur alongside the more deliberate or unusual metaphors. Metaphors in the cluster are mixed rather than linked to a single, overarching metaphor, as is again common in both text and talk (Cameron and Stelma, 2004; Kimmel, 2010). In this short stretch there are metaphors of STRENGTH *(strength, supporting)*, BETRAYAL, DEPTH *(deeper, draw from)*, CONNECTION *(share, with)*, SEEING *(picture)*, SCALE *(little, bigger)*, WORK, MONEY/VALUE *(contribution)*.

The discourse activity of the metaphor cluster centres on Jo explaining her reaction to other people's attitudes about her meeting with Pat. The metaphor *betrayal* gives their negative perspective on her decision to meet Pat. Jo defends herself against this view by turning it around, so that meeting Pat avoids another sort of *betrayal*, and by explaining that her father would encourage her to engage with Pat. The first use of the *betrayal* metaphors is the reported thinking of other people:

> 2502   . . . those . . who say I <u>betray</u> his memory.

The second reformulates and emphasises the content of this line:

> 2503   . . . (2.0) many will say that,
> 2504   I'm <u>betraying</u> him.

The reformulation shifts in several ways: to refer to what people *will say* (when Jo goes to Northern Ireland as she plans to do); in talking about the other people *those* becomes *many; I betray his memory* becomes *I'm betraying him*. By changing the object of *betrayal* from *his memory* to *him*, this last change seems to strengthen the accusation; *him* here is a metonymy for *his memory*, not a reference to the person himself. After stating *the deeper truth*, that her father would have supported her, Jo returns to *betrayal*, now relating it to herself.

> 2507   . . . (1.0) and <u>betrayal</u>,
> 2508   . . . (1.0) is actually more about,
> 2509   . . . me <u>betraying</u> myself,
> 2511   . . by not . . doing this <u>work</u>.

Doing this work is put forward as such an important obligation in Jo's life and conception of herself, that it becomes what must not be betrayed. In pushing forward this argument, the *betrayal* metaphor has been redeployed from the topic of her father to herself.

The metaphors of *betrayal* to talk about the disapproval of relatives of other victims (2502–2511) carry strong affective force through their cultural connotations of serious acts of disloyalty. When she describes the alternative as *the deeper truth that he is with me*, the metaphor *deeper* carries a sense of being more honest and more important to Jo. To describe her father as being *with* her echoes the idea of him *supporting* her in 2498;

in the poetics of place, physical proximity suggests or correlates with being available to help.

As with many clusters, this talk seems to arise around some discourse difficulty. The multiple, fairly long pauses suggest something painful or awkward is being said. We cannot know from the transcript whether the difficulty is more intrapersonal or interpersonal; it may be a difficult topic for Jo to talk about for herself, perhaps because she feels hurt by what these other people think, or it may be difficult to share with Pat.

In terms of the metaphor cluster's contribution to conciliation and empathy, several possible discourse actions might be seen as gestures of empathy. Firstly, because the talk is clearly difficult and troubled, we can know that Jo is making an effort to share her feelings about the topic. Secondly, we can note that, at line 2496, Jo uses a metaphor of *the big picture*, which was used earlier in the talk by Pat (see extract 3.1). As we will see in chapter 9, 'using the Other's metaphors' is a gesture of empathy that comes in various forms. The cluster contributes to conciliation by giving Pat access to Jo's feelings about this issue; through the cluster, Pat may know more about Jo's experiences and, through the affect attached to the metaphors, may be helped to 'feel with' Jo, and to enter into her perspective about other people's responses to their meetings.

Pat's response to Jo's explanation (from 2512) is to build on Jo's turn by asking a supportive question. It is as if Pat is here tentatively entering the perspective that Jo has just opened up. By doing this, Pat makes a gesture of empathy towards Jo that we might describe as 'thinking about the Other's feelings and attempting to describe them'. In the conciliation process, where the two started from extreme alterity of perpetrator and victim, having the knowledge and confidence to try to describe the Other's feelings suggests considerable progress. Offering a description of the Other's feelings through a question is a good way to be tentative and avoids asserting any right to know what those feelings might be.

FINDING METAPHOR CLUSTERS AND ABSENCES

When the spread of metaphors across a conversation is examined, their distribution is found to be uneven. Metaphors group together densely in some places, while elsewhere in they are thin on the ground. This phenomenon of metaphor clustering (sometimes called 'bursts') has been observed in various types of talk and written text: baptist sermons (Corts and Meyers, 2002); university lectures (Corts and Pollio, 1999; Low, 1997); school lessons (Cameron, 2003); newspaper reports (Kimmel, 2010); marketing discourse (Koller, 2003). Clustering appears to be a robust feature of metaphor use.

In the college lectures examined by Corts and colleagues, it was found that a metaphor cluster was often produced by several metaphors connected to a single overarching metaphor that was being used to make a topic accessible to students. So, for example, when a lecturer was explaining alcoholism in terms of a social game metaphor, a cluster emerged around that explanation as it was developed using extensions or developments of the social game metaphor (Corts and Pollio, 1999). This neat relationship of one big metaphor per cluster has not, however, been found in other types of discourse; instead, clusters often feature mixtures of metaphor types (Kimmel, 2010).

There is a statistical method for identifying clusters that picks out stretches of talk where the frequency of metaphors suddenly rises (described in Cameron and Stelma, 2004). Sudden rises in metaphor density can also be identified visually on a graph that plots successive totals of metaphor; here, a metaphor cluster appears as a sudden increase in the steepness of the line of the graph. Cameron and Stelma (2004) showed that visual inspection is sufficiently valid and reliable as a way of finding clusters, and that the complicated Poisson distribution statistics are not really necessary for qualitative metaphor analysis. When metaphors are underlined in transcripts, visual inspection can pick out episodes of talk with denser underlinings. An additional check of the metaphor density inside and outside the episode can then be made to confirm or remove clusters.[1]

Cluster analysis was carried out statistically and visually on the first two conversations in the dataset, where Jo and Pat are talking together without external mediation (reported in Cameron and Stelma, 2004). This exercise revealed that clusters are typically of two lengths: shorter clusters occurring on a timescale of about 5 intonation units, and longer clusters on a scale of between 20 and 50 intonation units, as in extract 5.1. Most shorter clusters occur inside a longer cluster.

The first conversation contained 21 longer clusters and 31 shorter clusters. The second conversation contained 22 longer clusters and 68 shorter clusters. The timescale of longer clusters was extended in the second conversation, from a mean length of 39 IUs to a mean length of 52 IUs, possibly because Jo and Pat were more relaxed with each other or because they revisited many topics at greater length. Clusters included about 42% of all metaphors, while covering about 30% of the talk.

Stretches of conversation were identified as 'metaphor absences' through the same procedures. There were 15 episodes with significantly fewer metaphors, often just 1 or 2, in the first conversation and 13 in the second. As we will see below, 5 of these metaphor absences were significant to the conciliation process.

ANALYSIS OF METAPHOR CLUSTERS

The analysis of clusters began by examining, in each cluster, which metaphors were used in connection with which topics, how the metaphors shift within the cluster, and whose perspective was being presented.

Topics of Metaphor Clusters

In the conciliation talk, it was found that most clusters featured a single discourse topic, rather than switching between topics. Unlike college lectures, there was seldom a single metaphor that was extended and developed to make a cluster; most clusters included metaphors from at least two different vehicle groupings (chapter 3), as we saw in extract 5.1. Metaphor clusters occurred during explanations of most of the key discourse topics that Jo and Pat cover in the conversations (figure 3.1). Systematic metaphor trajectories, including framing metaphors for the conciliation process, pass through clusters and continue outside of clusters (see extract 5.2 in the next section). In this and following chapters we also see how metaphor clusters occurred in talk about other key discourse topics, in particular:

- Jo's response to the her father's death as conciliation, rather than revenge;
- Pat's decision as a young man to join the IRA;
- the impact of the violence on Jo, her family and Pat.

Metaphor Shifting Inside Clusters

The various types of metaphor shifting, as described in chapter 3, are found inside clusters. Extract 5.2 shows the metaphor of *journey* being developed inside a metaphor cluster where Pat is talking about the moment where their lives collided, and how meetings like their own may help other people who are also prepared to *meet the other halfway*:

Extract 5.2	A cluster of journeys:
2–641 Pat	meet the other halfway.
642	. . . (1.0) in your journey.
643	it was from--
644	. . . (1.0) 1984,
645	when your father was killed,
646	or when I killed your father,
647	. . when the republican movement killed your father.
648	. . . (3.0) er,
649	my journey,
650	. . . (1.0) preceded that you were catapulted into this struggle.
651	. . I think,
652	er,
653	. . . (1.0) my journey preceded that.
654	. . . (1.0) but,
655	. . . (1.0) our journey began that moment.
656	. . . and here we are.
657	. . today.

658	sixteen years later.
659	seventeen years later.
660	. . . (1.0) it's quite a remarkable <u>journey</u>.

The interpersonal difficulty of this extract (which comprises the first half of the cluster) may stem from lines 645–47 where Pat reformulates the passive, non-agentive *when your father was killed,* to a form where he takes responsibility: *when I killed your father.* This statement of his personal responsibility is absolute, in syntax and in meaning, and perhaps sounds rather too stark as they sit side by side. It is reformulated and distanced slightly into a statement of collective responsibility: *when the republican movement killed your father,* and followed by a long pause.

Five uses of *journey* in this cluster describe first Pat's process, then Jo's, then the shared conciliation process: *your journey, my journey* (twice), *our journey, a remarkable journey.* The first metaphor, in 641, extends the *journey* metaphor by constructing the idea of *meet the other half way.*

Two instances of the interplay of metaphor and non-metaphor in the poetics of place appear in extract 5.2. While *half way,* in line 641, refers not to distance but to attitudes and so is metaphorical, *meet* may be both literal as well as metaphorical. The pronoun *here* in 656 is similar in having the potential to be metaphorical, referring to being engaged in conciliation together, but also literal, referring to being in the same physical place. It is connected back to *meet the other half way* as a vehicle reformulation or as an extension, referring to the event/place of meeting.

Extract 5.3, from slightly later in the same conversation, shows how the use of contrasting vehicles naturally occurs in discourse:

Extract 5.3	Finding and losing:
2–835 Jo	. . . (3.0) what about <u>your journey</u> to--
836	. . . (1.0) <u>re-find,</u>
837	. . <u>part of</u> your humanity,
838	that you <u>lost</u>.

The goal of Pat's metaphorical *journey* is spoken of by Jo as *re-finding your humanity,* which is then immediately developed as *that you lost.* The metaphors of *finding* and *lost* are contrasts that here describe the 'before and after' states. Such contrasts often contribute to the density of metaphors in clusters.

The Discourse Activity of Metaphor Clusters

Across the different kinds of discourse examined in empirical studies, metaphor clusters often seem to co-occur with some difficult discourse work; dealing with interactional difficulties seems to generate metaphors in larger numbers than usual. In the conciliation conversations, interactional difficulties might be interpersonal, e.g. embarrassing or painful to say, as when Pat talks about the killing of Jo's father in extract 5.2. Sometimes clusters resulted from difficulties in managing the discourse, as when a new topic needed to be started or a current topic closed down;[2] this is what generated the cluster including extract 5.3. A final source of difficulty came from content, as when an idea is complicated in some way these and needed analogies or comparisons to help explain.

Analysis of speaker and point of view in the metaphor clusters in the conciliation conversations showed that most were produced by a single speaker, with just three being jointly produced, in the sense that the other speaker produced more than just minimal supportive responses. Jo and Pat used metaphors in the clusters mostly to present their own point of view to the other. There were 22 instances in clusters where one of them presented their own point of view, 6 where they offered the other's perspective, and just 2 where a shared perspective was presented.

We can say, therefore, that a key discourse activity of metaphor clusters was to explain perspectives and experiences to the Other. There are many things that need to be explained to the Other in post-conflict conciliation if he or she is to come to understand you as a more whole and more complex human being, and if some reparation is to be made for loss. Both Jo and Pat came to the first meeting with things that they wanted to explain or to find explanations for: Jo wanted to understand why Pat had chosen to take violent action and wanted Pat to understand the personal consequences of that political decision; Pat wanted to explain the political situation so that Jo could understand why he had made that decision. Explanations do not concern just factual details but also the emotions and feelings that accompany experiences and/or the retelling of them, and the attitudes and values that might have been attached to the situations being explained or that now apply to them. The kinds of things that are being talked about are very likely to evoke intense emotions, although at the same time, the person one is sharing this with might be the very last person from whom one would expect or wish to receive emotional support. Metaphors in explanations may be particularly powerful if they activate simulations of emotions or embodiment in the listener, enabling the 'feeling with' aspect of emotional empathy to be developed.

Explanations of perspectives and experiences are, of course, not done once and for all, but are 'unfinalisable' in Bakhtin's term (Bakhtin, 1981). A complete and final explanation of past experience is impossible to formulate for another person, or even to know for oneself. Instead partial and incomplete explanations will be offered, and may be returned to reformulation or development at a later point. Each explanation is a product of its local discourse context as well as it historical source. Responses to explanations vary from minimal acknowledgement to asking further questions or, as we saw in extract 5.1, responding with support. Metaphors used in an explanation may be echoed in responses or contrasted.

Two new types of discourse activity were found in the clusters of the conciliation talk: argument through contrast with negative alternative scenarios and metaphor appropriation. In the first of these, metaphor cluster analysis revealed a particular form of argumentation threaded through the conciliation conversations and explanatory metaphor clusters, in which participants would explain or justify decisions by constructing a very negative hypothetical alternative through a series of metaphor contrasts that was then dismissed, briefly uniting the speakers in being able to share the dismissal. A series of such 'negative alternative scenarios' will be seen in the next chapter in Jo's talk about why she engaged in conciliation.

The second form of discourse activity found in clusters, metaphor appropriation, was another type of metaphor use across speakers. The movement of metaphors between speakers appears to be a significant indicator of achievement of the discourse goals of reconciliation. The particular type of metaphor movement that is labelled 'appropriation' occurs when a metaphor that has been the 'discourse property' of one speaker is taken over by the other. The original user is then in a position to refuse or allow the appropriation. Allowing the Other to use a metaphor that was previously one's own is a gesture of empathy that contributes to the larger process of conciliation, and is described in more detail in chapter 9.

Metaphor Clusters and Conciliation

Extract 5.1, as one of the few clusters featuring both speakers, conveniently illustrates how the discourse activity of metaphor clusters can be related to conciliation and empathy. It first shows Jo explaining to Pat her feelings about people who were not supporting her decision to meet him. In offering the explanation, Jo makes a gesture of empathy. The explanation that she offers opens up for Pat the opportunity to understand, not just what is happening, but how she feels about it. He then makes a reciprocal gesture of empathy with his question that seems to 'enter into' this perspective by acknowledging the feelings she has just shared with him. Explaining oneself to the Other and entering into the Other's perspective are two important aspects of empathy.

In line 650 of extract 5.2, we can see another gesture of empathy as Pat shifts slightly into Jo's perspective when he uses the phrase *catapulted into* to describe the effect of her father's killing with its VIOLENT ACTION metaphor. Although he shifts straight back into his own republican perspective with the collective metaphor of the Irish conflict, *the struggle*, we might see this as a small gesture of empathy following his statement of personal responsibility.

DISCOURSE ANALYSIS OF METAPHOR ABSENCES

As we have seen, people use metaphor when they say things that are in some way difficult, either emotionally difficult or dealing with ideas that are difficult to put into words. Many conventional ways of talking also make use of metaphor, so much so that it is difficult to avoid using metaphor. When we come across a stretch of talk without metaphor, its absence is conspicuous. The distribution analysis described earlier showed where particularly dense clusters of metaphor occurred but also when metaphor was more or less absent. Investigating these 'absences of metaphor' shows that talk without metaphor happens very rarely but, when it does occur, can be very powerful indeed.

When metaphor is absent, what is going on in the talking and thinking? We find two, very different kinds of discourse dynamics producing absence of metaphor. The identification process described in chapter 3 relies on finding a more basic meaning for a vehicle term, where 'basic' usually means more physical and more concrete. Where stretches of talk have no metaphor identified, speakers must be using words and phrases with their most basic meanings. They are not using the physical and concrete to refer to something more abstract but only to refer to the physical and concrete world. If they want to talk about emotions without metaphor, they must use vocabulary that describes the physical and concrete manifestations of emotions.

The statistical cluster analysis revealed 28 episodes of talk with little or no metaphor. On examination, some episodes had hardly any metaphor because they contained very little talk. There might have been hesitations and false starts, unfinished phrases and pauses. Other episodes contained talk about the physical and concrete world that concerned location or travel and had little to contribute to understanding conciliation, as the next section shows.

Absence of Metaphor: Talk about the Physical World

The first kind of talk that does not require the use of metaphor is talk about the concrete physical world with no metaphorical connections or analogies made from the concrete and physical to more abstract topics. Such stretches of talk occurred when Jo and Pat talked about the arrangements for their meeting, as in extract 5.4.

Extract 5.4   Making arrangements to meet, without metaphor:

1–1584	Jo	. . . and when I tried . . . (1.0) [just] to see you,
1585	Pat	[yes]
1586	Jo	I actually got a message that you didn't want to see me.
1587		which,
1588	Pat	hmh
1589	Jo	obviously was a mistake.
1590	Pat	yes sure.
1591	Jo	. . . um,
1592		. . . (1.0) so there was always the question,
1593		well,
1594		. . . I've no [idea--
1595	Pat	[but er],
1596		. . . I got on the phone immediately to people--

1597		er,
1598		. . . (1.0) <u>in</u> Dublin.
1599		. . and <u>in</u> Belfast.
1600		. . . saying to <X the people facilitate it X>.
1601		<X we knew X>.
1602	Jo	hmh
1603	Pat	so that the next time--
1604		er,
1605		. . . (1.0) er,
1606		. . . (1.0) it was--
1607		er,
1608		. . . Sir Anthony Berry's daughter,
1609		gets <u>in contact</u>.
1610	Jo	hmh
1611	Pat	. . please,
1612		you know,
1613		let's arrange it.
1614		. . you know,

Just three metaphors were identified in this stretch, all conventionalised: *in* referring to cities as containers; and *get in contact* meaning, not physical contact, but connecting by telephone. The rest of the language used refers to the physical world of *messages, phones, arranging* and physical acts of *seeing* and *saying*.

It seems in this instance that, not only were all referents physical and concrete, but also no figurative nuances were implied in using these words. Not all talk about the physical and the concrete is as literal as this extract. As we have seen, when Pat speaks about meeting Jo, he often uses phrases that include some physical action, for example: *sit down and talk* or *sitting in this wee kitchen talking to this woman for the first time whose father's dead*. In these examples, the physical actions and concrete location carry some symbolic or figurative sense. The significance of meeting and talking with Jo is emphasised by the contrast with the humble nature of the meeting place, and the fact that they sit down to talk seems to symbolise something about the end of their metaphorical journey. In extract 5.4 such symbolic or figurative nuances appear to be absent; the absence of metaphorical meaning is more or less complete.

In episodes such as 5.4, metaphor is not used because it is not needed; it is not needed because talk concerns simply the physical and the concrete, with no metaphor or symbolism explicit or implied, and with little or no affect or emotion involved: place without poetics. Talk about the physical world was one category of metaphor absence.

Absence of Metaphor: Bare Narratives

Removing this type of talk left two episodes in the first conversation and three in the second meriting deeper consideration because the speakers are talking about important matters without using metaphor.

These episodes all took the form of narratives, stories about something specific that had happened in the lives of Jo or Pat.[3] These narratives concerned the effect of violent action on people, both those at the core of the conflict and those removed by generations. Pat recounts narratives about Belfast at the time he decided to join the IRA; Jo recounts narratives about how the Brighton bombing still affects her family and also about telling her step brother and sister about their father's death immediately after the Brighton bombing. The narratives include talk about the physical world and about emotions. Without metaphor, these narrative episodes come across as particularly strong, and there is evidence that at least one of them reverberated in the hearer's mind long afterwards. I call these stories-without-metaphor 'bare narratives'. Unlike talk about other topics, bare narratives were not repeated across the discourse events. It may be that they are so difficult for both speaker and listener that once is enough.

In the chapters that follow, these metaphor absences are analysed in depth to explore how the speakers created bare narratives without metaphor and how this led to their strong impact, both in their own right and alongside the metaphor clusters that often occur close by.

CONCLUSION

This chapter has described the method for finding clusters and absences of metaphor distributed across discourse data, and has introduced the kinds of discourse activity that clusters and absences support.

Gestures of empathy have been identified in the cluster used in this chapter:

- Jo offered an explanation to Pat of her feelings about the situation with relations of other victims who disapprove of her meeting him;
- Pat entered into Jo's perspective to acknowledge her feelings.

Metaphor clusters may indicate perturbations in the complex dynamic systems of talking-and-thinking, and so are particularly rewarding for researchers to investigate. Even if a major disruption is not occurring, there is likely to be some difficulty at that point. Metaphor absences rarely signal interesting moments in the talking-and-thinking, but when they do, are found to produce bare narratives that have profound perturbation effects, as will be shown in chapters 7 and 8.

In the next chapter, equipped with the full toolkit of metaphor analysis, we examine the framing metaphor trajectory for the conciliation process, CONNECTION, and its contrast SEPARATION.

6 *CONNECTION* and *SEPARATION* in Conciliation

> "Only connect!"
>
> —E. M. Forster (epigraph to the novel
> *Howards End*, 1910)

Empathy and conciliation in a post-conflict situation are essentially about re-connecting what has been disconnected by conflict, about finding new ways to see and understand the Other as a more whole person who, while remaining someone who caused harm, can also be seen as a fellow human being.

Connections can be made through several modes:

- through the physical connection of meeting the Other and being able to see their face, their human-ness;
- through the connection of language: listening to the Other, asking questions and explaining oneself;
- through the cognitive connection of coming to understand the perspective of the Other before and during the time of conflict;
- through emotional connection with the Other: by hearing how it was for him/her, by seeing it on their face.

In this chapter, we first examine the systematic metaphor trajectory that framed the conciliation process in terms of CONNECTION and SEPARATION. In the second part, we see how Jo uses metaphors of CONNECTION and SEPARATION to think about herself after the death of her father, and how a desire for connection took her into the conciliation process. A feature of the talk examined in this chapter is the construction, through the use of contrasting metaphors, of hypothetical scenarios and metaphor clusters, which offer important discourse opportunities for Jo and Pat to push the conciliation process forwards.

CONNECTION AND SEPARATION

Metaphors of CONNECTING are frequently used in contrasting pairs, alongside metaphors of SEPARATION and often around the metaphorising of death as *loss*. Both Jo and Pat speak about the killing of Jo's father in terms of *losing* and *loss*:

174 Pat   . . . (2.0) you who've *lost* your father,

For Jo, the *loss* of her father entails a separation from him. However, a consequence of this *loss* is a *connection* to others who suffered in a similar way through the conflict (extract 6.1):

Extract 6.1   Connected through suffering:

1–135 Jo	<u>on</u> that day,
136	. . it was like suddenly I was . . <u>thrown into</u> the conflict.
137	. . . it was suddenly my conflict.
138 Pat	yeah,
139 Jo	. . and it <u>felt</u> like my heart was <u>broken</u>,
140	. . . <u>through</u> the conflict.
141	. . . (1.0) and,
142	. . . the <u>suffering</u> was . . my <u>suffering</u>.
143	I couldn't <u>separate</u> it.
144	I couldn't be <u>detached</u> anymore.
145 Pat	hmh
146 Jo	. . and that--
147	. . . (1.0) that um,
148	. . that <u>pain</u>,
149	that <u>loss</u>,
150	. . . was <u>shared by</u>,
151	. . by everyone.

The metaphor cluster that is extract 6.1 begins with a VIOLENT ACTION metaphor, *thrown into*, to describe how Jo's life was suddenly involved in the Irish conflict. While her own bereavement involves SEPARATION, from her father and in her *broken heart*, the emotional *suffering* (142) produced is connected to the suffering of others in the same conflict. Whereas before she might have been *separate* or *detached*, this was no longer possible; her *loss* was *shared*.

In terms of identity theory (Tajfel, 1981), the killing of her father initiated a new social identity for Jo. By sharing loss through conflict, she becomes a member of a new social group of people who have experienced similar events. This assumption of a new social identity is marked by negative metaphors of VIOLENT ACTION (*thrown into, suffering, pain*) and SEPARATION (*broken, separate, detached, loss*), but ends on the more positive note of CONNECTION with what is now *shared*.

CONCILIATION AS CONNECTION: A FRAMING METAPHOR

The systematic metaphor trajectory CONCILIATION AS CONNECTION brings together metaphors from across the talk, inside and outside of clusters, and provides a further framing of the conciliation process. However, rather than including metaphors explicitly referring to 'connection', the trajectory mainly features three main sub-groupings of metaphors that imply CONNECTING or SEPARATION. Two are ways of making connections across separation: BUILDING BRIDGES; BREAKING DOWN BARRIERS. The third is a precondition for connection: BEING OPEN.

Metaphors of BUILDING BRIDGES

The BUILDING BRIDGES metaphor entered the conciliation discourse as a theme of a poem that Jo wrote six months before meeting Pat in person, and that she read aloud to him in both conversations. Jo remembers clearly the origin of this metaphor, as she explains many years after the event in extract 6.2.

Extract 6.2	The origin of <u>building a bridge:</u>
4–93 Jo	by chance sharing a--
94	a taxi with a young man in London.
95	. . who. . erm.
96	. . who <u>shared with</u> me his brother had been <u>in</u>,
97	. . the IRA.
98	and . . erm.
99	he'd been killed by the British army.
100	and so,
101	. . we <u>shared</u> in that taxi,
102	. . erm.
103	. . a <u>dream</u> of a--
104	of a <u>world,</u>
105	<u>where</u> peace was possible.
106	. . and as I left that taxi,
107	. . the,
108	thoughts <u>came to</u> me.
109	. . that's one <u>thing</u> I can do.
110	I can <u>build a bridge across the divide</u> and--
111	. . and it was my first experience of--
112	of meeting someone who,
113	should've been the enemy,
114	but,
115	. . instead we <u>looked at</u> what we could <u>share,</u>
116	and our <u>shared</u> humanity,
117	and it was,
118	. . very <u>profound</u> experience.

Here again a contrast is made with metaphors of SEPARATION—*divide*—and metaphors of CONNECTING—*build a bridge, share.* The contrasting metaphors create two contrasting scenarios on a timescale of just several intonation units. In the 'divided' scenario, the fellow passenger in the taxi *should have been an enemy* because of his connections to the IRA (97, 113); in the 'connected' scenario, the focus was instead on what was *shared:* the taxi, the information about the brother, *our humanity* (93, 96, 101, 115, 116). In a move that is the reverse of Pat's shift from the political to the personal, Jo extends from her personal experience to broader politics when she talks of a *dream of a world where peace was possible* (105).

The construction of hypothetical worlds or scenarios becomes a recurring aspect of Jo and Pat's talk, and emerges as very productive in developing their understandings of each other. In this instance, Jo shows how a *dream* or hypothetical scenario can help motivate the conciliation process by serving as an ideal of a goal to aim at.

The BUILDING BRIDGES metaphor was developed in Jo's metaphor-rich poem to conceptualise both meeting Pat and the process of understanding his perspective. The poem asserts the possibility of this conciliation process. It has the title 'Bridges Can Be Built' and begins:

> Fires rage in my heart,
> The heat heals the pain,
> Bridges can be built.

As a metaphor, BUILDING BRIDGES emphasises the gap between self and Other as in need of *bridging*. Understanding is metaphorised as the *bridge*, and the conciliation process as *building the bridge*. In the conversations, outside of the reading aloud of the poem, the metaphor is used 21 times and remains close to the form in which it was first used. The verb *build* is used just once without being accompanied by *bridge;* the noun *bridge* is used in both singular and plural forms, but other aspects of *bridges* are not found. Although Jo remembered clearly when the metaphor came into her mind, she was unable when asked to elaborate the metaphor in terms of type of bridge or its appearance, suggesting that this metaphor was linguistic and conceptual, but did not have a visual dimension.

From being the 'discourse property' of Jo when it enters the conversations through the poem, the BUILDING BRIDGES metaphor is gradually taken on by Pat, who uses it four times in the first conversation and seven times in the second. Only Jo uses it in the radio interview, and extract 6.2 contains its only use in the more recent seminar. In one of his first uses, responding to the poem (extract 6.3), Pat incorporates the *bridge* metaphor into a JOURNEY metaphor and elaborates the vehicle term to emphasise the divide with *two ends:*

Extract 6.3   A bridge with two ends:

1–678 Pat   . . . (3.0) that's a very beautiful poem.
679   and er--
680   . . . (1.0) in the er--

681	the journey,
682	... (1.0) coming ... to a bridge,
683	... you [know].
684 Jo	[hmh]
685 Pat	... with two ends,
686	... (1.0) er--
687	... (2.0) that's--
688	... that's why this is so important,

The vehicle development in line 685 that speaks of the *bridge* as having *two ends* is a discourse move that enables Pat to distance himself slightly from Jo, while using her metaphor simultaneously makes an aligning move. In negotiating Jo's metaphor by emphasising one aspect of it when he uses it, Pat engages in one type of metaphor sharing.

By the time of the second conversation, the metaphor is more fully shared. Pat has adopted the metaphor, and extends it to talk about wider conciliation processes between other people caught up in violence:

2–573 Pat   all those bridges are there to be built

Later in the same conversation, Pat develops a political point about the causes of conflict by building a hypothetical scenario with contrasting metaphors in which *distances* and *barriers* are opposed to *bridges*. The importance of the negative scenario created by metaphor contrasts is that both speakers can agree on it as undesirable (1659).

Extract 6.4   Bridges, distances, barriers and exclusion:

2–1633 Pat	there's an inverse,
1634	to that er,
1635	... (1.0) you know,
1636	er,
1637	... (2.0) figure of speech
1638	you know,
1639	bridges.
1640	... bridges can be built.
1641	... and that is if you,
1642	.. actively--
1643	er,
1644	.. create,
1645	er,
1646	.. distances.
1647	... barriers.
1648	... or what are they?
1649	they are exclusions
1650	... (1.0) and er,

1651	. . a <u>thing</u> I believe absolutely fundamentally,
1652	is that er,
1653	. . . (1.0) if you <u>exclude</u> anybody's <u>voice</u>,
1654	. . . (1.0) you know,
1655	. . . you're se--
1656	you're <u>sowing the seed</u> for later violence.
1657 Jo	. . . (1.0) hmh
1658 Pat	. . and [er--
1659 Jo	[I] would agree.
1660 Pat	. . . (1.0) the <u>way</u> to counter that,
1661	. . . (1.0) is to <u>build bridges</u>.
1662 Jo	. . hmh
1663 Pat	. . . (1.0) the <u>way</u> to ensure it doesn't happen,
1664	is to <u>build bridges</u>.

The alternative hypothetical scenario, in which people are separated politically and in which separation inevitably leads to violence, is entered into with *if* at line 1641, and created with a sequence of three metaphors that work in contrast with, or *inverse* to, *building bridges: distances, barriers, exclusions* (1646–49). These metaphors suggest different kinds of SEPARATION on a SOCIAL LANDSCAPE, and as such would connect with JOURNEY metaphors (chapter 4). Each metaphor carries a negative evaluation as undesirable—in the physical world and thus in the social world, people do not want to be at a distance, to face barriers or to be excluded. A series of three such metaphors emphasises and exaggerates the undesirability of the scenario, creating an 'extreme case formulation' (Pomerantz, 1986).

In the construction of the alternative scenario, the topic of the metaphors shifts from the personal, in which the *bridge* is *built* between Jo and Pat, to the political, in which certain social groups are kept at a *distance* or *excluded,* and what is needed is CONNECTING between the groups. Pat develops this more political alternative scenario in his statement in lines 1651–56, with the argument that *excluding voices* leads to violence. The NATURAL WORLD metaphor *sowing the seed* adding a sense that violence is as inevitable as organic growth. With the idea of violence resulting from *excluding voices*, Pat alludes perhaps to Jo's opinion that people *not being listened to* led to conflict in Ireland (extract 4.19).

The construction in face-to-face talk of an extreme negative alternative scenario, or 'dystopian scenario' (Markova et al., 2007), leads almost inevitably to agreement between speakers on the non-desirability of that scenario. It seems likely that the speaker who constructs the scenario starts from a position of assuming the other is likely to agree, but by exaggerating makes agreement more likely. The alternative scenario constructs a discourse space where both parties can agree. Agreement from Jo is indeed what is received at 1659. Pat then proceeds to suggest a solution with the metaphor *build bridges* (1661), now in plural form.

The *building bridges* metaphor is undoubtedly important in the development of Jo and Pat's thinking about their conciliation processes because it offered Jo a way of imagining and verbalising what she wanted to achieve eventually. The lack of precise visual imagery attached to the metaphor perhaps reflects the lack of precise detail Jo could, at that time, imagine of the conciliation process, rather like the vagueness of the *something positive* to be brought out of the process. After some small negotiation, the metaphor is taken up by Pat and used by him. The affordances of the metaphor—to capture key aspects of the idea, to work successfully with a degree of imprecision, to be negotiated and to be extended in order to become more acceptable—enable Jo and Pat to use and adapt it helpfully. The adapting and the way they come to share use of this metaphor contributes to the overall conciliation process.

Connecting by Breaking Down Barriers

Barriers was one of the sequence of SEPARATION metaphor vehicles used by Pat in extract 6.4. Its contrast CONNECTING metaphor is *breaking down barriers*, a more violent alternative to *building* bridges, that does not connect by making contact across a gap but by removing the barrier that is the cause of SEPARATION. There were 13 uses of this metaphor type across the talk, first and more often by Pat. The metaphor of *breaking down barriers* has strong resonance with the physical *barriers* constructed during the conflict on the streets of Irish cities: loyalists and republicans made barriers of burning cars to divide the territory of the streets, and the British army constructed the road blocks to control the movement of both sides.

The metaphor is used in the first conversation when Pat talks about the usefulness of his filmed conversations with Jo (extract 6.5). It occurs in a metaphor cluster that also features the metaphor of CONCILIATION AS CORRECTING A PARTIAL OR DISTORTED IMAGE.

Extract 6.5	Reaching a wider audience:
1–1347 Pat	. . . (1.0) explain ourselves to--
1348	like a <u>wider</u> audience.
1349	and er,
1350	a <u>wider</u> audience,
1351	who have also been affected too.
1352	. . and who have . . only <u>dealt with</u> the misrepresentations.
1353	perhaps.
1354	will onl--
1355 Jo	. . . [hmh]
1356 Pat	[and--
1357	er,
1358	would only <u>see</u> . . . the stereotypes.
1359 Jo	. . . hmh

1360 Pat   . . . the--
1361   . . breaking down,
1362   . . you know,
1363   those barriers,
1364   . . was very important.

Metaphorical *barriers* can be mental blocks that prevent understanding or empathising taking place, and which must be removed as a pre-requisite of understanding the Other. In extract 6.5, Pat is concerned with *barriers* that are generated by people's misunderstandings or *misrepresentations* (1352), by *seeing* only *stereotypes* (1358).

In extract 6.6, Jo describes the *breaking down* of metaphorical *barriers* when victims of the Irish conflict meet with perpetrators at the Glencree Reconciliation Centre.

Extract 6.6   Breaking down barriers and sharing stories:

2096 Jo   <X where X> victims of all <u>sides</u> have been meeting,
2097   . . and--
2098   er,
2099   . . . (1.0) that is just about,
2100   . . . er,
2101   . . br- breaking down barriers,
2102   sharing stories,
2103   and--
2104 Pat   hmh
2105 Jo   . . . and through . . experiencing each other's stories,
2106 Pat   hmh
2107 Jo   . . . there's a real feeling of,
2108   . . . closeness and humanity of everyone,
2109   and,
2110   . . . (1.0) <X that's really felt X>.
2111   . . and er,
2112   . . . there--
2113   . . . there's been so much healing going on.

The removal of *barriers* is, except for one instance (in extract 6.7 that follows), spoken of across the talk as *breaking down,* as in line 2101. While other, less violent, options could be available, such as 'removing' or 'dismantling', it is this stronger vehicle that is chosen by Pat, and used by Jo. Once the *barriers* are *down, sharing* can happen (2102) and *closeness* (2108). As a CONNECTING metaphor, *closeness* also brings positive affect through its experiential link with physical and emotional warmth.

In the conversation after their fourth meeting, a metaphor cluster produced by Jo (extract 6.7) brings together BUILDING BRIDGES and BREAKING

DOWN BARRIERS metaphors, and also alludes to the metaphor of LISTENING
TO THE OTHER'S STORY.

Extract 6.7   Building bridges and breaking down barriers:

2–1547 Jo	. . . (2.0) building bridges is about,
1548	. . . (2.0) friendship.
1549	. . . and love.
1550	. . . and,
1551	. . . (2.0) not believing in the labels.
1552	. . . and breaking down those barriers.
1553	. . . (1.0) and that,
1554	to me,
1555	. . . (1.0) er,
1556	. . . (1.0) is,
1557	. . . the way forward.
1558	. . . (1.0) and if I,
1559	. . . (2.0) with you,
1560	. . . who,
1561	. . I have the most broken relationship,
1562	. . . (1.0) of anyone,
1563	. . in this world,
1564	. . . can find a way to,
1565	. . . let go of those barriers.
1566	. . . let go of the prejudice.
1567	. . . (2.0) and we can listen to each other.
1568	and build that bridge.
1569	. . . (2.0) and that,
1570	. . . (3.0) that is where I wanted to g--
1571	. . get to.
1572	. . . (1.0) at the beginning.
1573	. . . (1.0) after the Brighton bomb.

Breaking down barriers appears in 1552, produced whole, as if Jo is quoting Pat; she is certainly using the metaphor in the form he introduced it to
the talk. The metaphor is then split apart and the parts redeployed separately. What is *broken* is the relationship between the two of them (1561),
and the *barriers* are not broken down but are *let go of* (1565).

The extract also demonstrates how the framing metaphors assist in the
discourse, working as lexico-conceptual pacts that both parties negotiate
and sign up to, and can then use as a shorthand. For example, when Jo
says *we can build that bridge* (1568), she can use the word *bridge* to refer
to the conciliation that they each want, with the demonstrative pronoun
that metaphorically pointing to a topic in their shared discourse history,
what the two of them have previously talked-and-thought about. Achieving this through the conciliation process is spoken of as THE GOAL OF A

JOURNEY when Jo concludes *that is where I wanted to get to. . . after the Brighton bomb.*

BUILDING BRIDGES and BREAKING DOWN BARRIERS are metaphors that clearly belonged initially to Jo and to Pat respectively, each metaphor tying into the individual's personal history and experience. But, in each case, the Other adopts the metaphor, adapting it in some way to make it comfortable to use. To adapt or quote or allude to a metaphor brought to the discourse by the Other is called 'metaphor appropriation', and can act as a potential gesture of empathy. It is examined in more detail in chapter 9.

Being OPEN

The final group of metaphors linked to CONCILATION AS CONNECTION link into the metaphor *open* and its contrasts. The vehicle *open*, in various forms, was used more than 60 times across the discourse events, mainly as an adjective and with a positive evaluation: *I find you very open* (Pat to Jo). Being OPEN is a good way to be. Initially, the Other is described as just being *open*, without any complement term, but in the later conversations, they are also *open* to: *each other, you, me, the other person's story, the other's humanity.* In the interview, Pat emphasises how Jo was *very, very open* and Jo's *openness* required him to be *open and frank too.*

Being *open to* another person's feelings or ways of thinking implies both listening to them and accepting them, although not necessarily agreeing with them. *Open* is a slightly unusual as a metaphor in two ways. Firstly, adjectives are fairly rarely used metaphorically, compared with verbs and nouns (Cameron, 2003). Secondly, although its general meaning is quite clear, it is used throughout the data at this general level of meaning rather than being made more precise. Being *open* is a metaphor that relates importantly to the idea of empathy. To understand more about the metaphor, we need to see the contrasting metaphors that often occur near it. First though, this section of the chapter is concluded.

Summary of CONCILIATION AS CONNECTION

The various CONNECTION metaphors used to talk about the experience of meeting face-to-face in the conciliation process form a coherent and systematic pattern that can be formulated as CONCILIATION AS CONNECTION.

Both speakers frequently invoke the metaphor of *being open* as the key to the success of their meetings; being *open* allows connection and understanding of the Other, rather than refusing CONNECTION or blocking with BARRIERS. Sometimes violent measures are needed to OPEN up a situation. In the political and physical world, this was the justification Pat used for IRA activity. In the metaphorical world, BARRIERS to understanding are BROKEN DOWN by the impact of meeting face-to-face. Once channels are OPEN, CONNECTION can be made by BUILDING A BRIDGE and both contact and sharing become possible.

When metaphors of CONNECTION are used, they most often concern the part of the conciliation process that is about learning about and coming to understand the Other. In the initial model of empathy (figure 1.1), this would be part of 'deliberate empathy'. It emerges from the data analysis as absolutely core to the development of empathy, and so the phrase CONNECTING WITH THE OTHER will be adopted to describing the activity of emerging empathy in the revised model to be presented in chapter 10.

CHOOSING CONNECTION AS AN ALTERNATIVE TO SEPARATION

Three metaphor clusters in the data show Jo explaining her choice to engage in conciliation in response to the killing of her father. Each time she does this by constructing alternative scenarios that describe what her life could have been like had she chosen differently. Each time, the alternative scenario is constructed with metaphors of SEPARATION and CAPTIVITY, placed in strong contrast to CONNECTION and being OPEN.

The clearest example comes in the conversation after their fourth meeting, and is shown in extract 6.8:

Extract 6.8	Negative alternatives to being *open:*
2–2108 Jo	. . if I was--
2109	. . . was still angry.
2110	. . . (1.0) the only person I'd be <u>hurting</u>,
2111	would be myself.
2112	. . . (1.0) you know.
2113	. . . (2.0) and,
2114	. . . (1.0) I would be <u>stuck</u>,
2115	I would be <u>closed down</u>.
2116	my heart would be <u>shut</u>.
2117	. . . and I would've <u>lost out</u>.

The extract ends with a series of four metaphors that contrast with *open,* building a very negative scenario as a hypothetical alternative to engaging in the conciliation process. The metaphors *closed down, shut* (2115–16) clearly contrast with OPEN. *Stuck* (2114) suggests not being able to move. *Lost out* (2117) acts as a coda summarising and evaluating the previous lines, and links with the idea of *excluded* that we saw previously in extract 6.4. All these, together with *hurting* (2110), create very negative affect; they are each, in their basic meanings, quite violent and damage the person who experiences them.

As before, the alternative scenario, entered with *if* in 2108, features extreme case formulation, and seems so undesirable that it must surely be rejected. In this case, agreement is not sought from Pat; rather, Jo emphasises to Pat the strength of her determination to meet and talk with him—there was no real alternative.

The argument for engaging in conciliation is made in an episode, and metaphor cluster, in the conversation after their second meeting, extract 6.9. Here Jo sets out the choice between *blame* and *letting go of blame*. The hypothetical alternative is marked in bold.

Extract 6.9   Being *closed down* as an alternative to conciliation:

1–2333 Jo	. . . (2.0) I suppose for--
2334	. . . for me,
2335	. . it was that <u>clear</u> choice,
2336	you know,
2337	do I [. .] blame an enemy,
2338 Pat	[hmh]
2339 Jo	. . . (1.0) and <u>live with</u> that,
2340 Pat	[[hmh]]
2341 Jo	[[and the]] consequences of that,
2342	which would have meant,
2343 Pat	. . hmh
2344 Jo	. . that my heart would've been <u>closed down</u>.
2345 Pat	that's it,
2346	[exactly it].
2347 Jo	[and I] would've <u>suffered</u>.
2348 Pat	yeah.
2349	. . . X X X
2350 Jo	or,
2351	. . . (1.0) do I <u>look at,</u>
2352	. . . (1.0) <u>letting go of</u> blame.
2353 Pat	. . . hmh
2354 Jo	and <u>seeing</u> the causes <u>within</u> myself,
2355	and <u>within</u> my . . . (1.0) group,
2356	my <u>tribe,</u>
2357	<u>where I come from.</u>
2358 Pat	. . hmh
2359 Jo	. . and try to--
2360	to <u>heal</u> that.

The first half of the choice, the negative alternative, is signalled by a question (line 2337), in fact what turns out to be the first part of a two part question. The modal verb *would* is used three times in talk about hypothetical actions. In this alternative scenario, the metaphor of *closed down* is used (2344), with *heart* standing metaphorically for the emotional part of the self. The presentation of the alternative scenario concludes with *I would have suffered*, with a metaphor of physical pain applied to emotional effects. Both metaphors highlight the negative consequences of the alternative.

The actuality is presented from line 2352 with the second half of the question begun in 2337, *or do I look at letting go of blame.* The *letting go of blame* scenario is contrasted with the previously described alternative, both through the sense of freedom that is associated with *letting go* and through the idea of metaphorical *healing* of emotions rather than *suffering.*

In this episode Jo also explains that not blaming the enemy entails *seeing the causes within* both herself and her social group, which she calls *her tribe.* A SOCIAL LANDSCAPE / JOURNEY metaphor is evoked when she rephrases this as *where I come from*; her socio-cultural background is her starting point.

Shortly after extract 6.9, and closing down the discourse topic, Jo summarises with another alternative scenario (extract 6.10). The idea that blaming the enemy would mean having her *heart shut* (2401) is repeated. The extract ends with a strongly negative alternative from Pat.

Extract 6.10 Hatred as an alternative to conciliation:

1–2388	Jo	. . I had to <u>say</u>,
2389		no,
2390		I'm not going to repeat that cycle.
2391		. . . because even if I didn't,
2392		. . . (1.0) then,
2393		. . . retaliate by,
2394		. . . (1.0) <u>coming to</u> . . . use violence,
2395		. . just by me blaming,
2396		. . I'm perpetuating that <u>myth</u>,
2397		and that--
2398		. . . co--
2399		. . . the continuation of--
2400		of violence,
2401		is by having my heart . . . <u>shut</u>.
2402		. . . <u>to</u>--
2403	Pat	. . yeah.
2404	Jo	. . . to er,
2405		. . the group.
2406	Pat	[yeah]
2407	Jo	. . . and [I di-] didn't want to live my life . . like that.
2408	Pat	. . . [[hmh]]
2409	Jo	[[so]],
2410		. . . (1.0) that was sort of the motivation.
2411		. . it was--
2412		. . . (1.0) ho- how can I,
2413		. . keep my peace,
2414		and--
2415		. . . (1.0) if you like,
2416		my humanity.

2417 Pat	hmh
2418	of course.
2419 Jo	you know,
2420	um
2421 Pat	<X that's X>,
2422	<X hatred alone X>
2423	<X <u>see</u> what I mean X>,
2424 Jo	[hmh]
2425 Pat	<X [with] just hatred X>
2426	<X it'll just <u>eat away at</u> you X>.
2427 Jo	. . .[[hmh]]
2428 Pat	[[and it could]] never be enough,

As the episode concludes, Pat expresses agreement or, at least, understanding of Jo's argument, not just by explicit supportive comments like *of course* (2418) but by offering the strong negative metaphor *hatred eats away at you* (2425–26). Pat's use of the metaphor in reply to Jo, together with his use of it later in the narrative of 6.11 and the fact that Jo does not use it at all, suggests that it is a metaphor framing that Pat brings to the conversations, what Markova et al. (2007) would call an 'external framing'.

Many of the explanations in the conversations are sequential rather than interactional; i.e. one person presents an explanation and the other receives it. In this instance, Pat does not just receive the explanation, but picks up Jo's idea of *keeping her peace and humanity* and adds to it with his contrast with *hatred*. We can see this as a gesture of empathy: building on the Other's explanation or argument with one's own contribution. In conciliation, this dialogic dynamic is not to be taken for granted; as a discourse act that avoids simply receiving what is said, it reaches across alterity to express commonality with the Other.

Two similar explanations from Jo occurred in the conversation following their fourth meeting. One we have met as extract 6.8; the other is shown in extract 6.11 as follows. Just before the talk in extract 6.11, Jo had spoken of her determination to *build a bridge* with Pat and here she is explaining why she wants to do that in response to her father's killing. The talk in bold shows Jo constructing a brief hypothetical alternative as the choice she did not make.

Extract 6.11 Captivity as an alternative to conciliation:

2–278 Jo	. . . (1.0) because it's . . my <u>way</u> of saying
279	. . . I'm not going to let,
280	. . . (1.0) that [experience] of the bomb,
281 Pat	[hmh]
282	hmh
283 Jo	killing my father,

284 Pat   . . yes.
285 Jo   . . <u>put</u> me . . . <u>further,</u>
286   and,
287   and er,
288   <u>lock</u> me <u>in.</u>
289   <u>in there.</u>
290   . . . (1.0) <Q I'm a victim,
291   and there're baddies <u>out there.</u>Q>
292   . . . (1.0) but I wanted to <u>bring</u> that experience to--
293   . . . (1.0) <Q yeah.
294   . . . (1.0) that's a tragedy.
295   . . that's a <u>trauma</u> Q>.
296   . . . and now,
297   . . <Q how can I <u>bring something</u> positive <u>out of</u> this Q>.

The alternative scenario in 285–91 is constructed as a metaphorical location where Jo might have been placed by her *experience*. The location is created by a JOURNEY metaphor, *put me further* (285), and by three metaphors that express, not just SEPARATION, but SEPARATION BY CAPTIVITY: *lock me in, in there, out there*. Both metaphor types carry negative affect: the first with the conventional idea that distance is undesirable and the second with the highly negative connotations of being *locked in*, held against one's will, and isolated. These SEPARATION BY CAPTIVITY metaphors are strong and emphatic.

The quasi-reported speech in lines 290–91 does more scenario construction by being spoken as if from inside the place of captivity, and with a strong sense of fear and loss of personal agency. From line 292, we move out of the alternative scenario and back into Jo's world as she actually chose it to be. Again, quasi-reported speech is used to give the essence of this perspective, accepting the tragedy and moving on with agency to *bring something positive out of it* (297).

The extreme negative scenario is contrasted with actuality in two ways: through the metaphorical contrasts of *in there /out there,* and through contrasts in agency between being held captive and the active role of *bringing*. Inside the alternative scenario, in the hypothetical quoted speech, a simplistic social group differentiation is made into *victim* and *baddies* (lines 290–91). In actuality, Jo opts for the more complex route of understanding the humanity of the perpetrator.

Table 6.1 brings together the contrasting terms from the four extracts analysed in this section where hypothetical and negative alternatives to conciliation are presented. The metaphors contribute to an emergent dystopian metaphor scenario on the longer timescale, in which choosing blame rather than conciliation would, for Jo, feel like BEING ISOLATED IN CAPTIVITY, WITH AGENCY REMOVED, GROUPS DIVIDED AND DISTANCED, HURTING.

Table 6.1   Hypothetical Metaphorical Alternatives to Conciliation for Jo

Dystopian metaphor scenario	metaphorical alternatives	conciliation
SEPARATION BY CAPTIVITY	*put me further*	*bring something positive*
REMOVAL OF AGENCY	*lock me in there*	*out of it*
	live with	*letting go of blame*
	closed down	
	shut	
	stuck	
DIVIDE BETWEEN MY GROUP	*victim*	*seeing causes within myself,*
AND OTHER GROUP TO BLAME	*blame the enemy*	*my group*
AND DISTANCE	*baddies out there*	
HURTING	*hurting*	*heal*
	suffered	
LOST	*lost out*	*frees me*

Over the discourse events, repeated local use of contrasting metaphors contributes to the emergence of the alternative dystopian metaphor scenario suggested by table 6.1: the hypothetical SEPARATION BY CAPTIVITY scenario in which one is locked into anger, hatred or grief, with loss of agency and power. In contrast to this dystopian scenario, which is rejected, Jo chooses CONNECTION and BEING OPEN. The outcomes of the choice will, she believes, be HEALING rather than HURTING.

CONCLUSION

This chapter has elaborated a further framing metaphor for the conciliation process: CONCILIATION AS CONNECTION. Together with the framing metaphors discussed in earlier chapters: CONCILIATION AS CHANGING A PARTIAL OR DISTORTED IMAGE OF THE OTHER, CONCILIATION AS A JOURNEY and CONCILIATION AS LISTENING TO THE OTHER'S STORY, the metaphors worked together to help Jo and Pat talk-and-think about the processes of conciliation that they were engaging in.

Connecting by BUILDING A BRIDGE seemed to offer Jo a way to imagine and talk about the potential process for herself **in advance of doing it.** This is likely to be important for motivating participation in conciliation at a point when more precise goals may be unthinkable. By negotiating the metaphor so that it felt more comfortable to him, Pat found a way to share in its use.

BREAKING DOWN BARRIERS and BUILDING A BRIDGE were brought into the talking-and-thinking by Pat and by Jo respectively. Each negotiated ways to use the Other's metaphors in gestures of empathy where making use of similar metaphors indicates acknowledging commonalities with the Other.

Further gestures of empathy noted were:

- adapting, quoting or alluding to a metaphor brought to the discourse by the Other;
- adding to the Other's explanation or argument with one's own contribution.

Metaphor is found to offer participants in conciliation a useful discourse opportunity in the construction of hypothetical scenarios through contrasting metaphors that produce particularly negative alternatives. The negative evaluations of the hypothetical alternatives make it relatively easy for both participants to agree that these are undesirable—creating a discourse space where participants are able to agree on what is clearly not desirable may help build a positive climate for talking-and-thinking about more disputed issues.

We have seen how Jo used such dystopian scenarios to explain her choice to respond to the death of her father through conciliation rather than revenge, with the hope that the outcome would be *healing* rather than *hurting*. The metaphor of *healing* is examined in chapter 9.

CONNECTION as the preferred alternative to SEPARATION will be used centrally in the dynamic model of empathy in dialogue.

7 Becoming Involved in Violence

In 2009, explaining his motivation for engaging in conciliation, Pat uses the metaphor of *restoring* something of what has been *lost* (extract 7.1).

Extract 7.1	Conciliation as exploration of loss and restoration:
4–917 Pat	coming out of conflict,
918	you have to be open to this.
919	you have to go back,
920	and you have to,
921	. . . restore what's lost,
922	in some sense.
923	in some sense.
924	you are never going to be able to bring Jo's father back or other people,
925	that were killed back.
926	but we begin--
927	we can begin,
928	an exploration of the loss.
929	and somehow,
930	<X you know X>
931	recover something of our own loss.
932	. . because,
933	<X as I said X>
934	when you fight in a conflict,
935	part of you does close down.
936	. . . so it's restoring that.

Pat sees conciliation as *an exploration of the loss:* Jo's loss of her father and of his own loss of humanity that resulted from his youthful decision to join the provisional IRA and engage in violence. In this chapter, extracts from the dataset where Pat talks about his decision to join the provisional IRA are analysed to show how he explains this to Jo and something of Jo's response to the explanations.

The analytic tools used to reach these findings are those set out in chapters 3 and 5: close analysis of metaphor clusters for what metaphors do and the affect they bring into the discourse; analysis of the poetics of place and the interplay of metaphor with non-metaphorical language; analysis of the bare narratives without metaphor—how language in these episodes is used in the discourse activity. Gestures of empathy are identified and collected together.

Bare, metaphor-free narratives play an important role in Pat's explanations, vividly capturing what it was like for him in Belfast as a 19 year old newly arrived back from England. Pat is aware that some of his words may be painful for Jo to listen to, so his explanations are accompanied by metaphor clusters that show him taking her perspective in gestures of empathy. Jo's responses to Pat's explanations of how he came to join the IRA is, as we saw in chapter 5, one of LISTENING TO THE OTHER'S STORY. She does not, in fact, simply listen, but also pushes him to justify himself and shapes the use of certain metaphors.

RE-LIVING A VIOLENT TIME

The first bare narrative was told by Pat in the conversation at their second meeting in response to a challenging question from Jo which acts as perturbation event in the discourse. Asking the question is shown in extract 7.2. Jo takes a long time to formulate the question, which involves a shifting of perspectives. The preface to the confrontational question shows Jo apparently taking account of Pat's perspective and point of view, in lines 1183–95. A short metaphor cluster emerges as a result of the coda at 1192–95 where Jo summarises Pat's perspective on what led him to decide that violence was called for.

Extract 7.2   A challenging question:

1–1175 Jo	. . . hmh
1176	. . . (1.0) yeah.
1177	. . . (3.0) I've--
1178	. . . (2.0) wh--
1179	one <u>thing</u> I was--
1180	. . . (2.0) still <u>grappling with</u> this week,
1181	. . was--
1182	. . . er,
1183	. . . (2.0) understanding--
1184	. . . (1.0) very much <u>where you are coming from,</u>
1185	and,
1186	. . and . . you--
1187	the oppression,

1188	and the lack of rights,
1189	. . . and what the . . . British government did with internment,
1190	which I think was a--
1191	for you a major--
1192	. . . (1.0) sort of <u>catalyst point</u>.
1193 Pat	. . . hmh
1194 Jo	. . and <u>seeing</u> that,
1195	that's what <u>led to</u> Brighton.
1196	and,
1197	. . how <X it was wrong X>.
1198	. . . (1.0) and then,
1199	. . . (1.0) because of that,
1200	. . . then a <u>whole</u> lot more people,
1201	had their . . rights <u>taken away</u>.
1202	. . . you know,
1203	like my daughter,
1204	her--
1205	her right to a granddad,
1206	that--
1207	. . . and how you . . . <u>come to terms</u> with that,
1208	that,
1209	. . the rights of your group.
1210	. . . (1.0) were--
1211	were so--
1212	. . . (1.0) that was so important.
1213	. . . that it was worth <u>taking away</u> other people's rights.
1214	. . in order to . . <u>get</u> your <u>point</u> <u>across</u>.

In her preface to the question, Jo uses Pat's phrase *lack of rights* (1188) and offers a summary reformulation of the effect of internment as *a cata- lyst point*, a metaphor that describes Pat's moves to violence in terms of SCIENCE or the NATURAL WORLD, metaphors of a type that he has used several times. This using of Pat's metaphor is not as comfortable as it first appears because Jo then subverts the apparent gesture of empathy, turn- ing the perspective around to portray her daughter's loss of her grand- father as, in Pat's terms, the taking away of rights. The question, when finally formulated in lines 1207–14, appears to be an attempt to force Pat to confront moral issues around his actions by presenting them to him in his own terms. Evidence that this is a difficult question comes from the nature of Pat's response. Jo's question provokes from Pat a powerful description of the intensity of living in Belfast at the time and his per- sonal decision on how to respond to British army action (extract 7.3). The narrative is set in Belfast and begins with a particular street, New Lodge Road.

Extract 7.3   Six shot dead:

1–1252 Pat	. . . (1.0) on New Lodge Road for instance,
1253	you--
1254	you had--
1255	er,
1256	. . . (1.0) on top of the flats,
1257	. . . (2.0) you can have high storey flats.
1258	. . at the top of them there's army bases.
1259 Jo	. . [hmh]
1260 Pat	[helicopters] arriving and landing.
1261	. . there was a--
1262	. . . there was a man shot dead from them.
1263	. . . on one night there were six shot dead.
1264	. . . three from the flats,
1265	. . . (1.0) three others from--
1266	er,
1267	. . . (1.0) er,
1268	. . colluding forces.
1269	. . we think they were British military intelligence.
1270	and cars going past,
1271	few peo--
1272	six killed--
1273	people killed <u>in</u> one night.
1274 Jo	. . . hmh
1275 Pat	. . I mean,
1276	and there are so many other stories like that.
1277	. . in other areas all over,
1278	. . er like,
1279	what we'd call the nationalist Belfast,
1280	or the nationalist north.
1281	. . . (1.0) and,
1282	. . . you know,
1283	. . . (1.0) you have to fight that.

The narrative of six men shot dead in one night is told without metaphor (apart from one *in*). It begins with the setting: the road, the flats and the army bases with helicopters flying in and out. The crux of the plot is then told, and the narrative closes with a summary (1272–73) of the main point: *six people killed in one night.* As the narrative ends, the talk moves from this particular narrative exemplar back out to the more general justification for responding with violence in the final lines of the extract.

Alongside the stark absence of metaphor, two linguistic features contribute to the style of the story that Pat tells: the use of verbs and pronouns.

Using Verbs to Capture the Action

The narrative opens again with a setting, this time the *New Lodge Road* and the *flats*. The action is made vivid through contrast with the ongoing noise and activity that brackets it: *helicopters arriving and landing* (1260); and *cars going past* (1270). Against this background, and between these intonation units, there is the killing: *there was a man shot dead* (1262); *on one night there were six shot dead* (1263). The continuous verb tenses of the background activity with their *-ing* endings produce longer words that contrast with the shorter, stronger forms of the simple past tense action, *shot*. The impact of the action is increased by putting together the two short strong words with their hard consonant endings to create the chilling phrase: *shot dead*. The sound of the phrase seems to echo the rhythm of gunshot. In the next line, the phrase is repeated.

Shifting Perspectives, Shifting Pronouns

The pronoun shifting across the extract follows the discourse dynamics of presenting a specific story to illustrate a more general point, but also seems to capture a shift in persona as the story is introduced, recounted and closed. From 1252 to 1257, the subject pronoun is *you*, which is probably used for generic reference but might also create an effect of including Jo as listener. The lines that tell the crux of the story, 1258–73, are presented impersonally through the use of the existential *there*. This grammatical form avoids attributing agency but also creates a distance from the action, giving the feeling of Pat and colleagues watching from the street. When Pat uses the pronoun *we* in an inserted comment at 1269, he speaks from the perspective of a member of the IRA at that time reporting their collective opinion. This pattern of the impersonal, distancing *there* followed by *we* occurs again in the summary. Once again the *we* pronoun is used to present a group perspective, this time on how to describe the area of the city. The extract closes with a return to the *you* pronoun, as if Pat has now returned to his post-conflict persona in the conversation with Jo, leaving behind his former group identity.

The absence of metaphor, together with these other language choices, creates a direct narrative, short and to the point, and likely to have a strong impact on Jo. Such narratives can offer the listening Other access to the emotional history of the speaker, enabling emotional empathy, as well as new insights into how it is to be the Other through understanding more about formative events in their history. Entering into the perspective of the Other is done by recreating the setting and events in their stark, physical and concrete reality. Because telling and listening to bare narratives is potentially distressing, it might be expected to need some degree of familiarity with the Other, not only to be willing to take the floor for a longer period of time, but also to take the risk of such directness. My hypothesis here is that Jo's question acted as a perturbation that prompted Pat to move into this very different mode of discourse and produce this bare narrative.

MOTIVATION TO BE A MEMBER OF THE IRA

In the conversation after their second meeting, Pat does not go as deeply into his personal experiences and reasons for joining the IRA in the 1970s as he does a few months later, other than in the narrative just examined. However, a long metaphor cluster emerged around his talk about being involved in the IRA, which includes a comparison between his own motivation and that of a fellow member. The episode occurs as part of explaining to Jo how her father was chosen for political reasons and not because Pat was motivated by feelings of hatred.

The episode (extract 7.4) is a narrative which serves to contrast the motivations of the friend with those of Pat. It begins by setting the context as a time when Pat was thinking of leaving the IRA. Pat describes his intense emotions to Jo about how he felt at that point about participating in the conflict (*struggle*), with WATER metaphors used to emphasise his exhaustion at the time.

Extract 7.4   Motivations for being involved in violence:

1–2609 Pat	. . <u>in</u> conversation,
2610	. . . er--
2611	with a friend once,
2612	. . I was <u>at a</u> pretty <u>low ebb</u>.
2613	. . . and I was actually <u>at that stage</u>--
2614	er,
2615	. . . (1.0) prepared to <u>walk away from</u> the <u>struggle</u>.
2616	simply because I was--
2617	er,
2618	. . . (1.0) what X--
2619	totally fatigued and mentally <u>drained</u>.
2620	. . . (1.0) like you know,
2621	you're talking about thirty years,
2622	<u>at that [point]</u>.

The JOURNEY metaphor of being prepared *to walk away from* emphasises the seriousness of the situation, since this metaphor is conventionally used in reference to commitments and responsibilities that cannot be abandoned (Cameron and Deignan, 2006) and brings that import to its use here. Further emphasis of Pat's negative emotions is done in 2619 with the non-metaphorical *totally fatigued* and the metaphorical *drained*. The metaphors used to explain Pat's feelings may assist Jo to attune emotionally with him as a human being, despite him being engaged at that time in the conflict that brought her so much suffering.

Pat then proceeds to create an alternative scenario around the friend he has mentioned that enables him to explain what motivated people to engage in sectarian violence in Ireland. While, as we saw in the previous chapter, Jo explores dystopian alternatives to her chosen actions, Pat seems to explore alternatives by bringing other characters into the talk. The actions and emotions of these alternative characters are negatively evaluated, thereby rendering the alternative the more approved choice. Here, it is acting through hatred that is an alternative, appearing in the narrative through the friend's response to a question from Pat:

Extract 7.4   (ctd):

2625 Pat	I said to him,
2626	you know and,
2627	<Q how do you keep <u>going</u>? Q>
2628	. . . (1.0) and he says,
2629	I suppose just <u>off the cuff</u>,
2630	. . . <Q hatred Q>.

In the next stretch of talk, Pat expresses doubt about whether hatred could actually sustain as sufficient motivation for political violence, and then, in the next extract, he develops this idea through a short cluster of vivid and dramatic metaphors, in bold:

Extract 7.4   (ctd):

2660 Pat	. . I can honestly <u>say</u> <u>in my heart,</u>
2661	that I don't know any--
2662	. . . <X few X>--
2663	I know very very few people,
2664	. . . (1.0) that hatred was a <u>big part</u> of it.
2665	. . and those you could <u>say</u> to it,
2666	. . . <u>say</u> that it was,
2667	. . . wouldn't have lasted XX.
2668	. . . it's--
2669 Jo	[hmh]
2670 Pat	[it's] not enough to sustain,
2671	. . . during a <u>struggle</u> like this.
2672 Jo	hmh
2673 Pat	. . I don't think so.
2674	. . . you--
2675	you couldn't <u>keep up with</u> it,
2676	if it was just <u>driven by</u> that sort of--
2677	. . . (1.0) hatred that <u>gnaws away at</u> you.
2678 Jo	. . . [hmh]
2679 Pat	[you would] soon be <u>a casualty of</u> it.

The *hatred* that motivated the friend mentioned earlier now becomes exaggerated and emphatic through four negative metaphors that animate it, turning *hatred* into a relentless and dangerous entity. *Hatred* is first metaphorised as something moving much faster than the person feeling it, who is unable to *keep up with it* (2675) and then as something that *drives* the person who feels it (2676). Together these metaphors carry a sense of being chased into a state of distress and physical exhaustion. In 2677, a more intense metaphor, *gnaws away at you,* is applied to *hatred,* as if it were some malicious animal, like a rat (recalling the metaphors Pat used in extract 6.10). The outcome of the alternative of being motivated by hatred is summarised and emphasised in the final metaphor of the preceding segment, *you would be a casualty of it.* These increasingly unpleasant metaphors construct the extreme negative alternative scenario, of violence motivated by hatred. Pat's more rational (as it seemed to him at the time) political motivation is placed in contrast to this negative scenario.

A further short metaphor cluster contributes to a narrative coda as Pat reflects on his choices:

Extract 7.4   (ctd):

2682 Pat	. . . (1.0) <u>at the end</u> that ma--
2683	what does that <u>make</u> you?
2684	sort of,
2685	. . . a person that can do these <u>things</u> without hatred,
2686	is that a good <u>thing</u>?
2687	I don't know.
2688	. . there's a <u>cost,</u>

The final *cost* metaphor contributes to a systematic metaphor trajectory in which the effect of engaging in political violence is spoken of in terms of *price* or *cost*. This metaphor can be labelled, following Lakoff and Johnson (1999), as a MORAL ACCOUNTING metaphor, which is discussed further in chapter 8.

In being willing to try to explain his motivation for engaging in violence, Pat makes a gesture of empathy. The explanation is developed through the contrasted negative scenario, and added to by Pat's reflection on the *cost* of engaging in violence. We can see the evaluation that Pat makes of his choices as another kind of gesture of empathy that brings with it some acknowledgement of vulnerability: opening oneself to critical self-reflection on past choices and actions, and sharing that with the Other.

"BEING ON THE GROUND IN BELFAST"

When Jo and Pat talked after their fourth meeting, Pat spoke at more length and more deeply about his experiences in Ireland. He explained how their conciliation meetings had helped him to acknowledge feelings and experiences around deciding to join the IRA, and Jo then invites him to talk more about those experiences. There follows an extended sequence of metaphor clusters and metaphor absences as he recounts and comments on traumatic experiences from those times. Together these help to explain to Jo how he came to decide to join the provisional IRA, in terms of a JOURNEY ACROSS A LANDSCAPE metaphor.

By this point in the conversation, Jo had told several extended and embedded bare narratives (see next chapter), and it may be that this 'allowed' or prompted Pat to take the floor for similarly long retellings. However, as we see at the beginning of extract 7.5, Jo also explicitly invites him to do so. Stretches of the narrative use vivid metaphor-free language to convey the emotional impact of an event, with metaphor prefacing the narrative and then re-entering the talk in coda and reflection or comment.

> Extract 7.5   Being on the ground in Belfast:
>
> 2–2918 Jo   . . . (1.0) I'd like to hear some more of those . . [experiences],
> 2919 Pat   [ehm]
> 2920 Jo   if you'd like to . . share them now.
> 2921 Pat   . . . (5.0) I f--
> 2922   I--
> 2923   I'll talk about it in a very general way.
> 2924   it's just being on the ground in Belfast.
> 2925   and particularly the '72 period.
> 2926   er,
> 2927   . . . (3.0) I came a--
> 2928   I came--
> 2929   . . . (1.0) I was--

A web search of the phrase *on the ground* (2924) shows it to have military connections, as in *ground forces* (as opposed to air and sea forces), *boots on the ground* (meaning actual numbers of soldiers in action), extended to *commanders on the ground* (officers in action) and *eyes on the ground* (referring to air controllers working on land to control aircraft). The IRA described itself as an 'army', and this phrase is an example of how they adopted military vocabulary as part of the formation of their group identity.

Visual Scenes in Belfast

Immediately following extract 7.5, Pat describes how he joined the republican movement in the early 1970s. In line 2930 of extract 7.6, Pat appears to organise his narrative temporally, although in what follows he organises it geographically, telling of how he moved from Belfast to England and back to Belfast (2940). The phrase *the Falls*, mentioned in 2947, is the Falls Road in Belfast, a strongly republican area from where the IRA recruited many members.

Extract 7.6   I can remember seeing:

2–2930	let me start <u>at</u> the beginning.
2931	. . . I was born <u>in</u> Belfast.
2932	. . . but <u>at</u> four years of age,
2933	my father moved to . . . (1.0) England.
2934	brought the family <u>over</u>.
2935	and I grew up <u>in</u> England.
2936	I <u>spent</u>--
2937	er,
2938	fifteen years <u>in</u> England.
2939	so the formative years were there.
2940	. . . (2.0) returned to Belfast when I was nineteen.
2941	. . the troubles had just been starting.
2942	this is 1970.
2943	. . . (2.0) uhm
2944	. . . (1.0) and--
2945	er,
2946	I can remember seeing,
2947	. . <X the little wrecks X> <u>in</u> the Falls,
2948	see the petrol bombs,
2949	. . black.
2950	. . pitch black.
2951	<X night in X> Falls Road.
2952	but--
2953	you know the--
2954	. . . the arc of a,
2955	. . petrol bomb through the night.
2956	and it sort of <u>stuck</u>.
2957	you know.
2958	it was a very exciting . . time.
2959	. . . and then you see,
2960	the <u>spirit</u> of the people,
2961	and them <u>rallying</u> to it.
2962	. . . and,

Between lines 2946 and 2957, Pat describes night time activity in the Falls Road almost entirely without metaphor. The *wrecks* (probably of burnt out cars) and *the arc of a petrol bomb through the night* describe the visual scene in concrete physical terms, although the latter has a poetic form and sound. In the coda (from 2956), the scene was *exciting* enough to be *stuck* in his mind, with this latter metaphor emphasising the lasting impact of the memory. Added to the visual impact on the young man was the social impact that was also visible: *the spirit of the people* and their response, which may have been literal *rallying* as well as metaphorical *rallying* (2960–61).

In telling this narrative, Pat may help Jo to see through his eyes how it was to be 19 in Belfast at that time. By describing what was physically visible, he offers a visual explanation; it is as if the metaphor UNDERSTANDING IS SEEING is being enacted through language.

The bare narrative is followed shortly after by the metaphor cluster in extract 7.7. In this cluster, the metaphors are mainly connected into a systematic metaphor in which JOINING THE IRA IS A JOURNEY ACROSS THE LANDSCAPE. The LANDSCAPE in question is the socio-political landscape, with the IRA positioned in a particular location that Pat is working his way towards.

Extract 7.7   Feeling the ground out:

2998 Pat	. . . (3.0) my mind then,
2999	I was pretty sort of <u>left-wing orientated</u>.
3000	. . and I actually thought of <u>joining</u> the official IRA.
3001	and I'd <u>made</u> one or two--
3002	sort of er--
3003	. . . (2.0) tentative <u>openings</u> to people.
3004	who I knew were <u>connected</u> to <u>that way</u>.
3005	. . . (1.0) just to <u>feel the ground out</u>.

Within the JOURNEY ACROSS A LANDSCAPE metaphor that describes Pat's process of reaching the decision to *join* the IRA, the official and provisional IRA organisations are places or paths (*that way*) on a landscape that he is journeying across. On the socio-political LANDSCAPE, the *official IRA* is situated *left*, using a conventionalised metaphor; Pat's contacts are *connected to that way;* Pat is *orientated* to this direction. The nature of this JOURNEY or decision is explained through the affect attached to the metaphor *feel the ground out*, i.e. slow and painstaking.

The next metaphor cluster in this long 'story' (extract 7.8) also seems to take place on the socio-political LANDSCAPE. Events in Belfast make Pat realise that he has to make a move, and can no longer *stand back from* what is happening.

Extract 7.8   Setting the scene for a narrative:

3037 Pat	[. . . (1.0) <u>something</u> had to be done,
3038	and you just couldn't <u>stand back from</u> it.
3039	. . . (1.0) and I began to realise,
3040	that the people who are really exp--
3041	. . . (2.0) <u>giving</u> leadership in that district,
3042	. . . were the provisional IRA.
3043	. . . (1.0) and that's--
3044	. . . the district was pretty <u>solid</u> <u>behind</u> them.
3045	. . . and that's a pretty <u>powerful</u>--
3046	you know,

3047	it was a pretty <u>powerful</u> as a r- <u>recruiting sergeant</u>.
3048	. . . (2.0) and er,
3049	. . . I did eventually <u>join up</u>.
3050	. . . (2.0) but,
3051	before I <u>joined up</u>.
3052	. . . (1.0) there was <u>something</u> pretty traumatic happened to me.

By this time in his recounted history, Pat has come to know the socio-political LANDSCAPE and sees that the provisional IRA are supported by *the district* (3044), with the conventionalised LANDSCAPE metaphor of being *behind* someone indicating support. The *district* is a physical geographic metonymy in which the place stands for the people who live there and their allegiances and attitudes. *Standing back from* something carries, along with the notion of physical positioning at a distance, a sense of reluctance to take action and an attitudinal value that disapproves of the reluctance. Into this mix of LANDSCAPE metaphors, Pat adds the metaphor of the *recruiting sergeant*, which stands for any factor that encourages people to join an army, or here, a political organisation that thinks of itself as an army.

The end of this metaphor cluster leads into another episode of metaphor absence in which Pat recounts the *traumatic* experience of being taken off the street by the British army.

A BARE NARRATIVE: "BEING LIFTED"

Pat talks a little more about how the conditions at the time led him to join the IRA and then tells a story about *something pretty traumatic that happened* to him—being taken to the British army barracks for questioning, or *being lifted*.

Being Taken to the Barracks

The verb *be lifted or be lifted up*, which here means being taken by force to the army barracks, is based on metonymy, because part of an action, the physical *lifting*, is used to refer to the whole action. They are underlined as metaphorically used on the assumption that no physical *lifting* was involved. The lack of agency in both metonymic and metaphorical senses contrasts with the agency of Pat on the socio-political LANDSCAPE.

Extract 7.9   Being lifted[1]:

3057	. . but I remember being <u>lifted</u>--
3058	. . . and brought to Girdwood Barracks.
3059	which was the sort of main interrogation centre,
3060	*at* that time.
3061	. . . (1.0) before Castle really <u>got going</u>.

3062	Castlereagh really <u>got going</u>.
3063	. . . (1.0) and I was <u>lifted up</u> with about--
3064	. . I think about twenty thirty other men,
3065	out of a drinking club.
3066	. . . (2.0) and er,
3067	we all got the--
3068	sort of,
3069	obligatory kicking in the back of a Saracen.
3070	I mean,
3071	I remember,
3072	I still got the scars on my hands.
3073	. . . (1.0) er,
3074	. . . then,
3075	. . . (1.0) I remember--
3076	er,
3077	. . . (3.0) details <X been X>--
3078	. . from the moment I was in Girdwood,
3079	I remember--
3080	er,
3081	. . . (1.0) the contempt.
3082	. . . (1.0) you know,
3083	er,
3084	the RUC,
3085	and the special branch had for you.
3086	. . . it was just sheer contempt.
3087	it was like they were <u>treating cattle</u>.

After the early metaphors, the story continues without metaphor until 3087 where Pat emerges from recalling memories to comment to Jo on how it felt at the time with a metaphorical comparison: *it was like they were treating cattle*.[2] The comparison emphasises the negative and depersonalising effect of the experience, that acted as a step on the way to further violence.

The Sights and Sounds Inside the Barracks

Pat returns to the story to state his belief in the innocence of those *lifted* that night, before proceeding to speak about his personal experience, extract 7.10, again letting Jo understand his experience through his recalled visual and aural memories in a bare narrative.

Extract 7.10   Pat's experience in the barracks:

3099	. . . (1.0) we were put in cubicles.
3100	and then you <u>spent</u> the next six hours,
3101	you slept like in this cubicle,
3102	and had those--

3103	what would you call it now,
3104	plasterboard with all the perforations in it.
3105	. . . (1.0) you know,
3106	sort of--
3107	er,
3108	. . . (1.0) machines.
3109	. . . (2.0) and there was a--
3110	. . . one of those--
3111	er,
3112	. . . (1.0) her Majesty's Government's sticky labels,
3113	that you put on these er brown envelopes.
3114	and it was upside down,
3115	and somebody's . . . put,
3116	. . . (2.0) sixteen,
3117	number sixteen.
3118	so I was number sixteen,
3119	in this row of cubicles.
3120	. . . (1.0) and er,
3121	. . . (1.0) you are <u>made</u> to s--
3122	. . . you know,
3123	just,
3124	look at this wall.
3125	. . . hours <u>on end</u>.
3126	<u>at end</u>.
3127	occasionally you'd hear people,
3128	who'd say to you,
3129	who somehow would--
3130	. . . because remember we're <u>lifted</u> out of the club.
3131	and if someone had taken drink and all,
3132	. . they'd <u>nod off</u>.
3133	and then there would be an almighty . . rattle,
3134	and a scream.
3135	or <u>something</u>.
3136	that says,
3137	. . <Q Jesus what's happening Q>.
3138	. . . well,
3139	that--
3140	that <u>sobers</u> you <u>up</u>.

The description of the conditions in the barracks focuses on specific and visual details of the cubicles, such as the plasterboard with perforations and the sticky labels with numbers on. Being able to recall such small details of place with such clarity after more than 20 years indicates the vividness of the experience at the time, as does the second part of the description which switches from visual detail to aural detail: *rattle and a scream* (3133–34).

The bare narrative about *being lifted* describes how Pat's experience of being deprived of agency made him feel reduced to a number: *so I was number 16* (3118). His landscape is reduced to the *wall* that he is *made to look at* (3124–28), with only the disembodied sounds of a *rattle* or *scream* reaching him.

In the short coda at 3140, *sobering up* possibly refers to more than recovering from the effects of alcohol, to understanding their position as being more serious. This change in understanding is mentioned again in a reflection on the experience produced shortly after the narrative and leads into a metaphor cluster (extract 7.11). Here, Pat explains how his understanding of the British position changed as a result of his treatment when *lifted*.

> Extract 7.11 A very powerful enemy:
>
> | 3146 | I think-- |
> |---|---|
> | 3147 | what I learned from it, |
> | 3148 | though, |
> | 3149 | is this, |
> | 3150 | . . . is this, |
> | 3151 | . . . (2.0) this is known about. |
> | 3152 | this has been sanctioned. |
> | 3153 | . . . ehm, |
> | 3154 | . . people have been trained, |
> | 3155 | . . . for this duty. |
> | 3156 | . . . (1.0) this is a very powerful enemy, |
> | 3157 | we're <u>facing here</u>. |
> | 3158 | . . . (1.0) this didn't-- |
> | 3159 | somebody didn't <u>concoct</u> this. |
> | 3160 | . . . (1.0) this has <u>come from a long</u> . . history of it. |
> | 3161 | you know, |
> | 3162 | a <u>long</u> experience of <u>dealing with</u> . . natives, |
> | 3163 | etcetera. |
> | 3164 | . . . (1.0) and I <u>find</u> that very <u>powerful</u>. |
> | 3165 | . . . and, |
> | 3166 | . . . (4.0) it scared me. |
> | 3167 | . . . very much. |
> | 3168 | when I got out. |
> | 3169 | . . . I <u>lost</u> the <u>appetite</u> for <u>joining</u> the republican <u>movement</u>. |
> | 3170 | . . . for a couple of weeks anyway. |
> | 3171 | . . . it took me a time to sort of er-- |
> | 3172 | . . . <u>transcend</u> the fear. |

At the beginning of this extract, a series of statements use the passive voice: *this is known about* (3151); *this has been sanctioned* (3152); *people have been trained* (3154), climaxing in the statement *this is a very powerful enemy* (3156). The passive voice does not specify agency and in these statements hides the specifics of the institution or people who were *knowing, sanctioning* and *training*. The grammar reflects how it probably felt at the time; the men who were *lifted* came into contact with the end result of this *knowing, sanctioning* and *training* without seeing the people in control or power.

The words used in the phrase at 3156, *a very powerful enemy we're facing here,* contrast strongly with those at the start of the narrative where the republican men were together in a drinking club. The way they were treated and positioned by their treatment has contributed to 'militarising' the situation. The metaphor of *facing here* further develops the metaphor of DECIDING TO JOIN THE IRA AS MOVING ACROSS A LANDSCAPE, with words that more basically describe physical position being used to refer to a political situation and state of mind. British soldiers are an *enemy,* dehumanised in being spoken of as a singular entity positioned on this landscape; republicans are also spoken of as a group, using the *we* pronoun, and metaphorically positioned as *facing* their enemy, as if in readiness for conflict.

In the metaphor cluster that begins at 3157, the effect of being taken in by the British soldiers is described as *powerful* (3164), Pat admits to *fear* (3172) and to feeling *scared* (3166) by it. But the effect is also temporary, as implied by the metaphor in the coda to the narrative, *I lost the appetite for joining* (3169), and eventually Pat Magee joined the provisional IRA.

The story of 'being lifted' recalls a single event inside the larger succession of violent events. It cannot exonerate Pat from any of the responsibility that he must take, but it does illuminate the cycle of dehumanising and escalating violence that he was part of. It demonstrates how memory holds on to the sounds and sights that accompany fear and trauma, and how retelling the physical actuality of an experience can convey emotions and impact to the listener.

LOOKING BACK ON BEING A MEMBER OF THE IRA

Explaining oneself to the Other can be particularly difficult when dealing with specific acts of violence that affected the Other, directly or indirectly. In extract 7.12, we see how, even when engaged in this tricky discourse activity, Pat manages to make some gestures of empathy that acknowledge Jo's perspective. The first such gesture comes at line 360 with the adjective *uncomfortable.* By choosing this word, Pat enters into Jo's perspective to describe and sympathise with the feelings she might have experienced. He makes this gesture of empathy in advance of the difficult explanation of the IRA perspective on the bombing and why Jo's father was involved.

Extract 7.12   He was a legitimate target:

1–358 Pat	I've never <u>lost sight</u>,
359	. . of what the purpose was.
360	. . . (2.0) one of the <u>uncomfortable things</u>,
361	about that is that.
362	. . . (1.0) er,
363	and er--
364	I know it must have been <u>uncomfortable</u> for you to listen to.
365	. . but I think you do understand it.
366	. . . but then you can speak for yourself.
367	. . . Jo,
368	. . . (1.0) that,
369	. . . (2.0) Brighton,
370	. . . (1.0) <u>from our perspective</u>,
371	was a justified act.
372	. . . (1.0) your father,
373	and I don't--
374	. . I don't know if your father even spoke *out* about the war.
375	er I'm *led to* believe that he had--
376	. . . he--
377	he <u>made</u> no <u>contributions</u> to,
378	the sort of <u>debate on</u> it.
379 Jo	. . hmh
380 Pat	. . . but he was--
381	er,
382	. . . (2.0) he was a <u>part of</u>,
383	. . you know the,
384	. . . (1.0) you know,
385	. . . (1.0) the political elite.
386	the . . Tory government.
387	etcetera.
388	. . . and er,
389	he must've been--
390	er,
391	. . . (2.0) <u>supported</u> decisions <u>made</u> in regard to Eire,
392	and affected people's lives <u>on the ground</u>.
393	. . . (2.0) and er,
394	. . . (1.0) if--
395	. . . (1.0) <u>in</u> that sense.
396	. . you know that--
397	. . . (1.0) there's that <u>cruel</u> word.
398	. . you know,
399	um,
400	<u>cruel</u> expression.
401	. . he was a legitimate <u>target</u>.

402	. . . (2.0) meeting you though.
403	. . . (1.0) I'm reminded of the fact that he was also a human being.
404	. . . (1.0) and that he was your father.
405	. . . and that he was your--
406	. . . (1.0) your daughter's,
407	. . . grandfather.
408	. . and that's . . all <u>lost</u>.

Towards the end of the episode, extracted as a metaphor cluster, another such gesture is made. Line 401 carries a summary of the IRA perspective on Jo's father: *he was a legitimate target.* The metaphor of *target* invokes a violent dehumanising in which the person is reduced to an object aimed at. In anticipation of how this will sound to Jo, Pat leads up to it from line 393, with long pauses and with another metaphor *cruel* that evaluates, from Jo's perspective, what he is about to say. The repeated *cruel* prepares her for what she will hear.

The episode could have been completed at 401, but Pat continues with a further reflection evaluation, giving his view of the IRA perspective as it was back in the 1980s. The lines from 402 to 408 rehumanise the man who had been seen as a *target,* re-describing him in the most human way possible, through family relationships: *your father* and *your daughter's grandfather.* The phrase that concludes the episode, *and that's all lost*, poignantly summarises from Jo's perspective in a gesture of empathy.

CONCLUSION

The extracts in this chapter together try to explain to Jo how it felt to be Patrick Magee at that point in his history, through explicit description, through narratives told without metaphor and through the metaphors. The principal emerging systematic metaphor of DECIDING TO JOIN THE PROVISIONAL IRA AS A SLOW, CAREFUL JOURNEY ACROSS A LANDSCAPE suggests a decision that was thought through as well as influenced by traumatic experiences.

In some of the episodes metaphor was hardly used, in bare narratives where words are used with their most basic, physical and concrete, meanings. In these episodes, descriptions of places and actions, of what was seen and what was heard, work to create vivid and memorable accounts through a different kind of poetics of place. Affect, emotions and feelings are not absent from these narratives; on the contrary, they seem to be heightened by being implied through their physical manifestations: the rattle and scream of a fellow prisoner or listening to threatening noises in dark streets. These strong descriptions of the physical world allow the Other to share the physical experience, and thereby come to share some understanding of the feelings and emotions, through mental simulation. While metaphor can be a vivid way of explaining emotions to the Other, bare narratives offer a different type of access to emotions. The language used in Pat's bare narratives sometimes gives a bleak poetic feel to the account. Words and phrases are often monosyllabic, in repeated or parallel structures. Where narratives end in codas, these usually feature metaphor.

Too many such episodes would probably be unbearable for participants. Metaphor in conciliation talk seems to help protect participants somewhat from emotionally painful memories as they recount them, offering a perceptual distance from the trauma (Kirmayer, 2004). On the other hand, direct, metaphor-free talk seems to have a role in pushing the discourse system forwards in coming to terms with the reality of the Other's life.

The following gestures of empathy were noted around the episodes in this chapter:

- speaking from the Other's perspective;
- using metaphors preferred by the Other to confront them with their perspective;
- Pat, as perpetrator, being willing to try to explain his motivation for engaging in violence, even when that involves recalling traumatic experiences;
- Pat, as perpetrator, opening himself to critical self-reflection on past choices and actions, and sharing that with the Other;
- giving the Other access to the physical realities around key events;
- anticipating the effect of one's words on the Other.

Jo's assertive and subversive use of empathy (the first two bullet points) created a perturbation event in the discourse by confronting Pat with a difficult moral question and prompting the emergence of the first bare narrative.

8   The Impact of Violence

> the feelings that were there at the beginning.
> the pain.
> and the loss.
> and the anger.
> and the grief.
>
> —Jo Berry (in conversation with Pat Magee, 2001)

In this chapter, the tools of metaphor analysis are employed to explore how Jo and Pat speak of the consequences of Pat's decision to join the provisional IRA and commit to the use of violence.

The most significant way in which Jo explained the impact of the violence on her and her family was through two bare narratives, prefaced and concluded with metaphor-rich episodes. In the first of these, she tells of her daughter's reaction to her meeting with Pat Magee, using the child's voice to confront him with the human reality of his actions. This recounting affects Pat deeply, at the time, and afterwards, and we examine how Jo's use of language might have produced that effect. In a further extended narrative with hardly any use of metaphor, Jo tells of how it felt when she went to tell her brother and sister that their father had been killed. These direct explanations and narratives force Pat to engage with the personal and human consequences of the violence.

For his part, Pat talks about the dehumanisation that accompanied his move towards violence as a *price* that he had to pay, and about the *weight* of the responsibility he has to carry. In response to a question from Jo, he also speaks of the emotional impact of his IRA membership. In contrast to the absence of metaphors in Jo's explanations, Pat's talk about the various impacts on his own life employs several metaphors that form emergent systematic trajectories.

Attempting to explain such terrible times and feelings to the Other is a gesture of empathy in the conciliation process because it requires considerable investment to open oneself up to relive traumatic memories. Such explanations enable the Other to understand better and seem to result in more sensitive perspective taking.

THE PAIN AND LOSS OF VICTIMS OF VIOLENCE

From the start of the meetings with Pat, Jo speaks of her feelings around the death of her father with strong metaphors, often as *pain* and *loss* as in the extract opening this chapter. These metaphors relate emotional states to PHYSICAL SUFFERING, with other metaphors of this kind using words like *casualty, wound, hurt, trauma,* and to SEPARATION, where her father's death leaves Jo feeling very isolated, poignantly expressed at one point as *I was crying in a desert.*

As Jo *walked the footsteps of the* bombers, learning more about Ireland and meeting other victims, she began to feel less isolated, and the same metaphors of PHYSICAL SUFFERING and SEPARATION are applied to other victims (extract 8.1).

Extract 8.1   Shared pain:

1–146 Jo	. . and that--
147	. . . (1.0) that um,
148	. . that <u>pain,</u>
149	that <u>loss,</u>
150	. . . was <u>shared by,</u>
151	. . by everyone.
152	. . . you know an--
153	and after that,
154	. . . (1.0) um--
155	the <u>pain on</u>--
156	<u>on every side</u>.
157	. . you know,
158	. . I <u>felt</u> it.

Jo's process of conciliation, illustrated by this sharing of metaphors across both sides of the conflict, had started long before she met Pat, initiated by the commonality of grief.

Metaphors of *pain* were put into a sub-grouping within VIOLENT PHYSICAL ACTION together with the contrasting metaphors of *healing*. A connected metaphor trajectory emerged from these around EMOTIONAL DAMAGE PRODUCED BY CONFLICT IS PHYSICAL INJURY AND EMOTIONAL RECOVERY IS HEALING. Some of the metaphor vehicles are shown in table 8.1.

The PHYSICAL INJURY and HEALING metaphors also connect into metaphors that see the immediate experience of the bombing as violence to the emotions, such as *I knew I was going to wreck his life,* used by Jo to describe how she felt when she had to tell her brother about his father's death in the bombing, and Jo's description of how it felt to lose her father through a politically motivated action: *it was like suddenly I was thrown into the conflict.* The HEALING metaphor connects the idea of emotional recovery from conflict by connecting it to recovery from physical injury or illness. This important metaphor is discussed further in chapter 9.

Table 8.1 Elements of the Systematic Metaphor Trajectory EMOTIONAL DAMAGE
PRODUCED BY CONFLICT IS PHYSICAL INJURY AND EMOTIONAL RECOVERY
IS HEALING

topic	vehicle items	example metaphors
EMOTIONAL DAMAGE	pain	to deal with the anger and the <u>pain</u>
	hurting	people that are <u>hurting</u> still from Brighton
	casualty	you would soon be a <u>casualty</u> of it (hate)
	cruel	that <u>cruel</u> word . . . legitimate <u>target</u>
	raw	it's <u>raw</u>
	trauma	that's (bombing) a <u>trauma</u>
	wound(s)	Brighton's given me a <u>wound</u>
	suffered	I would've <u>suffered</u>
RECOVERY FROM EMOTIONAL DAMAGE	healing	a <u>healing</u> experience for me
	strength	that just gave me so much <u>healing</u> and <u>strength</u>

THE IMPACT ON JO'S DAUGHTER

We follow the theme of the impact on Jo's daughter from its first appearance as a narrative in Jo and Pat's early conversation through its retelling by Pat three months later to his comments on it in the radio interview two and a half years later. Even nine years later, Pat recalls Jo talking about the impact of his violence on her daughter. In this section, we explore how Jo's words had such a powerful effect on Pat.

"I want to tell him that was a bad thing he did"

In the conversation after their second meeting, Jo Berry told Pat Magee about her young daughter's reaction to the news that she was meeting with him, in a stretch of talk that formed a bare narrative almost free of metaphor. Jo was reporting what had happened before she left the house for their meeting. Extract 8.2 shows the beginning of this narrative which is constructed by bringing together reported dialogue. The stretches of talk enclosed in triangular brackets <Q. . .Q> are imagined or remembered speech, of other people and, sometimes, of oneself.

Extract 8.2   Jo tells Pat about her daughter's reaction to their meeting:

1–449	. . . (1.0) before I . . . left this morning,
450	I decided to tell my children,
451	. . that I was going to meet you.
452 Pat	hmh

453 Jo	. . . (1.0) and I told my seven year old.
454 Pat	yeah
455 Jo	. . . and she said,
456	<Q I want to come.
457	. . I want to tell him,
458	. . . that was a bad <u>thing</u> he did,
459	to kill my mum's daddy Q>.
460 Pat	hmh
461 Jo	<Q I want to tell him Q>,
462 Pat	hmh
463 Jo	. . . <Q can I come? Q>
464	she said,
465	and I said,
466	<Q well no,
467	. . but you can write it down,
468	or I'll tell him Q>,
469	. . <Q no Q>.
470	she said,
471	<Q I must come and tell him Q>.
472 Pat	hmh

As in a classic oral narrative (Labov and Waletzsky, 1967), Jo begins by setting the scene, *before I left this morning,* and introducing the characters, herself and *my children.* When the action of the story begins, she focuses on the reaction of one of the children, *my seven year old* (453). Her reaction is told through quoted or reported speech (shown enclosed in <Q Q> brackets) which allows the language to be very simple and very direct. By quoting the speech, it is as if Jo can herself tell Pat in her daughter's words, "That was a bad thing you did".

The only metaphor that would be identified in this extract is the use of *thing,* with its basic meaning of a concrete object, to refer to the action that killed Sir Anthony Berry.

Creating a Narrative through Quoting a Child

This short episode had a huge effect on Pat, evidenced by his referring to its impact in the meeting two months afterwards and in the radio interview two and a half years later. The impact is created by using the quoted speech of a seven year old child to confront Pat with the consequences of his decision to use violence. Just the idea of a seven year old child thinking about her grandfather being killed creates an impact; we expect that young children should be kept safe from such horrors, whereas she had to face the killing of a close family relation. Her description of this as *a bad thing he did* (458) in reply suggests that she has not only thought about Pat's action, but has judged it. The straightforward and forthright judgement of a seven year old contrasts good and *bad*. Her response is made still more poignant by her description of Pat's action as *to kill my mum's daddy*. She could have referred to him as *my grandfather*. Instead, by describing him as *my mum's daddy*, it sounds as if she herself is mentally confronting Pat. At the same time, the phrase demonstrates empathy towards her mother, with the childlike term *daddy* suggesting that the daughter was imagining herself in her mother's place. For Pat hearing this, the suggestion is that his action has caused pain to the child as well as to the mother, and that this child is willing to confront him and tell him so.

The language of the child that Jo reports is simple in several ways. The words are very short and mostly monosyllabic, many with consonant endings, both hard: *want, bad, did,* and soft: *tell, kill.* These last two form 'half rhymes', a poetic effect of consonance across final consonants. A further poetic effect comes from the interplay of the hard and soft consonant endings. Children do tend to use these kinds of words first in their language development, but, by the age of seven, would also have available longer and more complex words; Jo has made a choice to use words like this, perhaps not consciously, and they contribute to the impact of the episode. The clauses are also simple, in that several of them have a basic syntactic structure of I + modal + verb: *I want to come; I want to tell him; I must come and tell him,* with an absence of pre-modification as in *to kill my mum's dad.*

The child's talk builds up over the extract through parallelism, i.e. repetition of very similar forms, to a climax at line 471 with *I must come and tell him.* This brings together what she has previously said separately: *I want to come; I want to tell him,* with the change from *want to* to *must* emphasising her determination and sense of moral imperative.

The impact of this episode comes from several interrelated features of language use in the narrative. Jo's bare narrative presents Pat with the personal consequences of his political action through the voice of a seven year old child who, despite her family tragedy, displays empathy for her mother and resilience. It would be difficult not to be moved by this.

Jo And Her Daughter Dealing with the Tragedy

After telling the narrative as in extract 8.2, Jo reverts to her own voice to summarise and comment on what she has told (extract 8.3).

Extract 8.3   Summarising and commenting on the narrative:

473 Jo	. . . you know,
474	she really wants to tell you,
475	and at age seven she <u>feels</u> furious.
476 Pat	. . . [so she does].
477 Jo	. . . [she's been] . . . cheated.
478	and,

479	. . . (2.0) and yeah,
480	I can hold her when she cries,
481	and,
482 Pat	[hmh]
483 Jo	be with her when her <u>loss</u>,
484	. . . (2.0) and I <u>feel</u> I can show her,
485	. . . (1.0) <Q yeah,
486	. . . that was a tragedy.
487	that is a tragedy Q>.
488	. . . you know,

Her summary (473–77) emphasises her daughter's feelings by adding *really* to a re-voicing of the daughter's words in *she really wants to tell you*, and a restatement of her daughter's age: *at age seven.* The words *furious* and *cheated* describe her daughter's feelings; whereas before, the listener had to infer her daughter's feelings from the reported speech, here it is made explicit, again serving to emphasise that aspect of the narrative. Pat demonstrates his attentive listening with his comment in line 476.

From 480, we are back in Jo's perspective, as she tells us how she comforts and responds to her daughter. However, Jo does not just respond by describing their situation as *a tragedy,* as we see in extract 8.4; she explains to her daughter how she is trying to turn around the tragedy into something positive.

Extract 8.4   Turning *tragedy* around, and a coda to the narrative:

489	. . <Q and yet,
490	. . I'm . . . becoming friends,
491	and talking,
492	and understanding,
493	and together we are <u>looking at ways</u> in which,
494	. . . that needn't happen again Q>.
495	. . . (1.0) you know,
496	and--
497 Pat	. . . (1.0) hmh
498 Jo	. . <Q no that's what it's about Q>.
499	it's [not]--
500 Pat	[yeah]
501 Jo	it's not--
502	. . er,
503	. . . it's not easy,
504	it's still . . . <u>live</u> <u>in</u> my [family],

In lines 486 to 498 Jo seems to be imagining that she is speaking to her daughter. This time, the quoted speech is not presented as a retelling of something that has actually happened but more as a generalisation of 'the kind of thing' that she says on such occasions. Although it is less specific, it has a similar effect, of moving the listener into the world of the speaker. The quoting allows Pat to hear what it's like when Jo is with her daughter and, furthermore, allows him to hear how she talks about him to her daughter. The coda, or closing sequence, of the narrative begins at 501 as Jo presents an affective summary of how it is now in her family, using the metaphor *live*. At this point, something interesting happens as metaphor is used in a gesture of empathy. Extract 8.4 continues with a short sequence in which Pat offers another metaphor to describe the pain and loss still *live* in Jo's family:

Extract 8.4 (ctd):

504 Jo	it's still . . . <u>live in</u> my [family],
505 Pat	[<u>raw</u>].
506 Jo	it's <u>raw</u>,
507	it's [<u>raw</u>].
508 Pat	[<u>raw</u>]

When Pat responds with the connected metaphor *raw,* he reformulates the affect that Jo has just expressed and seems to offer the vivid metaphor to Jo. She accepts the offer by repeating it twice, with the final repetition echoed by Pat. The offering of the metaphor suggests that Pat has been listening closely to Jo's narrative and is trying to enter into her perspective; this gesture of empathy shows him responsive to the affective import of the narrative. The episode that started with speaker and listener in very different places—Jo telling the story and Pat listening to it—concludes with them coming together in the metaphor.

The bare narrative with which Jo confronts Pat with the human consequences of his decision to use violence through her daughter's words acts as a perturbation event in the complex dynamic system of their talking-and-thinking. Things are different as a result of this episode, and the effect continues for years afterwards.

The Long Term Impact of the Narrative Using a Child's Voice

In their conversation together three months later, Jo asked Pat if he remembered her telling him about her daughter's reaction. Pat's metaphorical response indicates the power of that episode: *they're imprinted on my mind*. He then proceeds to tell Jo what he recalls, extract 8.6.

Extract 8.6   Pat retells the narrative:

2–944 Pat	you said to me that--
945	er,
946	<Q before,
947	. . . I came to meet you,

948	. . . (1.0) my seven year old daughter says,
949	. . . (1.0) <Q you tell him he's a bad man Q> Q>
950	. . . (1.0) and er,
951	. . . (1.0) well that's <u>something</u> I'll have to <u>carry</u>.
952	. . . (2.0) what I do want to know er--
953	. . . what did you say to her.
954	after meeting me that time.

A significant moment occurs in 949, where Pat quotes Jo quoting her daughter, or more precisely, Pat misquotes Jo's quoting. First, it is significant that the retelling includes a quote of the quote, suggesting that the impact lay in 'hearing' the child's voice through the quoting. Secondly, there is a significant change from the original formulation. Looking back at extract 8.2, we see that the words Jo actually attributed to her daughter were: *I want to tell him that was a bad thing he did*. Not only do we lose the daughter's expressed desire to tell him herself, but, more importantly, the negative focus has changed from the action to the agent. Pat calls himself *a bad man*, whereas Jo's daughter had described Pat's action as *a bad thing*. To separate what someone has done from who they are as a human being is often seen as a necessary for forgiveness or reconciliation. It seems that Jo's daughter, or Jo as rapporteur, may be able to do this more easily than Pat himself.

Pat's rather brief retelling uses the simple language and short words of the original, and also avoids metaphor until its coda in 951. Here, Pat comments on how the daughter's opinion affects him, describing it as *something I'll have to carry*. Metaphorically, her opinion is seen as some kind of concrete object that cannot be discarded but has to be 'carried' as Pat continues his life.

Extract 8.6, taken from the radio interview, shows Pat reflecting on the consequences of his decisions for Jo and her family. The interviewer brings up the topic and Pat comments on the affect of the bare narrative Jo had presented him with two and a half years earlier:

Extract 8.6   Pat reports the impact of Jo's narrative (2003):

3–579 Int	and Pat
580	whenever Jo mentions her daughter
581	and
582	how she <u>feels</u> about you
583	you seem to be very affected
584	by the daughter's opinion of you
585 Pat	well
586	that is very true
587	that is because you're suddenly
588	aware of another <u>dimension</u> to the suffering you've caused
589	you know
590	you're aware of the fact that Jo's daughters

591	will never know their grandfather.
592	beforehand
593	I could say
594	well
595	<Q Brighton
596	you know
597	that's <u>clear cut</u>
598	that was an attack on the British
599	political <u>establishment</u> Q>
600	you know
601	<Q I shouldn't have any misgivings about that Q>
602	but when you're <u>come face-to-face</u>
603	you know
604	<u>directly</u>
605	with people you've <u>hurt</u>
606	it does change the <u>matter</u>

Pat reports that what *suddenly* changed his understanding was *coming face-to-face . . . directly . . . with people you've hurt* (602–5). After that experience, he is no longer able to only think of the bombing as a political act. The impact of *coming face-to-face* with the consequences of his decision is seen across the talk. Sometimes it is spoken of through metaphor—as something to be *confronted,* something *there's no way around, no hiding from. Coming face-to-face* is a metonymy here, because there was a literal coming face-to-face with *people you've hurt.* However, it may also work as metaphor, with the extra meaning of not being able to turn away from or ignore consequences, of being forced to be *aware* of what it meant to a child (589–91). The metaphorical meaning derives from the metonymy but is here separable from it. Returning to the bare narrative that Jo told in extract 8.3, it seems that her voicing of her daughter's anger served to make Pat *face* the human consequences of the bombing. The particular presentation of the narrative through the direct words of a seven year old seems likely to have made this a face difficult to forget. In 2009, Pat again mentions Jo's talk about her daughter (extract 8.7).

Extract 8.7   Pat reports the impact of Jo's narrative (2009):

4–851	Pat	during the <u>course</u> of the conversation,
852		you become aware of the,
853		you know,
854		the <u>dimensions</u> of that <u>hurt.</u>
855		. . you know,
856		Jo woul--
857		would've talked about her . .erm.
858		her daughters,
859		and . . erm.

860	how they never met their grandfather.
861	(2.0) .. a--
862	I started to get this <u>picture in</u> my head,
863	.. about this person I killed.
864	.. Jo's father.
865	that was totally lacking before.

Jo's explanation about the impact on her daughter has contributed to the rehumanising of the Other for Pat. Through their conversations, Jo's father changes over time from a *target* or a *cipher,* as Pat describes the image he had in 1984, to a *person* with a family.

While metaphor is often held to be particularly memorable, the bare narrative that Jo told, with its retelling and recalling over time, show that language can be memorable without metaphor.

THE IMPACT ON JO'S SIBLINGS

Bare narrative also appeared when Jo explained to Pat what happened immediately after the bombing.

"we just . . . all cried and screamed together"

In the second conversation of the dataset, Jo describes, without using metaphor, how she told her half brother and sister about their father's death on the day of the bombing. This story is embedded within a longer narrative about how Jo's feelings changed over the years so that she currently feels much stronger, described as being *healed,* although certain occasions will bring back painful memories. One such occasion was the recent wedding of her half sister; this event brought back memories from about 17 years earlier of going to find her sister, who was then still a schoolgirl, to tell her about her father's death.

Preparing to Break the News

The metaphor-free story is prefaced with a LANDSCAPE metaphor, used by Jo to capture how it felt preparing herself, extract 8.8.

Extract 8.8	Getting into a space:
2174	. . . (1.0) we had about ten minutes,
2175	before we had to go,
2176	.. and I went outside.
2177	. . . (2.0) walked <u>down</u> Portobello Road.
2178	. . . (1.0) London.
2179	. . . (2.0) and I knew,

2180	. . I had to <u>get in</u> a <u>space</u>,
2181	. . . (2.0) <u>where</u> I could go and tell them.
2182	they were . . fourteen,
2183	and sixteen.
2184	. . . (3.0) I just walked <u>down</u> the road.
2185	I remember just saying,
2186	. . . (1.0) <Q dad's dead.
2187	. . dad's dead Q>.
2188	. . . over and over again.
2189	. . loudly.
2190	. . and people were looking at me,
2191	and I didn't care.
2192	. . . (4.0) and I just needed that time.
2193	. . . (1.0) to prepare myself.

This extract is itself a short narrative, beginning with the setting in time and place, and with a 'plot' that is Jo's mental and emotional preparation. The problem that needs to be solved in this brief narrative is *how to get in a space where I could go and tell them*. The spatial metaphor describes finding a 'frame of mind' as a *being in a space*. The physical action of *walking down the road* while speaking aloud seems to be intimately connected with reaching this mental state. Jo quotes herself at the time saying the short phrase *dad's dead*, which coincidentally echoes Pat's words in extract 7.2, *six men shot dead*.

Telling Her Brother in a Study

Jo and her twin sister first went to find their half brother at school to tell him the news (extracts 8.9–12). Metaphors of *wreck* and *destroy* are used as Jo contemplates the effect of what she's about to say, but after that metaphor disappears, leaving the listener faced with the bare narrative.

Extract 8.9   [He] just went white:

2204	. . . (1.0) and the housemaster knew me.
2205	. . . (3.0) he prepared a study for us to tell him.
2206	. . . and I looked at him.
2207	. . . (1.0) and I knew I was going to <u>wreck</u> his life.
2208	. . . (2.0) I knew the words I was going to say would--
2209	. . . (2.0) was going to <u>destroy</u> him for quite a <u>long</u> time.
2210	. . . (4.0) I told him,
2211	. . . (2.0) he didn't mention dad's name,
2212	. . for about another eight years.
2213	. . . (1.0) or maybe <u>longer</u>.
2214	. . . (2.0) he just looked at me,
2215	and then he just said,

2216	. . . (2.0) <Q you told me,
2217	. . . dad was okay Q>.
2218	cos I'd rung him up earlier,
2219	to say that I thought he was g- okay.
2220	. . . (1.0) and then he just didn't say a word.
2221	and he got in the car.
2222	. . . just <u>went</u> white.

The physical setting begins this extract as they meet in a room that had been prepared for them. Long pauses frame most of Jo's utterances in this extract. The brother's reaction is characterised by silence, refusing to talk about his father for a long time afterwards and, at the time, not saying a word. The description of the scene and of his physical reaction is very stark, summarised in the three final words *just went white* (2222), each word a single syllable, each ending with a hard *t* consonant, the lack of colour in his face echoing the lack of description.

Telling Her Sister in a Car Park

In contrast to the prepared study, Jo had to tell her half sister the news in a less private place and deal with a reaction that is far from silent.

Extract 8.10   [S]he screamed and she cried:

2223		we went to my . . half sister.
2224		her boarding school.
2225		. . . (2.0) and they hadn't even prepared a room for us.
2226	Pat	[hmh]
2227	Jo	we had to [tell her] in the car park
2228		with all the other girls there.
2229		. . . (4.0) and my half-sister,
2230		. . . she s--
2231		. . . (2.0) she screamed.
2232		. . and she cried.
2233		. . . (3.0) and there was nowhere for us to go.
2234		. . we just . . all cried and screamed together.
2235		. . got back in the car.
2236		. . . (2.0) the two of them . . huddled at the back.
2237		. . . (1.0) and we drove to--
2238		. . . to London.
2239		to their aunt.
2240		my step mother's sister.

Again, this narrative begins with the physical setting, the harsh and public setting of the school car park. The girl's reaction is again physical but this time loud and persistent: *she screamed and she cried*. The same verbs are repeated in reverse order when her sisters join in: *we just all cried and screamed together.*

The Poetics of Place: Thematic Interplay of the Physical and Emotional

Physical place emerges as a theme across the narratives. Each of the actions takes place in a different physical place: walking down the road, in a prepared study, in the car park. With line 2233—*there was nowhere for us to go*—the theme takes on a metaphorical resonance. On the one hand, this phrase is prosaically literal; the only private place is their car in the car park. On the other hand, the metaphorical sense of being *lost* or stranded fits exactly to their emotional condition at the time. In the metaphor scenario that is evoked, in which an emotional state is a physical place, the emotions have become so intense that they are as if lost inside them. In the physical world, they *got back in the car* with brother and sister *huddled at the back* as they drove back to London. It feels as if, metaphorically, the siblings take refuge in the small enclosed space of the car where there may find some small emotional comfort from each other's physical presence.

There is no metaphorical expression to be found in this stretch of talk but as we have seen there may be metaphorical meaning emanating from the thematic interplay of the physical and emotional. Absence of metaphor in narratives like this creates strong, direct retelling of pain; metaphorical resonances may strengthen the effect still further. The listener is given access to the speaker's perspective directly and viscerally through the unmitigated language of loss and grief.

The Long Term Impact of the Violence

There was a coda to this embedded story, extract 8.11, in which, as so often happens, metaphor is used to summarise and convey affect.

Extract 8.11   I carry that wound:

2241	. . . (3.0) and I--
2242	. . . (1.0) I <u>carry</u>,
2243	I <u>carry</u> that <u>wound</u>.
2244	. . . (1.0) of being the one with my twin sister.
2245	we <u>shared</u> it.
2246	. . and till I die of knowing,
2247	. . . (1.0) ho--

Although left uncompleted, Jo's words here described the painful memory of telling her brother and sister about their father's death with the metaphor of a *wound* that she must *carry* for the rest of her life. There is an interesting parallel to Pat's description earlier in extract 8.5 of the impact on him of the narrative about Jo's daughter as *something I'll have to carry.*

Losing and Being Lost in an Emotional Landscape

The painful and direct narratives of extracts 8.9–11 were embedded in Jo telling Pat how she felt at her half sister's wedding. Talk about this wedding precedes and follows the extracts used previously, and gives further evidence of a metaphorical theme, in which physical places correspond to mental and emotional states; words related to *loss* and *being lost* are used by Jo to describe how she feels when overwhelmed with grief or painful memories.

> Extracts 8.12   Metaphors of being <u>lost</u> and <u>loss:</u>
> 2145   and it doesn't mean that,
> 2146   . . . (1.0) I haven't . . <u>felt lost</u> since then.
>
> 2272   . . . those <u>feelings</u> of <u>loss came back.</u>
>
> 2286   . . . that <u>loss</u>--
> 2287   . . . it <u>feels</u> like it's <u>part of</u> my humanity,
> 2288   to still <u>feel</u> that <u>loss.</u>

Being emotionally 'grounded' or not *feeling lost* correspond metaphorically to being sure of one's physical place or space. Emotional distress corresponds metaphorically to feeling lost or having nowhere to go, being unable to cope in physical space. The metaphorical theme is extended to the conciliation process which is described as requiring *safe places* in which people can talk to each other (in the 2003 radio interview, extract 4.14). The physical places referred to in this chapter and the previous one—flats in Belfast, Portobello Road in London, a college study, the car park—mark significant moments in the history of the two speakers, as of course does *Brighton,* which is how they often refer to the bombing. The places come to stand for or symbolise the events that took place within and around them, metonymically extending the metaphorical theme.

THE IMPACT OF VIOLENCE ON PERPETRATORS

During conflict, perpetrators experience violence from several directions. Their actions cause death and injury to victims, and emotional suffering to victims' families. They also witness the death and injury of their fellow combatants, some of whom may be close friends or even family. The dehumanisation and desensitisation that Pat speaks of may numb perpetrators' responses to their own losses at the time, but the conciliation process brings a degree of rehumanising, and this may evoke emotions as events are recalled.

In their conversations, Pat speaks about the impact of the violence on him, both as he was aware of it at the time and how it affected him years later as he comes to know Jo through the conciliation process. Conciliation forces him to confront the consequences of provisional IRA violence and acknowledge his share of responsibility for them. He also talks about the emotional effect of the deaths of fellow combatants. Metaphor is much used and the analysis of clusters allows insights into the impact of the violence on Pat.

Violence and Dehumanisation

The dehumanising process begins when a perpetrator decides on violence, as we saw in the last chapter. It has to continue throughout conflict and its consequences, as traumatic events are experienced.

In 2009, Pat described the process of dehumanising as *closing down* some *part* of what it means to be human, and *functioning* from what remains active (extract 8.13). Metaphors of PARTIAL SEEING describe the results of this *closing down*, as we briefly saw in chapter 4.

Extract 8.13   Dehumanisation as PARTIAL SEEING:

4–761	Pat	I think when you're in a--
762		involved <u>in</u> conflict,
763		and you are involved <u>in</u> violence.
764		. . . <u>part</u> of you,
765		has to <u>close down</u>.
766		in order just to <u>function</u>.
767		. . . erm.
768		and--
769		. . er.
770		and be violent.
771		<u>take</u> life.
772		you--
773		you--
774		you h--
775		you are <u>forced</u> to <u>wear these blinkers</u>.
776		and <u>see</u> the world in very <u>black an</u>--
777		<u>and white terms</u>.
778		<X I mean X>
779		that's totally,
780		the opposite of empathy.
781		I mean,
782		that is <u>closing</u> of <u>aspects</u> of,
783		the humanity of others.

784	<u>seeing</u> them,
785	<u>purely in</u> . . erm.
786	. . a dehumanised <u>form</u>.
787	and th--
788	and it's only <u>at that level</u>,
789	that you're capable of,
790	. . erm.
791	. . of . . erm.
792	. . being involved <u>in</u> violence.

PARTIAL SEEING metaphors begin in line 775 with the deliberate and strong metaphor of bring *forced to wear blinkers.* (*Blinkers* are put around the sides of a horse's eyes so that it can see only what is directly in front of it and is not distracted or disturbed by what else is happening.) The person wearing metaphorical blinkers does not need to think about issues outside of the violent activity of direct concern, such as the human consequences of that activity. In 776–77 this is reformulated as *see the world in black and white terms,* another mode of PARTIAL SEEING, this time with colour removed, and with the result that the world is conceptually simplified into opposites, such as friend/enemy or good/bad. A third reformulation of this PARTIAL SEEING idea comes in 784–86, *seeing them [others] in a dehumanised form.* Here the metaphor of *form* affects the object of vision rather than the agent, reducing the full humanity of the Other to a mere shape and removing the human consequences of violence from the picture.

A perpetrator dehumanises both Self and Other in this process, moving into a simplified world where people on the other side of the conflict become *form, cipher* and *target.* We can note the removal of agency, and responsibility, in the metaphor *forced* (775). The perpetrator's own choices, as well as various factors and influences, lead to this happening, but the metaphors remove the notion of choice.

The *closing down* in the dehumanising process is contrasted with the *opening up* of the conciliation process (chapter 6). Likewise, PARTIAL SEEING metaphors are replaced with metaphors of FULLY SEEING to describe understanding the other as a complex human being (extract 8.14).

Extract 8.14   Rehumanising the Other:

4–862 Pat	I started to get this <u>picture in</u> my head,
863	. . about this person I killed.
864	. . Jo's father.
865	that was totally <u>lacking</u> before.
866	there was n--
867	nothing <u>here</u>.
868	. . you know.
869	. . . erm.

870	he was just--
871	again,
872	he was a cipher.
873	. . but then over time,
874	I started to build up this picture.

The *picture* that Pat *builds up* comes from things that he learns about Jo's father during their conversations. There is an extra twist in this— Pat explains that as he comes to 'admire' qualities in Jo, he also realises that some of these may be family traits inherited from the very man that he killed. The more detailed the *picture* of the victim, the stronger the impact on Pat.

The *price to pay* for violence

In chapter 4, we began to understand how metaphors of JOURNEYS and SEE-ING work together in the talk, when acknowledging the consequences of violence is spoken of as *coming face-to-face* and *confronting,* and we see how this is done in extract 8.15. Here, Pat again uses the idea of PARTIAL SEEING to describe dehumanisation as *losing sight of* the other person's humanity. A further metaphor comes into play to refer to the consequences as a *price*.

Extract 8.15   Coming face-to-face with the price of violence:

2–878 Pat	. . . (1.0) you can stand over your actions,
879	on an intellectual level.
880	. . justify the past.
881	. . . past actions.
882	. . . (2.0) but when you start losing sight of the--
883	. . t- the--
884	the fact that you're also harming a human being.
885	. . . (1.0) you lose sight of that,
886	or ignore it,
887	or you find it easier to ignore it.
888	. . . that's . . always had a price.
889	. . . (1.0) and some way,
890	well down the line.
891	. . . (1.0) you know,
892	you're going to come face-to-face with that price.

We have encountered the idea of the MORAL ACCOUNTING metaphor in extract 7.3 when Pat reflected that there must be *a cost* to his rational motivation for joining the provisional IRA. Extract 8.16 provides a further example from this systematic metaphor, in which the consequences of dehumanisation and violence is *a price to pay*

Extract 8.16   The perpetrator's humanity as the price:

1–1173 Pat   because it's always <u>a price to pay</u> for it.
1174   . . . <u>in terms of</u> my humanity.

Other metaphors from the domain of ACCOUNTING include *the bottom line* which Pat uses in extract 8.17 to express his unshakeable conviction that armed conflict in Ireland was necessary. *The bottom line* in ACCOUNTING refers to the final sum of income after subtracting all expenses. There is nowhere to go from this point; the sums are finished.

Extract 8.17   The bottom line:

1–924 Pat   that--
925   you know,
926   the <u>bottom line</u>.
927   . . . (1.0) er--
928   . . . (1.0) the <u>struggle</u> was necessary

Tracking the MORAL ACCOUNTING metaphors through the dataset provides an insight into what Pat has to deal with in accepting, as part of the conciliation process, his individual responsibility. It also suggests that the metaphor of MORAL ACCOUNTING may stem from cultural and childhood religious influences.

When questioned in 2009 directly about whether religious affiliation had influenced their participation in conciliation, both Jo and Pat said that, although brought up as Christian, they no longer felt this influenced their lives. However, Pat's language in the radio interview, and more particularly, his metaphors, tells a somewhat different story.

The interview was an early Sunday morning show with a Christian perspective. The host asked Pat if he felt that his 14 years in prison made him feel that *you paid your debt*. His reply in extract 8.18 picks up the metaphor of *debt* as he talks about his responsibility for hurting people through the IRA violence.

Extract 8.18   Purging the debt:

3–661 Pat   I <u>bear the weight</u> of the fact that I've <u>hurt</u>
662   other human beings
663   and
664   I mean
665   I'm always going to <u>carry</u> that
666   and there's no <u>way</u> of
667   <u>purging that debt</u>
668   as <u>far</u> as I'm concerned
669   not <u>in</u> this life anyway

Responsibility is *a weight* that Pat must *bear* (661) and *carry* (665) for the rest of his life. It is also a *debt* that can never be fully paid. The *purging the debt* metaphor derives from Catholic beliefs about the need for a person's sin to be removed, or purged, before entering heaven. Pat's use of the phrase here has resonances with the metaphors of sin as *debt* found in Catholic pronouncements on purgatory, the metaphorical place where:

> redemption is brought about in the sacrifice of Christ, by which man *redeems* the *debt* of sin and is reconciled to God. (Pope John Paul II, 1994; italics added)

These metaphors of sin as *a debt* to be *redeemed* have become conventionalised beyond the religious group where they originated, but they may not have lost all their power for Pat. In his next question (extract 18.19), the radio interviewer asks Pat a further question about his responsibility. The interviewer again employs a MORAL ACCOUNTING metaphor that Pat picks up in his answer:

Extract 8.19   An account will be taken:

3–678	Int	do you think
679		in an afterlife
680		in another life
681		you will be called to account
682		for what you've actually done?
683	Pat	I wouldn't say I'm a particularly religious person
684		I say in the last few years
685		about that—
686		more things
687		XXX
688		on the plane of the spiritual
689		than any time in the past
690		and yes
691		I do think that somewhere along the line
692		there has to be some form of account taken
693		and you will have to—
694		you know
695		stand over your actions

The use of the MORAL ACCOUNTING metaphors suggests that Pat's Catholic upbringing may have contributed to his conceptualisations of what his personal responsibility entails, even though he may no longer be an active member of the church.

The final example of *the price to pay* metaphor is also an instance of metaphor sharing (extract 8.20). In the conversation after their fourth meeting, about 20 minutes into the conversation, Jo opens a new topic, using what had until then been Pat's metaphor.

Extract 8.20   Refinding humanity:

2–665 Jo   [you] said that,
666   . . . (2.0) the <u>price</u> that er--
667   . . . you <u>paid</u>,
668   for <u>taking up</u> violence,
669   was <u>part</u>--
670   . . . <u>partly losing</u> some of your humanity.
671 Pat   . . hmh
672 Jo   . . . and that now you're . . <u>refinding</u> that.
673   . . . (1.0) <u>through</u> . . other meetings with--
674   . . . (1.0) ehm,
675   other victims,
676   and loyalists,
677   and,
678   <u>through</u> meeting me.
679   could you tell me more about,
680   . . . what that <u>feels</u> like.

It is not unusual in conversation for a speaker to summarise, as Jo does here, something the other person has said in order to ask a further question. In the context of conciliation, Jo's use of Pat's metaphor signals a gesture of empathy.

A Perpetrator's Pain and Loss

As Pat responds to Jo's encouragement to talk more about his feelings and emotions, the metaphors become stronger and Pat uses some of the metaphors of *pain* and *loss* that Jo has been using to describe her grief.

JOURNEY metaphors are used (extract 18.21) to talk about how he coped with the deaths of friends during the conflict; *carrying on* depicts the determination to continue on the JOURNEY of the conflict.

Extract 8.21   Carrying the pain:

2–3243   . . . (1.0) I remember attending the funerals,
3244   and,
3245   . . . one of them,
3246   the . . coffins had to be weighted.
3247   because there was just a leg in one of them.
3248   that sort of <u>thing</u>.
3249   . . . and--
3250   er,
3251   . . . (2.0) you just <u>carry on</u>.
3252   there's a sort of obligation.
3253   well,

3254	. . <u>carry on,</u>
3255	you're not going to be <u>put down</u> by this.
3256	. . you weren't even thinking about it.
3257	you <u>carry on.</u>

. . . .

3288	. . . (2.0) <u>carrying on</u> is a means of--
3289	er,
3290	. . . (2.0) you know,
3291	er,
3292	. . <u>dealing with</u> it I suppose.
3293	that--
3294	that--
3295	that sense of--
3296	er,
3297	obligation to,
3298	that you have to <u>carry on.</u>
3299	. . . you know,
3300	you can't <u>walk away from</u> this.
3301	. . . (1.0) but there's--
3302	there's so many republicans.
3303	I know,
3304	that are <u>carrying</u> that <u>pain.</u>
3305	. . . (1.0) and er it's--
3306	. . . (3.0) sometimes there's an <u>outlet</u> for it.

The *pain* is something to *carry* on the JOURNEY, but is carried internally. A poignant parallel is made between the carrying of the nearly empty coffin, symbolising the violent death of a colleague or friend, and the carrying of *the pain* of grief at such deaths. The WATER metaphor *outlet* (3306) emphasises the internalised nature of the grief, and connects to the physical reality of tears.

Jo encourages Pat in this conversation to talk about his emotions. Her curiosity about this aspect of his involvement in violence produces some insights that allow her then to see him more completely as a human being.

After Pat had explained to her how he had once broken down in tears during the conflict, Jo posed a direct question about emotions (extract 18.22). It is a measure of how the conciliation process had advanced in the previous months that Pat would share this event with Jo, and that she would then follow up with a further question, much more personal than questions in their earlier meeting. By asking about his emotions, Jo is at the same time acknowledging Pat's humanity. The long pauses at the start of each intonation unit suggest that this might have been a difficult question both to ask and to answer.

Extract 8.22   Have you cried?

2–3350 Jo   . . . (3.0) have you cried since then?
3351 Pat   . . . (3.0) only <u>at</u> a personal <u>loss</u>.
3352   . . . (1.0) never . . for a republican <u>thing</u>.

Pat, however, does answer, and his response following on from extract 18.22 produces a long metaphor cluster containing two short clusters inside it. He explains how, at IRA funerals even when carrying coffins, he did not express emotion through crying, as there was a job to be done, which is expressed through reported speech (3375), followed by an evaluative comment about this attitude: *let's just get on with it* (3376), and reflects on how this might affect the people involved in the long term:

Extract 8.23   At what price?

3375 Pat   . . . (1.0) <Q let's just <u>get on with</u> it.Q>
3376   . . . (1.0) but <u>at what price?</u>
3377   you know,
3378   <u>what price?</u>
3379   er <u>in</u> the <u>long</u> term.
3380   . . . (1.0) and again,
3381   to <u>go back at</u> some earlier remark I <u>made,</u>
3382   <u>in terms of</u> your own humanity.

Pat's use of the MORAL ACCOUNTING metaphor here takes the form of the question: *at what price?* Although this is probably self-reflection rather than a question directed at Jo, by formulating the metaphor as a question, Pat potentially opens a space in the discourse where he and Jo may be able to agree. He then goes on to speculate that people involved in the Irish conflict as republicans over a long period of time will have much emotion that they have never expressed. The answer to Jo's question about crying, and the metaphor cluster, is concluded with a coda (extract 18.24) that again invites Jo to share his evaluation, this time using the form *just imagine that:*

Extract 8.24   The welled-up pain:

3402 Pat   . . . (1.0) and they're still <u>there</u>.
3403   . . . (1.0) just imagine that--
3404   er,
3405   . . . (2.0) imagine the <u>welled up,</u>
3406   . . . (1.0) <u>pain there</u>.

What Jo is invited to *imagine* here is the *pain* that IRA members have not so far expressed, and is therefore kept inside them or *welled up* (3405). This is a further step in the spreading the application of the PHYSICAL SUFFERING metaphor of *pain:* from Jo's own grief, to the grief of other victims (extract

6.1), and here to the grief of perpetrators who have lost fellow combatants in the conflict. In her response (extract 18.25), Jo asks a question of Pat, employing the metaphor *let out* that contrasts directly with his *welled up* and recalls *outlet* from extract 18.21. Her response implicitly allows the application of the PHYSICAL SUFFERING metaphor and, with it, the humanisation of the IRA members.

Extract 8.25   Letting out grief:

3407 Jo	. . . (2.0) and do you think there'll <u>come</u> a time <u>where</u>,
3408	. . . (1.0) it's safe enough,
3409	for those people,
3410	and for you,
3411	to . . . (1.0) <u>let out</u> those tears.

When Pat applies the *pain* metaphor to the emotions that might be felt by perpetrators of violence, as he does in 3406, he is both taking a risk and making a gesture. Being willing to use the Other's metaphors is, in a way, a gesture of empathy that reaches across alterity. At the same time, it takes the risk of attributing humanity to the perpetrators of violence and that may offend the victim. A reciprocal gesture allows the Other to use the metaphors and thereby lets the metaphors become shared resources in the talking-and-thinking.

CONCLUSION

At the end of this chapter reporting metaphor analysis findings about the effects of violence, we have ended where we started, with the inevitability of *pain* and *loss* as a consequence of violence. However, by talking together, Jo has come to understand how Pat also suffered *pain* and *loss*. Her curiosity about Pat's emotions during and after the conflict lead her to ask questions, and to finding human commonalities across their alterity. Through the same process, Pat has come to understand the depths and breadth of the suffering experienced by Jo and her family as a result of his actions.

The appearance of MORAL ACCOUNTING metaphors suggests that the conciliation process offers Pat some ways of making amends.

Bare narratives have again proved particularly strong and direct ways to convey emotions, as Jo described her family's reaction to of her father's death. The emotional resonance of the physical world is a theme that we have observed in metaphors and in metaphor-free talk. In Jo's bare narratives, as in Pat's stories about Belfast and prison in the previous chapter, specific places seem to resonate with the emotions of what happened in them.

Gestures of empathy observed in this chapter are:

- Both Pat and Jo attempt to explain traumatic events and emotions to the Other.
- Both are willing to open themselves up to relive traumatic memories.
- Pat, as perpetrator, invites Jo to imagine the suffering of his colleagues: Jo, as victim, acknowledges that they suffer.
- The same metaphors of *pain* and *loss* are applied to experiences of both victim and perpetrator.
- Pat, as perpetrator, offers a metaphor to enter into the Other's perspective.
- Jo, as victim, uses Pat's MORAL ACCOUNTING metaphor to ask a question from inside his perspective.

Explanations of traumatic events and emotions enable the Other to understand better and to connect with the human being behind the label of victim or perpetrator. Each can come to see that the Other has been hurt and that they have experienced similar, if not comparable, emotions and feelings. Becoming aware of the Other as human and as suffering seemed to lead to an increase in sensitivity about the Other's perspective, demonstrated in the offer of metaphors across alterity, immediately and over the long term. In the next chapter, we see how taking the risk of using the other's metaphor can be understood as an act of appropriation, and how metaphor appropriation contributes to empathy and conciliation.

9   Appropriating the Other's Metaphors

> I was aware from speaking to certain people,
> how you--
> saw this as a journey
> > —Pat Magee (second meeting with Jo Berry, 2000)

Metaphor analysis has revealed the range of metaphors used in the concilia-tion talk and how they changed as time went by and Jo Berry and Pat Magee came to understand each other better. In chapter 3, the research question was asked: how does metaphor contribute to the conciliation process and to the dynamics of empathy? In this chapter the dialogic uses of metaphor are examined: how do Jo and Pat use each other's metaphors, and what does this movement of metaphors across alterity show about the conciliation process?

Both Jo Berry and Pat Magee picked up metaphors from each other and used them in their own or new ways. There were several occasions where one of them seemed to deliberately re-shape metaphors first produced by the other. The discourse dynamics approach insists on the connectedness but also on the uniqueness of each individual and of each moment of talk— you can never step into the same river twice, to quote the ancient Greek philosopher Heraclitus of Ephesus. Each metaphor produced in the flow of talking-and-thinking is a distinct discourse action, ruling out as simplistic the idea that speakers come to 'share' metaphors or to use 'the same' meta-phors. Instead we can think of metaphors as being 'appropriated'.

Calling the movement of metaphors across speakers 'appropriation' draws on ideas from socio-cultural theory, where appropriation is: "tak-ing something that belongs to others and making it one's own" (Wertsch, 1998, 53). For Bakhtin, appropriation was one of the main processes by which we acquire language and meaning, or as he terms it: 'the word'[1]:

> Prior to this moment of appropriation, the word does not exist in a neutral and impersonal language ... but rather it exists in people's mouths, in other people's contexts, serving other people's intentions: it is from there that one must take the word, and make it one's own. (Bakhtin 1981, 293–94)

ANALYSING THE APPROPRIATION OF METAPHORS

Two ways of examining the appropriation of metaphors across alterity are applied in order to understand how such movement contributes to concilia-tion. The first describes how a speaker uses metaphors previously voiced by the Other; the second explores the gestures of empathy that may be offered in the process.

This chapter gathers together the various types of metaphor appropriation that occur in the local moment of talk, some of them met in previous chapters, to analyse them in terms of double-voicing and gestures of empathy across alterity. It concludes with a close study of the appropriation of the metaphor of *healing* and its particular relevance to the conciliation process for Jo and for Pat.

Metaphors and Double-voicing

To assist in the analysis of the movement of metaphors, the Bakhtinian notion of double-voicing is used (Morson and Emerson, 1990). Double-voiced discourse features the words of another in some way, and contrasts with single-voiced discourse in which a speaker directly and straightforwardly produces an utterance without any reference to others' words. In metaphor appropriation, a particular type of double-voicing occurs, where the metaphorically used words of the Other are re-voiced. The voicing of metaphors is often more prominent than the voicing of literal language for two reasons. Firstly, the vehicle terms of metaphors stand out from the ongoing flow of talk, and so can be tracked across the conversations. Secondly, the affect of metaphors that we have noted throughout the book, their emotional or evaluative meanings, is often highly individual and so incorporating the metaphors of the Other will often be of significance in the unfolding conciliation process.

Extract 9.1 illustrates metaphor voicing. The moment of talk is taken from the longer extract 8.4 as Jo formulates a coda to her bare narrative about the impact of the bombing on her daughter. Pat offers Jo a new metaphor as an alternative way to summarise the affective meaning, which Jo accepts and uses.

Extract 9.1 (from extract 8.4):

504	Jo	it's still . . . <u>live in</u> my [family],
505	Pat	[<u>raw</u>].
506	Jo	it's <u>raw</u>,
507		it's [<u>raw</u>].
508	Pat	[<u>raw</u>]

What superficially appears here as substitution and repetition can be understood more deeply in terms of voicing. Line 504 is a single-voiced utterance from Jo, with the metaphor *live* describing how loss and grief is still felt. Pat's offered metaphor in 505 is a single-voiced utterance that reaches across alterity to find another way to describe Jo's family's feelings from inside Jo's perspective. Entering into her perspective with the metaphor *raw* is an act of creative understanding (Bakhtin, 1970, cited by Morson and Emerson, 1990). When Jo says *it's raw* in line 506 and again in 507, these utterances are double-voiced; Jo words echo Pat's. Furthermore, Jo is accepting, not contesting, Pat's metaphor; in orienting to the same discourse goal, her double-voiced utterance is said to be 'unidirectional' with his. This is not always the case with metaphor double-voicing, as we will see. Pat's final, overlapping utterance is again unidirectional and is now (doubly) double-voiced, incorporating Jo's acceptance of it.

Analysing the various shades of double-voicing in metaphor appropriation will help in understanding their dialogic importance. Analysing the gestures of empathy made in these double-voiced utterances will help in understanding the dynamics of alterity across which Jo Berry and Patrick Magee speak, the Otherness that each perceives in respect of the other.

Gestures of Empathy in Metaphor Appropriation

Pat's first gesture of empathy is his reaching across alterity to offer the alternative metaphor, *raw,* that tries to capture Jo's family's feelings from Jo's perspective. The second possible gesture of empathy is Jo's appropriation—acceptance of Pat's suggested metaphor, followed by her re-use of the word. Pat's repetition would be a possible fourth gesture of empathy in this short stretch of talk.

TYPES OF METAPHOR APPROPRIATION

Using the Other's Preferred Metaphor Alongside One's Own

In chapter 6 (extract 6.7), Jo uses three metaphors, one after the other. The first is her preferred CONNECTION metaphor *building bridges;* the second uses the term *labels* to refer to simplistic categories; and she then uses Pat's preferred metaphor of *breaking down barriers.*

> Extract 9.2 (from extract 6.7):
> 1547 Jo   . . . (2.0) building bridges is about,
> 1548   . . (2.0) friendship.
> 1549   . . . and love.
> 1550   . . . and,
> 1551   . . . (2.0) not believing in the labels.
> 1552   . . . and breaking down those barriers.

Jo's use of Pat's metaphor is a double-voicing, bringing his voice into her utterance, and the double-voiced metaphor is used unidirectionally, aligned with her discourse activity.

The double-voiced metaphor appears also to be a gesture of empathy towards Pat, indicating awareness of his perspective. However, using the Other's metaphor in this kind of double-voicing may not simply be a gesture of empathy towards the Other. The unidirectional double-voicing presents Pat, as listener, with a glimpse of himself working alongside Jo in the *building of bridges*. The temporary crossing of alterity done with the double-voiced metaphor may itself offer a slender rope slung across the divide that may in time support a stronger bridge.

Adapting the Other's Metaphor

In chapter 6 (extract 6.3), Pat adapted the metaphor *bridges can be built* that was in the poem that Jo had just read aloud (extract 9.3). He reformulated the metaphor as: *a bridge . . . with two ends,* emphasising the fact that they were still divided even though engaging in conciliation.

> Extract 9.3 (from extract 6.3):
> 682 Pat   . . . (1.0) <u>coming</u> . . . <u>to a bridge,</u>
> 683   . . . you [know].
> 684 Jo   [hmh]
> 685 Pat   . . . with <u>two ends,</u>
> 686   . . . (1.0) er--
> 687   . . . (2.0) that's--
> 688   . . . that's why this is so important

In using Jo's *bridge* metaphor, or part of it, in line 682, Pat is doing double-voicing, but this time the voicing is not unidirectional because he is making the metaphor work for his own discourse intention at this point, highlighting their alterity rather than what they share. This is an example of 'varidirectional' double-voicing (Morson and Emerson, 1990, 150) of metaphor. This metaphor appropriation may mark a slight gesture of empathy made in taking up the Other's metaphor, even though it was then adapted to better fit Pat's own perspective.

Using the Other's Metaphors to Ask a Question

There are two occasions on which Jo, who often takes a lead in managing the discourse, prefaces a question to Pat with double-voiced metaphors that show she is entering into his perspective. One was seen in chapter 8 (extract 8.20, shown below in extract 9.4), where Jo prefaces a question to Pat about his feelings with a reference back to his metaphor: *the price that you paid for taking up violence.*

> Extract 9.4   (from extract 8.20):
> 2–665 Jo   [you] said that,
> 666   . . . (2.0) the <u>price</u> that er--

```
667              . . . you paid,
668              for taking up violence,
669              was part--
670              . . . partly losing some of your humanity.
671 Pat          . . hmh
```

This appears to be a straightforward double-voiced metaphor, quoting what Pat had said earlier. There is a small change of topic and direction from its earlier uses, e.g. extract 8.15, in that Jo here uses it to contextualise the question she is about to ask about the affective side of that dehumanisation. The double-voicing involves a gesture of empathy as Jo recalls and reuses Pat's metaphor.

The double-voiced metaphor, and its accompanying gesture of empathy, brings Pat's perspective into the talk. By doing this in the preface to her question, Jo at the same time shows her willingness to *hear* Pat's perspective while also making it more difficult for him to avoid answering the question that will follow. This kind of alignment through metaphor double-voicing of the person asking the question with the person asked may lead to more willing, more complete or more open responses.

Using Metaphor Preferred by the Other to Enter Their Perspective and Ask a Difficult Question

A less straightforward use of the aforementioned technique was seen in chapter 7 (extract 7.2), where Jo confronted Pat with a difficult question about how he *comes to terms* with taking away the right of her daughter to a grandfather through the bombing, given that he had told her that the Irish conflict was justified from his perspective by the denial of rights to Catholics in Northern Ireland.

In a long preface that sets up the question, Jo uses Pat's vocabulary of *lack of rights* in a (non-metaphorical) double-voicing that, as previously, brings his perspective into the talking-and-thinking and makes it difficult for him to avoid answering. She also uses a SCIENCE metaphor of *catalyst point* which enhances the impression that she is entering into Pat's perspective in this stretch of talk, through a kind of distant double-voicing. This time, however, the double-voicing is much more confrontational and pushes the talk into quite different direction. Jo's question, shown in extract 9.5, directly asks for a justification of her father's killing.

Extract 9.5 (from extract 7.2):

```
1-1207 Jo        . . . and how you . . . come to terms with that,
1208             that,
1209             . . the rights of your group.
1210             . . . (1.0) were--
1211             were so--
1212             . . . (1.0) that was so important.
```

1213   . . . that it was worth <u>taking away</u> other people's rights.
1214   . . in order to . . <u>get</u> your <u>point across</u>.

The double-voicing of the *catalyst* metaphor may appear as a mild gesture of empathy, even to Pat, but, along with the double-voiced vocabulary of *rights,* is used by Jo in order to encourage him to apply his own moral judgements to his own actions in a quite confrontational move. The double-voicing may make it difficult for Pat to avoid the direct implications of the question.

Adopting the Other's Metaphor for One's Own Use

Pat refers twice to *breaking that cycle of bitterness* as he talks about the importance of not further dehumanising the enemy. Near the end of the talk, he offers this metaphor to Jo as a way of describing their future goals, and Jo adopts it:

Extract 9.6   [B]reaking the cycle of violence:
2–3732 Pat   . . . (1.0) [it's <u>breaking</u>] the <u>cycle</u>,
3733   isn't it.
3734   er,
3735 Jo   yeah.
3736   . . . (1.0) yeah,
3737   it's <u>breaking</u> the <u>cycle</u>.
3738   . . . and that's what we were doing.
3739   <X by X> saying,
3740   . . . (1.0) we're go--
3741   we're <u>breaking</u> the <u>cycle</u> <u>through</u> us meeting.

Having accepted the offered metaphor at 3737, she redeploys the vehicle to refer to their own conciliation process in 3741. A little later, a redeployment shifts the metaphor to refer to her own role in conciliation, after reiterating her sense of responsibility for the conflict:

Extract 9.6 (ctd):
3848   . . . (1.0) I'm <u>part of</u> a . . tradition that has caused . . . (1.0) injustice.
3849   . . . (2.0) and I want to <u>break</u> that <u>cycle</u>.
3850   . . . (5.0) and that <u>frees</u> me,

By this point, it seems that Jo has adopted Pat's metaphor and is comfortable using it for her own concerns.

Adopting the other's metaphors and using them for your own topics seems to be a powerful signal of increased empathy between speakers who start from very different perspectives. The *breaking the cycle* metaphor is fairly neutral; adopting more emotive or personal metaphors is another matter. In the conciliation conversations, very personal metaphors were used on either side of the divide without necessarily moving into the space between where they become personal to both.

STRONG APPROPRIATION OF METAPHORS

The use of metaphors across speakers appears to be a useful indicator of achievement of the discourse goals of conciliation. Some metaphors, like *building bridges* and *breaking down barriers* mentioned earlier, are appropriated after some local adaptation. Metaphor cluster analysis revealed a new dialogic dynamics that I have called 'strong appropriation of metaphor'. In strong appropriation, a metaphor that was previously used by just one of the speakers for a topic personal to them is taken through a process in which its use by the Other is sanctioned for application to a topic personal to the Other. The strength of the appropriation lies in the tight ties between the metaphor and the user; the process of appropriation requires bold discourse action and good judgement as to whether the appropriation will be sanctioned. In Bakhtin's terms, the double-voicing is strongly varidirectional.

Strong appropriation of metaphor requires evidence of previous close 'ownership' and of the strength of the step of 'taking and making one's own', in using the metaphor vehicle term with a changed and highly personal metaphor topic. It is also of interest to check for evidence, implicit or explicit, of the appropriation being sanctioned by the original 'owner'.

To find instances of strong appropriation of metaphors, the data was checked first for those that shifted across speakers, and then for a shift in topic. Out of 155 metaphors that shifted across speakers, only 8 were candidates for strong appropriation, and only 4 of these had sufficient evidence of prior 'ownership' to warrant a claim of strong appropriation. The phenomenon is thus not found on a large scale, but when it happens, it appears to be important to the conciliation process and the dynamics of empathy.

Strong Appropriation to Disarm the Power of a Metaphor

Jo appropriates three metaphors from Pat, the most interesting of which is *struggle*. The definite article *the* preceding the noun *struggle* marks it out as a conventionalised way of talking within the particular social group. The metaphor became a highly charged marker of republican social identity because, in the socio-cultural context of Ireland, *the struggle* or *the armed struggle* is the term used by republicans to refer to the conflict with Britain over the years, as when Pat says, *the struggle was necessary*. To use this phrase in Britain or Ireland would clearly mark out the speaker as sympathising with the republican cause.

It is not insignificant then that, in their fourth meeting, Jo appears to appropriate the metaphor and change the topic to refer to Pat's difficulties as an individual, rather than as a republican while also making a statement about how she sees Pat's identity (extract 9.7).

Extract 9.7   Appropriation of *struggle*:

2–242 Jo   the less,
243   . . . (1.0) I am <u>seeing</u> you,
244   . . . (1.0) as the perpetrator.
245   . . . (1.0) and,
246   . . the more,
247   . . . I am <u>seeing</u> you,
248   . . . er,
249   . . . (1.0) someone who's--
250   . . . (3.0) had,
251   . . . a lot of <u>struggle</u>,
252   . . . (1.0) and a lot of reasons to do what you've done.
253   . . . (2.0) and the more,
254   I am <u>feeling</u>,
255   . . . (1.0) <u>part of</u>,
256   . . . that <u>struggle</u>.
257   . . . (1.0) and that,
258   . . it's a joint responsibility.
259   . . . (2.0) that is not,
260   . . . (1.0) that I am the victim,
261   and you're the perpetrator.
262   . . . (1.0) but that we're <u>part of</u>,
263   . . . (1.0) a community,
264   a society.

The extract begins with a reassigning of identity in which Pat is rehumanised from *perpetrator* to a more full human being. The metaphor appropriation happens in two steps that are shown in bold, the first being fairly unremarkable and the second more striking. It is marked by a noticeable amount of fairly long pausing, suggesting tentative talk. In Pat's 'ownership' of the phrase up to this point, *the struggle* had referred only to the Irish conflict as seen from the IRA perspective. When Jo speaks of Pat as someone *who's had a lot of struggle* (251), she shifts the topic to the difficulties of Pat's life in addressing perceived injustices. Alongside this shift in topic from the political to the personal, the double-voicing of *struggle* involves a slight change in form, from *the* to *a lot of*.

When she allows, in 252, that he had *a lot of reasons to do what you have done,* she is making a gesture of empathy and creative understanding in trying to imagine Pat's view of the world, entering into his perspective as she fills out this revised discourse identity.

The second step in the appropriation of *struggle* is a much bigger and more dramatic one, and takes place from 254 to 256. A further double-voicing in 256 wrenches the topic into a new direction as Jo positions herself *as part of that struggle*. Whereas the previous topic shift stayed within Pat's general direction, this topic shift is very strong. The metaphor of *struggle* as it is now used must lose its power as a marker of Pat's social identity, together with its affective force that contributed to justifications of republican violence. It is, as it were, disarmed, and restored to a less harmful use.

The potential gesture of empathy that Jo makes here by suggesting that she aligns herself with the more general political (but not republican) goals of improving the Irish situation is rather overwhelmed by the boldness of her metaphor appropriation.

A further perspective and identity shift is made from 258 to 262 as Jo suggests that she and Pat might find a common social identity to replace the opposition of *victim* and *perpetrator*. She positions the two of them in the same *community* or *society* with *a joint responsibility*. This re-positioning offers a change in the nature of the alterity between them, with some part of their Otherness able to be dissolved and become commonality.

Pat's response does not come immediately but a couple of minutes later (extract 9.8) when he seems to refer back to the shift in social identity made in extract 9.8.

Extract 9.8:

2–426	Pat	you mentioned about--
427		er,
428		. . or you <u>recognised</u> the--
429		the fact that I'm,
430		. . . more than a perpetrator.
431		. . I think that anybody who's <u>come through</u> the <u>struggle</u>,
432		. . . (2.0) that applies to.

It is not clear whether *the struggle* in 431 is a double-voicing of Jo's words in extract 9.7, or a revoicing of the original socially marked metaphor. The surrounding talk shows that the *anybody* referred to in line 431 refers to people in general rather than IRA members, and so suggests that *the struggle* may be less tightly applied than before Jo's appropriation. However, by returning to the original marked form, and as happens in several places throughout the conversations, Pat is showing some reluctance to enter a joint perspective with Jo.

Several later uses in the same conversation go beyond the marked form of *the struggle* to something more like a double-voicing of Jo's disarmed metaphor, as when Pat speaks of people in working class areas as showing *dignity in their struggle*. In extract 9.9, where Pat reflects on improving the situation for Irish people, he uses the word *struggle* twice in close proximity.

Extract 9.9:

2–542 Pat	. . . what was really needed.
543	. . . (1.0) and that was an end to the discrimination.
544	and the--
545	the poverty,
546	and all those <u>things</u> that,
547	. . you know,
548	you need to <u>tackle</u> now <u>in the end</u>.
549	you don't even wait to--
550	<u>see</u> it as an <u>end</u>.
551	it's an <u>onward thing</u>.
552	. . but that that--
553	. . that <u>struggle</u> for justice and rights,
554	etcetera,
555	is--
556	. . . (1.0) was best facilitated <u>through</u> that nationalist <u>struggle</u>.

The first use of *struggle,* in line 553, seems, because of its broader topic, like a unidirectional double-voicing of the first appropriated metaphor in extract 9.7. In 556 it is used again with its narrower, social group identity marker, sense.

Jo's rather bold discourse move helps to 'disarm' the metaphor of *struggle* of some of its potency, by shifting it from being solely a marker of republican collective identity to functioning also in a more innocuous sense of effortful activity. Her attempt at disarming the metaphor required strong appropriation, and appears only partly successful. After the attempt at appropriation in extract 9.7, the metaphor is used with its shifted broader sense and its less harmful identity marking. However, given the power of its meaning within republican circles, it is not surprising that the original use persists.

The Strong Appropriation of *Healing* as Metaphor

A strong appropriation of the metaphor of *healing* made by Pat shows, not just a bold discourse action, but also a moment of connecting across difference in the conciliation process. As with Jo's appropriation of *struggle*, this strong appropriation happens in two steps in markedly tentative talk, the first step being fairly unremarkable extension and small shift of direction, and the second a more striking personal application.

Ownership of the metaphor vehicle *healing* can be traced to Jo's uses of it in the poem that she brought to the meetings and read aloud to Pat (extract 9.10).

Extract 9.10   Use of *healing* in Jo's reading of her poem:

1–591 Jo	the heat <u>heals</u> the pain
609	I will speak <u>out</u>,
610	for the <u>healing</u> for the world,
660	I feel that my heart <u>heals</u>,
661	as Ireland <u>heals</u>.

The poem connects *healing* and *heals* to three different but connected metaphor topics: to recovering from her personal grief at the killing of her father, which was metaphorised as *pain* and *loss* (table 8.1); to a general sense of recovering from suffering as a result of conflict; and to national socio-political recovery from the particular conflict. As seen in chapter 8, Pat also uses *pain* to describe the feelings of Jo and other victims from quite early in the conversation. In her poem, Jo speaks of *the pain of your war*, redeploying this vehicle from her personal topic of emotional damage caused by the bombing to a Pat/IRA-related topic, thereby allowing that perpetrators may also suffer as a result of conflict. The application of *healing* to perpetrators takes a little longer and occurs through a rather more explicit process of metaphor appropriation which is now described.

In response to Jo's reading of the poem, Pat picks up the metaphor vehicle *healing* and, in a double-voicing, extends it to refer to the recovery of other victims of the violence (extract 9.11):

Extract 9.11   Extending *healing* to other victims of violence:

1–690 Pat	I am hoping it will be--
691	er,
692	. . . (1.0) it can <u>act as</u> a--
693	a--
694	a <u>lesson</u> or an example,
695	. . . that somebody else can--
696	er,
697	. . . (1.0) er--
698	<u>gain something</u> from it.
699 Jo	. . hmh
700 Pat	. . . and er,
701	. . <u>move on in</u> their own,
702	. . you know,
703	. . <u>healing</u> process.

The vehicle *healing* is redeployed to the topic of the process experienced by an unspecified *somebody else* (695), in a relatively uncontroversial first shift. Pat's double-voicing of Jo's metaphor might also act as a gesture of empathy.

The moment of strong appropriation occurs later in this conversation as Pat talks about how he feels meeting Jo and listening to her pain, shown in extract 9.12. Until this point, only Jo has used the vehicle *healing* to talk about personal emotional recovery, from grief at the loss of her father. With hesitation and some long pauses, suggesting some unease, Pat uses the *healing* vehicle for the first time in reference to himself at line 1145, redeploying the vehicle to a topic personal to him, and being severely changing the 'direction'. The sequence of appropriation is shown in bold.

Extract 9.12   The strong appropriation of *healing*:

1–1132 Pat	. . . be <u>confronted</u>,
1133	. . <u>with</u> your <u>pain</u>.
1134	. . . that's a consequence that--
1135	er,
1136	. . . (3.0) you know,
1137	I suppose I deserve.
1138	. . . (2.0) you know,
1139	. . . (1.0) and—
1140	er,
1141	. . . (2.0) seems very--
1142	how do you <u>put it</u>,
1143	er,
1144	. . . (2.0) maybe that's <u>part of healing</u> too,
1145	**. . my <u>healing</u>.**
1146 Jo	**your <u>healing</u>.**
1147	. . [yeah].
1148 Pat	[yeah].
1149	. . . (1.0) you know,
1150	er,
1151	. . . (2.0) it's--
1152	er,
1153	<u>something</u> I have <u>to go through</u>.
1154 Jo	. . . hmh
1155 Pat	. . . if I'm going to sort of--
1156	er,
1157	. . . (1.0) really <u>retain</u> my humanity.

By double-voicing the *healing* metaphor while re-directing the reference from Jo to himself, Pat implies that he has also suffered emotionally in some way. From his talk at the end of this extract (lines 1153–57), it is clear that the suffering he refers to occurred as a result of engaging in politically motivated violence, and not, as for Jo, as a result of the violence itself. Here is the varidirectional double-voicing of metaphor, accompanied by change of personal reference, purpose and intention, that marks strong appropriation.

The appropriation of *healing* is a striking discourse move—by speaking of himself as also in need of *healing*, Pat as perpetrator of the violence is presenting himself as having similar needs to those of Jo who suffered as a direct result of the violence. Not only has the metaphor so far been owned and voiced by Jo, but socio-cultural conventions support this ownership; *healing* is conventionally used metaphorically in discourse about victims of abuse or violence, rather than about the perpetrators. Being *healed* through the conciliation process is thus part of Jo's social identity. Pat's hesitations and pauses suggest that he is, at some level, aware of this. He also seems to make a gesture of empathy and creative understanding in advance of the metaphor appropriation, in 1133–37 where he 'enters into' Jo's perspective by speaking of *the consequences that I deserve*. While claiming, as a perpetrator of violence, an entitlement to a healing process could be seen as bold, or even as unjustifiable, it may also be seen as a measure of the success of their meetings that Pat feels able to do so, and Jo's response shows that he judged the action well.

Looking at the precise choice of words, we see again a shift in form in the double-voicing: Pat's first mention (1144) uses a generic form, *part of healing*, in advance of the more specific, 'owned' form used in the next line, *my healing*. When Jo responds with *your healing*, she appears to sanction the metaphor appropriation; the personal pronoun *your* allows Pat's ownership, and her intonation on the recording at line 1146 indicates that she is accepting rather than questioning.

Some time later, at the end of the same conversation (extract 9.13), Pat's use of the *healing* metaphor in a short metaphor cluster seems to refer simultaneously to both types of emotional damage: Jo's recovery from grief at the death of her father and his recovery from the effects of engaging in violence.

Extract 9.13   Conciliation and two types of *healing*:

1–2731	Pat	. . . the process,
2732		. . . (1.0) that we're <u>in</u>.
2733		. . . (1.0) that er--
2734		it has . . . provided--
2735		er,
2736		. . . <X sort of er X>,
2737		. . an opportunity,
2738		a <u>window</u>.
2739		to . . <u>reflect on</u> the past.
2740		and that's a <u>part of</u> that [healing] process.

The strong appropriation has, over the course of the conversation, loosened the tie of the metaphor to its original use within the perspective of one speaker and allowed its re-voicing from within the perspective of the other. In the conciliation context, with the potentially large degree of alterity between speakers, this may be a significant shift.

Strong appropriation allows a speaker to display alignment with the other, while at the same time carving out a new discourse niche for themselves. The original 'owner' may permit or resist the appropriation of 'their' metaphors, but, if allowed, appropriation of metaphors is an important signal and measure of increasing alignment between participants, and particularly of the rehumanisation of a former enemy.

THE METAPHOR(S) OF HEALING IN POST-CONFLICT CONCILIATION

We stay with the metaphor of *healing* in this final section of the chapter to consider its application in conciliation.

Table 8.1 brought together metaphors in the trajectory labelled EMOTIONAL DAMAGE PRODUCED BY CONFLICT IS PHYSICAL INJURY AND EMOTIONAL RECOVERY IS HEALING. The EMOTIONAL DAMAGE metaphors—*pain, wound, casualty* and so on—were elaborated in chapter 8; here, we turn to the contrasting metaphors that portray and construct EMOTIONAL RECOVERY as HEALING.

The systematicity of this pattern of metaphors lies in what I would describe as the 'socio-cultural explanatory theory' that ties them together. It is, I suggest, broader than a relational analogy, more cultural than a schema, and has more explanatory power than a story or scenario. By bringing together the elements of the explanatory theory, we see how different are the metaphors of *healing* as applied to Jo and to Pat.

The basic, physical sense of *healing* involves a return to health from a bodily sickness or disease. Metaphorical or symbolic *healing* applies to sickness that is not (or not only) physical. Humans have developed healing practices, often symbolic, to address afflictions that may be physical, emotional, interpersonal, social and/or spiritual (Kirmayer, 2004). According to Kirmayer, transformation is central to the various models of sickness and healing constructed by different religions, cultures and traditions; the person undergoing healing is transformed from one who feels in some way 'sick' to one who feels 'healed'. Thus, in western medical science, physical disease is healed through surgery or drugs, whereas Christianity heals moral sickness from sin through prayer, and psychotherapy heals psychological conflict through behaviour modification or insight (Kirmayer, 2004, 35).

In post-conflict conciliation, *healing* is used metaphorically to refer to emotional, interpersonal and social transformations of the individuals concerned.[2] Jo seeks *healing* from the *pain* and *loss* she felt at her father's death in the bombing, and speaks of this as a transformation of her feelings (extract 9.14).

Extract 9.14   The *journey* of transformation:

1306	... (1.0) and the journey's ... been an inner journey.
1307	... (1.0) of transforming the--
1308	. . the feelings that were there at the beginning.
1309	. . the pain.
1310	and the loss.
1311	and the anger.
1312	... (1.0) and the grief.
1313	... (1.0) and,
1314	. . discovering that they can be transformed.
1315	... (1.0) ehm,
1316	... through the heart.
1317	... (1.0) into,
1318	compassion and empathy.

Although the same metaphor vehicle is used, the *healing* is in each case different and the process is inevitably asymmetric, since Pat's actions were the cause of Jo's affliction. Pat's *healing*, as we saw in the previous section, is to rectify his *loss of humanity,* and although there may be a refinding of humanity, his responsibility for the death means that there cannot be a parallel transformative process: *there's no way of purging that debt* (extract 8.18). Even for Jo, there is a continuity of *pain;* although her feelings may change, there can be no recovery in the sense of a return to how things were before Brighton. Both Jo and Pat talk about how they must *carry* the effects of the violence with them for the rest of their lives, as we saw in chapter 8. In extract 9.15, Jo speaks about accepting the ongoing *pains* and *wound.*

Extract 9.15   The ongoing outcomes of the violence:

2–2287	... it feels like it's part of my humanity,
2288	to still feel that loss.
2289	that I'm okay,
2290	feeling those pains.
2291	and,
2292	. . it's okay to cry.
2293	... (1.0) and to--
2294	. . to feel that--
2295	... (4.0) it's like,
2296	. . Brighton's given me,
2297	... (2.0) a wound that,
2298	will mean I'll always keep my humanity.

2299   . . . because--
2300   . . . (3.0) it's [there].

Just after this, Jo makes an explicit statement of transformation, marked by a change of metaphor inside the metaphor cluster (extract 9.16). The new metaphor is the *gift* of empathy, compassion and understanding that comes as a reward for her striving to understand the reasons for the violence.

Extract 9.16   The *gifts* of Brighton:

2315 Jo   [and] also,
2316   I can <u>see</u> the <u>gifts</u>,
2317   . . . (1.0) I can <u>see</u> the <u>gifts</u> that Brighton's <u>given</u> me.
2318   . . . (1.0) you know,
2319   I--
2320   the <u>amount</u> of compassion that I can <u>feel</u>,
2321   compared to before.
2322   . . . (1.0) the <u>amount</u> of understanding,
2323   . . . (1.0) that I have for other people.
2324   . . . (1.0) I--
2325   I don't <u>feel</u> I'm scared of anyone's <u>pain</u>.
2326   . . . (1.0) I can <u>listen</u> to people's <u>pain</u>.
2327   . . I can <u>listen</u> to their <u>struggles</u>.
2328   . . . (1.0) I can understand . . people's . . . anger and violence.
2329   as I've . . <u>come to terms</u> with my own anger and violence.
2330   . . . (1.0) and that's--
2331   . . I <u>feel</u> that's <u>given</u> me an--
2332   an empathy.
2333   and,
2334   . . . (2.0) that's a <u>gift</u> that I--
2335   I <u>treasure</u>.

No such *gifts* await Pat Magee. Instead he seeks to contribute to *restoration* as a way of making some amends for the hurt he has caused.

Table 9.1 brings together the metaphorical ways in which Jo and Pat describe their two separate but interconnected processes of *healing*. As we have discussed, the various metaphors indicate the cultural and religious influences on how they think about conciliation and its healing effects.

It is clearly insufficient to propose a single systematic metaphor CONCILI-ATION IS HEALING. Instead, two separate metaphors interrelate: CONCILIATION FOR VICTIM IS HEALING and CONCILIATION FOR PERPETRATOR IS HEALING. As summarised at the top of table 9.1, Jo's HEALING, as victim, is grief transformed to understanding, compassion and empathy, and of strength found to deal with ongoing loss. Pat's HEALING, as perpetrator, is a rehumanising and finding a way to live with the ongoing responsibility for the death of another human being. Meeting with Jo, and being accepted by her as sincere in his efforts at conciliation, seems to be an important factor in this latter search.

Table 9.1 Explanatory Theory of Metaphorical HEALING

HEALING	CONCILIATION	
	Jo	Pat
The topic of metaphorical *healing*	grief transformed to understanding, compassion and empathy, and strength found to deal with ongoing loss	*rehumanising, and finding a way to live with the ongoing respon sibility for the death of another human being*
sickness, symptoms	*pain* *loss* *hurting* *casualty* *cruel* *raw* *trauma* *wound(s)* *suffered*	*losing humanity* *part of you has to close down* *forced to wear blinkers* *losing sight* *a price to pay*
place for healing	*safe spaces* *places* *sitting down with those who did it*	*sitting there* *a space where you can really talk openly*
healing actions	*being open* *not closing down / shutting off* *hearing the Other's story* *take responsibility for . . . the not listening*	*breaking down barriers* *come face-to-face* *being heard* *drawing a line under..* *purging that debt* *offer myself*
transformations	*see the gifts that Brighton's given me frees me*	*see in our true lightunderstand . . . what we've come through*
expectations for recovery	*coming to terms* *moving on* *reached a place* *it's part of my humanity to still feel that loss* *Brighton's given me a wound*	*there's no way of purging that debt* *something I'll have to carry* *restoring* *working together for whatever purposes*

CONCLUSION

Metaphor appropriation is a discourse action that adopts a metaphor used by the Other and adapts it to serve one's own intentions and within one's own perspective. The Bakhtinian concept of double-voicing has been combined with identifying possible gestures of empathy to examine the various ways in which metaphors are appropriated across speakers and across alterity.

Metaphor appropriation has been shown to often involve creative understanding or entering into the perspective of the Other, to offer a metaphor to the Other or to use a metaphor from the Other's discourse world. Sometimes appropriation is subversive in using appropriated metaphor to shift the talk into the Other's perspective in order to encourage response to questions or to activate the Other's moral order in order to ask for justification of violence and confront the Other with the reality of the consequences.

Gestures of empathy are made locally both with and around metaphor appropriation. The appropriation may itself serve as a gesture of empathy. In other cases, gestures of empathy smooth the path for metaphor appropriation.

Infrequent but significant instances were found of strong appropriation involving major shifts in the use of the metaphors. In each case, the appropriated metaphors were tightly connected to their first 'owner' and constructive of their social identity. Hearing a metaphor re-voiced across alterity by the Other and re-directed to their contexts and intentions would seem to be particularly demanding in a conciliation situation. Strong appropriation of metaphor would seem to require significant gestures of empathy from both participants: from the first owner who sanctions its transfer to the Other, and by the Other who sufficiently values the metaphor to want to appropriate it.

Strong appropriation of metaphor has the power to perturb the discourse dynamics, and shift the course of the talking-and-thinking into new directions. What was strictly personal, often emotively so, is shaken up and becomes available to the Other. For example, by allowing Pat to become a person also in need of *healing,* Jo not only makes a gesture of empathy that reaches across alterity but dramatically changes the texture of that alterity.

Analysis of the explanatory theories underlying the metaphors of *healing* used by Jo and Pat highlighted how their different starting points as individuals led to two very different meanings for the metaphors. The metaphors are not independent since *healing* for each of them results from their conversations; the intersection of the separate metaphors occurred through, and is marked by, appropriation.

10 Metaphor, Reconciliation and the Dynamics of Empathy

> I feel that's given me an--
> an empathy.
> and,
> that's a gift that I--
> I treasure.
>
> —Jo Berry (fourth meeting with Pat Magee, 2001)

At the time of writing this final chapter, it is 10 sssyears since Jo Berry and Pat Magee first met, and 25 years since the Brighton bombing killed Jo's father. When the bomb went off in 1984, Jo and Pat were complete strangers, unaware that they were on opposite sides of a political conflict with a long history, and that they were about to be connected by an act of violence. Today,[1] the final stages of devolved power have been agreed in Northern Ireland between former loyalist and republican enemies; the conflict has evolved into a kind of peace, for the time being at least. How stable this peace will be remains to be seen; it seems stable enough currently not to be disrupted by occasional acts of violence. It is to be hoped that the stability of the peace is strong enough to absorb the tendency to violent action that runs through all societies, particularly when young people are underemployed or disenfranchised, and that nothing acts to fan the old conflict back into flames and violence.

Alongside these wider social changes, Jo Berry and Pat Magee have reached a kind of stability in their complicated relationship. While meeting and talking together is always stressful and exhausting because of the emotions evoked, the impact of the early, most powerful, meetings has been worked through to a calmer phase. Jo and Pat have proved themselves to be unusual and special people through their repeated willingness to engage with each other and to allow their talk together to be scrutinised and analysed.

This penultimate chapter summarises what has been revealed about the conciliation process, and the dynamics of empathy within that process, by employing metaphor analysis.

SUMMARY OF METAPHOR ANALYSIS

Metaphor has been investigated as discourse activity, integral to talking-and-thinking and understood as a complex dynamic system on multiple socio-cognitive dimensions. Metaphor analysis combines close scrutiny of metaphors with analysis of lexical, syntactic and rhetorical choices in immediate dialogic action, and, on a longer timescale, the contribution of metaphors to narratives, justifications and explanations as they are presented and re-presented.

The process of metaphor analysis began with the identification of metaphors in the transcribed conversations. Each metaphor was examined for its role in local discourse activity. The identified metaphors were assembled into semantically linked groupings around key discourse topics, producing systematic metaphor trajectories across the conversations,[2] including framing metaphors for key topics. Distributional analysis showed episodes of talk with metaphor clusters or metaphor absences. These three levels of metaphor analysis —local, emergent and distributional—were combined in hermeneutic and interpretive processes to understand how metaphor was used by Jo Berry and Pat Magee as they talked together over the years and how it contributed to their developing empathy.

HOW METAPHOR CONTRIBUTES TO THE CONCILIATION CONVERSATIONS

Metaphor has played an important role in helping each person to come to understand the Other more deeply and more fully through the conciliation process of talking-and-thinking together. The Other, who was distanced and dehumanised through the conflict and the violence, comes to be known through and with metaphor in the discourse activity of the conversations.

The study has found that metaphor contributes to the conciliation process and supports the development of empathy in the following ways:

- Metaphor motivates and guides participation in conciliation.
- Metaphor enables discourse encounters with the Other.
- Metaphor allows access to the emotions of the Other, and is also affectively protective.
- The poetics of place demonstrates how symbolic and metaphorical interaction between experience and physical place activates emotional resonances, and has implications for post-conflict reconciliation. Each of these is now summarised.

Metaphor Motivates and Guides Participation in Conciliation

Jo Berry's guiding metaphor for the process that we have called here 'conciliation' was *I can build a bridge across the divide* (extract 6.2). She voiced this metaphor to herself long before she met Pat Magee, and it contributed to the development of her ideas as she visited Ireland and tried to arrange a meeting. It continued to be used throughout the conversations: picked up and adapted by Pat; complemented by other CONNECTION metaphors; extended to talk about other meetings; related to other conflicts.

The idea of *building a bridge* offers an excellent example of how metaphor functions in talking-and-thinking, and is best understood as discourse activity. Despite its concrete nature, *building a bridge* was not an image metaphor for Jo, in that she reported no visual images linked with the words, nor was it particularly specific, in that she reports thinking of no particular type of bridge or divide. The words of the metaphor were what tied it to her developing ideas of conciliation; the level of the metaphor, neither too general nor too precise, provided the best fit in terms of flexibility and usefulness to support Jo's thinking and to work in dialogue with Pat.

Jo also understood, from soon after her father's killing, that she *wanted to bring something positive out of* this negative experience, and what she brings from the conversations and meeting is some peace for herself through new ways of understanding the causes of violence, what she calls *the gifts of Brighton*. Metaphor serves here to summarise the abstract idea of turning a negative experience into a positive one, emphasising the unexpected good that she has found. Together with the *building a bridge*, these metaphors seem to have supported Jo's participation in the conciliation process by giving her a positive long term vision of what might be possible.

Pat Magee's metaphors for the process have been more changeable, perhaps reflecting the way he himself has made multiple adjustments through the process. From initially offering *a platform* to convey *the republican message*, the process became *a breaking down of barriers*, and most recently a means of *restoration of loss*. The one metaphor that stands out as consistently important to Pat is the idea of *being open*. He values Jo's openness and tries to reciprocate by *being open* himself. Again, the metaphor serves as to guide participation in the conciliation process, not so much as a goal but as an attitude of mind to attain.

Metaphor Enables Discourse Encounters with the Other

The study has paid particular attention to the dialogics of metaphor: not just how individuals use metaphors, but how metaphors work between participants.

As has been found in other types of discourse activity, metaphors serve particular functions in dialogue. Some metaphors are particularly vivid and memorable, so serve to offer opportunities to reach deeper understanding of the Other's experiences and argumentation, and to be able to return to build on this in subsequent talk, as demonstrated by systematic metaphor trajectories. Some metaphors also work through simulations and somatic markers to help share the perceptual experiences of the Other. Metaphors often feature in codas to narratives, offering the Other a packaged and memorable summary of what happened and what was felt about what happened.

The particular discourse activity of post-conflict conciliation conversations has featured metaphors in other dialogic roles. The appropriation of metaphors across speakers marked small, and more significant, developments of empathy. Highly negative metaphors were used to construct alternative dystopian scenarios that enabled participants to come together in dismissing possible attitudes and values: to agree that being *open* was better than being *locked into bitterness,* for example. In this way, metaphor contributes to solving a key problem of reconciliation conversations—how is it possible to find any commonality with the Other across alterity opened up by violence? In the flow of discourse activity, metaphors can create an alternative discourse space where participants can align with each other. This discourse space is constructed through language, where talking-and-thinking can take new directions.

Metaphor Allows Access to the Emotions of the Other, and Is Also Affectively Protective

The importance of the affective in metaphor as discourse activity has been repeatedly and emphatically demonstrated by this study. Most of the metaphors in the conversations do not just contribute to talking-and-thinking about ideas but also reveal something of the emotions, attitudes and values of those who use them.

Many of the topics discussed in the conversations were difficult for Jo and for Pat. Painful memories were recalled and re-lived in telling to the Other; listening to the stories of suffering is also hard to bear. Jo had to cope with revisiting the terrible time around her father's killing while still living with his absence. Pat had to deal with the effect of taking responsibility for the suffering that he was faced with. Simple metaphors of MOVEMENT and JOURNEYS, of PARTIAL SEEING and of CONNECTION and SEPARATION helped to express deep and difficult feelings. The same metaphors offered ways of crossing the divide between Jo and Pat, and of entering into the Other's perspective, through appropriation and shifting.

The absence of metaphor in the emotionally powerful bare narratives of chapters 7 and 8 demonstrated how metaphor is crucial in distancing and protecting speaker and listener from the most visceral experiences of emotional pain. While metaphor allows access to the emotions of the Other, it is also affectively protective in distancing people from the trauma of relived memories.

The Poetics of Place

In these particular post-conflict conversations, the interplay of metaphor with physical places has been an important source of affective impact. Through the poetics of place, the emotional resonances of geographical sites significant to participants have been brought into the dialogue to be experienced by the Other. Traumatic human experiences are linked into the places where they happened—city streets, army barracks—and the places where the experiences were emotionally assimilated—city streets again, car parks, kitchens. The connections between the, often literally, concrete and the affective develop symbolically and eventually come to work as metaphor.

While metaphor theory has stressed the origin of much metaphor in the body and common bodily experience (Gibbs, 2006a; Lakoff and Johnson, 1999), the poetics of place pushes embodiment out into the environment, demonstrating our need to retain connection with the specificity of the larger physical world (McGilchrist, 2009; Merleau-Ponty, 1962). The actualities of the conflict tie emotions into particular physical reality. In the case of conflict in Ireland, the reality was urban territories and fighting on the streets. Loyalists and republicans were living in separated areas of cities like Belfast, so that roads and areas become metonymically associated with opposing sides of the conflict. British soldiers sent to stop or prevent fighting became the third enemy in the conflict, trying to take over the streets, with all the associations those streets had come to contain.

The particular embodied realities of Jo's and Pat's experiences of violence echo through their conversations. It seems probable that the poetics of place will be significant in discourse activity following violence or conflict. There are social implications for how changes to environments can contribute to moving on from conflict, but there are also implications for reconciliation dialogue. Visual images of places may be helpful if sensitively used, since they are likely to activate emotional and symbolic meanings, bringing them into the open to be adjusted, rendered less toxic or less painful. The actual physical places in which people meet for post-conflict conversations matter. From Jo and Pat's talk, these places must, above all, and in contrast to conflict situations, feel *safe*.

A DYNAMIC MODEL OF THE DEVELOPMENT OF EMPATHY THROUGH POST-CONFLICT CONVERSATIONS

The model of empathy set up in the first chapter and the dynamic model sketched out in chapter 2 are combined and extended from the findings of the research into Jo and Pat's conversations, and displayed in figure 10.1.

After preparing to meet, the data have revealed how Jo and Pat engage in developing empathy moment by moment in the conciliation process, and how empathy emerges on a longer timescale as new stabilities in their understandings, attitudes and feelings as a result of talking together. The left hand side of figure 10.1 shows the discourse activity as alternating periods of continuity talk and perturbation talk. This is where the local action of empathy happens, seen in this book as arising from various gestures

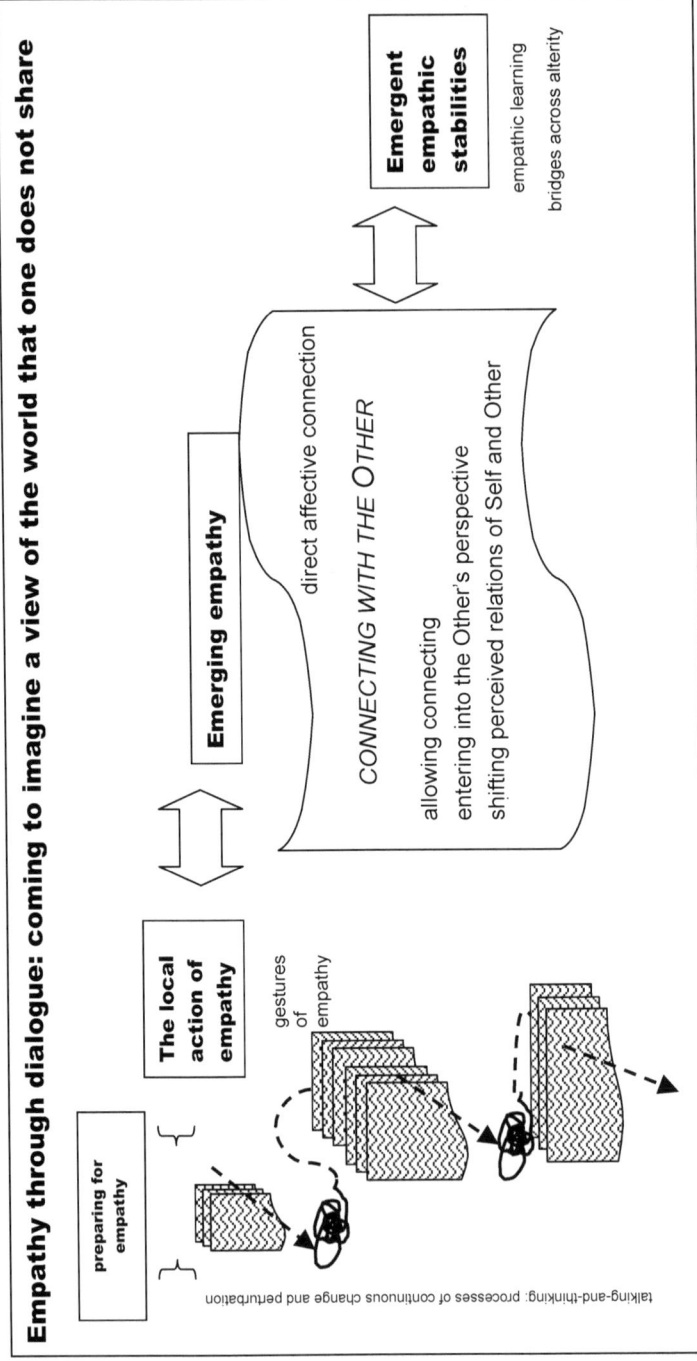

Figure 10.1   A dynamic model of the development of empathy through post-conflict conversations.

of empathy. The centre of the diagram shows empathy as emerging from local activity, building and developing as time goes by, through continuous accumulating understanding and through sudden revelations or changes. The bottom right of figure 10.1 shows the stable outcomes of the process of engaging in empathy.

In operating at these different scales, empathy is like any other complex human cognitive and affective process that concerns others—loving and hating, worrying about, taking care of, teaching. Each of these involves small local actions that give rise to and come out of longer term emotions, feelings and decisions. And, because the process involves relating with another person, it is, like these other processes and as Jo and Pat repeatedly demonstrate, always dialogic, although not necessarily symmetrical; the parties involved may act and feel quite differently but they are connected by the process they are involved in until one or other opts out. [3] Emerging empathy is thus to be understood in terms of connecting with the Other, as in the banner shape that represents the nature of emerging empathy in the middle of figure 10.1. The use of the word 'connecting' directly results from the metaphor analysis and the importance of the poetics of place; it feels appropriate to describe empathy metaphorically in terms of physical contact, particularly in a context where empathy attempts to repair a conflict that has violently separated people from each other.

To understand how connecting with the Other has been done in the reconciliation conversations, gestures of empathy were collected and analysed. The analysis produces three categories of gestures of empathy, that seem to contribute differently to emerging empathy as connecting with the Other: allowing connecting; entering into the Other's perspective, and shifting how the Other is perceived. These more deliberate process of empathy work alongside the automatic empathic process that is now labelled 'direct affective connection'.

The final level in the dynamic model concerns long term changes to the understanding and connection between Self and Other. What is known about the Other accumulates; what is felt towards the Other stabilises and various outcomes are no longer likely to be reversed. These affective and cognitive outcomes in the development of empathy are described as 'emergent empathic stabilities'.

The research findings are now pulled together and the four levels of the dynamic model of empathy discussed.

Preparing for Empathy

At the 'entry level' of empathy, participants need to be prepared for empathy. We have seen the different ways in which Jo Berry and Pat Magee prepared for meeting each other. They also mentally prepared differently. Jo was driven by her determination, personal ethics, and world view; she used metaphor to imagine process and outcome; she met other victims first which helped broaden her perspective; she learnt about the conflict which increased her openness to the possibility of empathy. Pat entered conciliation prepared to explain political motivations but the first meeting with Jo brought about sudden and dramatic change in his attitude to the process; he became more open and willing to talk about the personal as well as the political.

Preparing for empathy is important in advance of meeting but it continues throughout. Each development in empathy is also a preparation for the next development.

The Local Action of Empathy

The local action of empathy operates on a timescale of seconds and minutes and has been examined through Jo and Pat's moment by moment talking-and-thinking together. Metaphor cluster analysis provided potentially significant episodes of discourse activity that were examined in particular detail. Just over half of all metaphors occurred outside metaphor clusters, and each use was examined in the discourse activity.

The 'gesture of empathy' was introduced as a dialogic unit[4] of activity to describe local actions that are an affordance for connection with the Other. Every act of communication is, of course, in some way a gesture of empathy (McGilchrist, 2009) but the gestures of interest here are those that, as it were, take a step further towards the Other. Each gesture made by one participant has a possible dialogic counterpart action by the Other, even if this is only allowing the gesture to be made—you can't walk in the other person's shoes if they do not allow it.

Gestures of empathy made in episodes of continuity talk were sometimes interrupted by sudden changes in discourse activity that shifted empathy to a new phase through some kind of perturbation. Such perturbations included the bare narratives told by Jo about her daughter's reaction to her meeting Pat and by Pat about being detained by the British army as a young man; direct questions posed by Jo about Pat's use of violence and his justifications for doing so; Pat accepting responsibility for the consequences to Jo of the violence; and Jo accepting a degree of collective responsibility for the political causes of the Irish conflict.

Collected together from the preceding chapters, gestures of empathy can be divided into three types, each contributing differently to emerging empathy and connecting with the Other. These categories, and the role of metaphor in the discourse activity they include, are now summarised and discussed.

Emergent Empathy: Allowing Connecting

These gestures of empathy give the Other access to one's thinking and feelings about the past, the present and the future. They include:

- offering an explanation of one's feelings about events and situations to the Other;
- attempting to explain traumatic events and emotions to the Other;
- being willing to open oneself up to relive traumatic memories;
- being willing to try to explain reasons for engaging in violence;
- opening Self to critical reflection on past choices and actions, and sharing that with the Other.

Giving the Other access to one's thinking and feelings involves being willing to recall and describe past events and situations that may have been extremely traumatic. Explaining these to the Other is likely to cause renewed pain that must be prepared for and dealt with. A perpetrator has to be willing to try to explain what led to the violence happening, and this opens up multiple sources of difficulty. It will be painful for the victim to hear, and may make them angry or more hurt. Honest appraisal of decisions and justifications made many years earlier may face the perpetrator with what seems like an almost impossible choice, between standing by what was decided in the face of the personal pain it caused or re-assessing decisions and then having to live with the guilt. Allowing connection therefore benefits from personal strength and support from the Other, or from a mediator if present.

In the process of allowing connection with the Other, metaphor offers multiple alternative ways of expressing oneself, and of hiding and highlighting particular aspects of what is said (Lakoff and Johnson, 1980). Metaphors that express affect (*pain, raw, betray, purge debt*) give the Other access to one's emotions and feelings. Contrasting metaphors used to construct alternative dystopian scenarios were particularly helpful in explaining stance or decision.

Emergent Empathy: Entering into the Other's Perspective

Gestures of empathy that involve creative understanding of the Other attempt to understand the world view of the Other through what is known about their experiences and emotions. Entering the Other's perspective has been carried out in several ways, including:

- anticipating the effect of one's words on the Other, and mitigating them;
- acknowledging the Other's feelings, through choice of word or phrase;
- offering the Other a summary of what has been heard;
- adding to the Other's explanation or argument with one's own supporting contribution;
- speaking as if from the Other's perspective in the preface to a question.

Entering the Other's perspective is a more strongly empathic process since it involves applying what has been learnt about the Other to what one says and does. Pat Magee and Jo Berry show, throughout the data, a great deal of respect and care for the other's feelings while they are in conversation. Some metaphors enter the discourse activity as the 'discourse property' of one or other speaker, as it were from one side of the alterity; their affective or semantic content clearly marks them as belonging to the perspective of one speaker and so, when used by the other speaker, they offer a clear indication of creative understanding. Adapting, quoting or alluding to a metaphor brought to the discourse by the Other can demonstrate or suggest an entering into the Other's perspective.

Emergent Empathy: Shifting the Perceived Relation of Self and Other

A group of gestures of empathy were found that seem to mark a shift in the relations between Self and Other. These include:

- repositioning the Other, formerly an enemy, as someone with a story to tell, and taking time and effort to listen to what the Other has to say;
- as 'victim', exploring the political causes of the conflict and taking some responsibility through social group affiliation;
- as 'perpetrator', acknowledging the dehumanising of the enemy, and taking time and effort to come to see them as a more full human being;
- acknowledging that both Other and Self have suffered from the violence of the conflict.

Gestures of empathy that allow connection and enter into the Other's perspective change understanding of and attitudes towards the Other. Gradually or suddenly, perceptions shift. The gestures in this category are local, specific actions that position the Other and/or the Self differently. Changes in metaphor and appropriation of metaphor can mark this kind of gesture.

Emergent Empathy: Direct Affective Connection

Bare narratives, and their descriptions of the emotions of grief, anger and fear, proved to have particularly potential for powerfully evoking automatic emotional empathy through perceptual simulations and somatic markers that allow some kind of experiencing of the visceral impact being described by the Other.

Emergent Empathic Stabilities

The fourth level in the dynamic model concerns long term affective and cognitive changes to the understanding and connection between Self and Other, described as 'emergent empathic stabilities'. The emerging empathy detailed earlier leads to changes in the understanding and the alterity between Self and Other. It also leads to changes in understanding of the Self. What is known about the Other accumulates and what is felt towards the Other stabilises, although remains open to further change.

Emergent Empathic Stabilities: Empathic Learning

Through dialogue, Jo and Pat have come to know about each other's history. They have experienced tellings and retellings of key events, and shared some of the emotions around these events. Their experience in dialogue has led to a familiarity with each other's ways of using language and metaphor. We can describe this development as 'empathic learning'.

Automatic or emotional empathy lets you learn about the Other's feelings and emotions. There is much else that can be learnt: about their history and their social group affiliations; about their experiences and reactions to them; about their reasoning and justifications for action or decisions. The metaphor, developed mainly by Pat, that best fits the idea of empathic learning is of coming to see a full picture of the Other. Conflict and violence require and force limited and partial attention to the humanity of the Other; a *distorted image*, a *caricature* or a *glimpse* is all that can be permitted. Post-conflict conciliation fills in and corrects the image of the Other as a person with human emotions and responses to experience. The empathic learning they have achieved means that simple labels, such as victim and perpetrator, are no longer sufficient. Each now knows the other as a specific person, with families and in the wider socio-cultural world (extract 10.1).

Extract 10.1   That's what it's all about:

4–1163 Jo	Pat said,
1164	that,
1165	he realised now that he could,
1166	he could have sat down with my dad and,
1167	had a cup of tea.
1168	and . . erm.
1169	those words just sort of <u>shook</u> me,
1170	and <u>made</u> me realise that,
1171	actually that's what it's all about.

Empathy may be work of the imagination but the more that is learnt about the Other, the more effectively that imagination can work.

Empathic learning in reconciliation needs to counter the effects of engaging in violence that continue to influence both perpetrator and victim. Once the Other takes shape as a person through empathic learning, it becomes increasingly difficult to keep them distanced and dehumanised.

The study has shown how dehumanising worked on multiple dimensions for Pat Magee: he experienced dehumanising at the hands of the British army; he engaged in dehumanising of IRA enemies; by disallowing the humanity of people like Jo's father who became a *cipher* or *legitimate targets* rather than *father or grandfather,* he feels to have lost some of his own humanity. The conciliation conversations have contributed to countering some of the effects of that experience.

Empathic learning has an enormous task in changing the ideas, attitudes and values of participants in reconciliation. Individuals have turned to violence and conflict as a result of a nexus of influences: visceral responses to danger and threats to territory; groups that offer to meet the human need for approval and acceptance; political promises to address social issues; long histories of difficult relationships between groups. The question arises for future research of how strong empathic learning generated by reconciliation has to be in any given context to outweigh these influences and their lasting effects.

Emergent Empathic Stabilities: Bridges Across Alterity

Empathic learning is accompanied in the post-conflict conversations by an attitudinal 'moving toward' the Other, marked by the expression of increasing commonalities, and described, in homage to Jo Berry's vision and determination, as 'bridges across alterity'. The bridges across alterity are manifested in the commonalities they now find with each other and their continuing, complex relationship.

Their conversations have revealed and developed certain commonalities with each other, or across their social groups, that cover values, attitudes and judgements of behaviour. Pat admitted to sharing with his former enemies the tendency to dehumanising. Jo has said that she recognises a desire to hurt and blame inside herself, and that she cannot rule out the possibility that growing up in different circumstances might have led her to violence. Through their shared and individual journeys, Jo and Pat have come to agree that violence should not be necessary to solve political problems and injustices, and work together on various projects to advance that. It is in the pursuit of these new, shared goals that we find the most convincing evidence of success for the conciliation process they have engaged in.

The nature of the emergent relationship between Jo Berry and Pat Magee is intriguing. It continues to evolve. In 2003, they spoke of each other as *friends* but in 2009 found that label harder to accept when asked directly about the development of the relationship between them. As Jo said, "If friends are people who care about each other, then yes. But it's more complex than that." Pat speaks of "reaching a level of understanding with Jo", of admiring and respecting her. Friendship seems at once appropriate and inappropriate as a description of the bridge they have constructed between them. The emotional ambivalence that Halpern and Weinstein (2004) described as accompanying post-conflict reconciliation is what makes 'friendship' inappropriately simple to describe Jo and Pat's relationship; the killing of Jo's father leaves an alterity that can never closed but must be worked into a form that can be lived with.

The feeling of emotional ambivalence was described by Jo (extract 10.2) recounting an incident when empathy suddenly switched into ambivalence as she became aware of the contradictions involved in understanding the Other. The incident is contextualised in terms of place in the opening line.

Extract 10.2   Like a computer kind of dying:

4–1239 Jo	we were sitting at a table,
1240	and there was Pat ,
1241	and somebody who'd,
1242	been <u>in</u> the British Army,
1243	and someone who'd been <u>in</u> the loyalist paramilitary.
1244	. . . and I just looked at,
1245	three of them.
1246	. . . and just had this sense,
1247	<X sort of X>
1248	looking into their eyes,
1249	all three of them,
1250	actually,
1251	. . . I could've been all of them.
1252	I could be their sister.
1253	<X you know X>
1254	that . . erm.
1255	they were all right,
1256	<u>from their perspective.</u>
1257	and a--
1258	I think *part* of my,
1259	sort of,
1260	brain,
1261	. . just,
1262	sort of,
1263	<u>went,</u>
1264	you know,
1265	<@ couldn't cope @>
1266	<@ it was <u>like a computer kind of dying</u> @>
1267	because,
1268	. . it's very hard to think that it was,
1269	more about,
1270	the heart,
1271	I want to <u>make</u> sense,
1272	but it was like,
1273	a heart,
1274	. . empathy.
1275	<X because I understand it there X>
1276	but not necessarily with,
1277	my thinking.

For Jo, this kind of empathy—understanding the Others' perspectives 'from the heart', as she puts it—is not always compatible with rational or logical thinking. Coping with this ambivalence will remain as one of the difficulties of engaging in conciliation and developing empathy. When Jo and Pat reflect on their meetings, they mention both the rewards and the difficulties, the highs and the drained exhaustion they feel. But working and talking together feels to be valuable enough to outweigh the problems. The relationship is not just between the two of them but includes, as a third factor, the discourse activity that has enabled their empathy to develop and that continues.

11 Images of Empathy

This book is based on rigorous analysis of the detail of a process, combined with holistic understanding of that process which has come from seeing the participants in action in a range of different situations, meeting and talking with them. Writing it has not been straightforward. The linear nature of text argues with multi-dimensional and holistic understandings. The topic is so compelling that I had wanted something other than an academic text, that would be accessible to a wider audience. But I also wanted students of metaphor and other researchers to be able to follow my method and replicate the rich experience I have had with other data relevant to our human condition. There have been more versions of chapters written, and destroyed than was the case for any of my other books. Eventually, the content settled itself into chapters and sequence. The style became academic regardless of my wishes.

But in the opening and closing chapters of a book, a writer has more freedom of expression, and so I ask the reader to indulge me in this unconventional final chapter. I wanted here to bring together what I have learnt about empathy and conciliation from the years engaged with the work. I intended, when I sat down to compose it, that I would draw on metaphors of JOURNEYS, CONNECTIONS, SEEING MORE CLEARLY, HEALING and so on, select from them to produce a metaphorical model of empathy. This I imagined would be like painting a picture of empathy with the metaphors as a set of colours. I am a painter, sometimes and not often enough, and knowing the process of painting leads me to recognise similar processes in writing. Instead, what happened was indeed something like painting, but more creative, and I think more interesting.

I present three images of empathy, in the form and order in which they were composed. The first two appear exactly as they hit the keyboard and screen; the third is crafted into a final version. Each image is accompanied by a commentary, as if taking a step back from the image that emerged and reflecting on the composing process, and on how to shape or re-shape the image.

IMAGES OF EMPATHY (1)

empathy in the moment as connecting with the Other

understanding the Other through this connection and through listening, really hearing—experiencing—the stories, feeling with the story teller, living the events again through their telling, of the places, the noises, the human sounds of screaming and silence, the rattles of fear and the clanging of prison doors, the freedom of the streets and the closing down of the streets confining of personal space, of place to be free to think.

The walking, walking, walking down city streets to forget and to remember. Walking on to ferries, into strange rooms, meeting sad people, lost people, finding people who understand.

Walking, on and on, in the hope of finding something or someone that will unravel the mess.

the physical presence of the Other, the silences, the coffins, and the memories crowding empty rooms, forcing themselves between you, filling the space, urging you on.

flickering human feelings across the table, sorrow, remorse, hurt—do you see them or imagine them? act on them anyway, act as if and it may come to be.

Commentary on *Images of Empathy* (1)

Writing this was so much like painting that it was uncanny. The first impetuous throwing down of the words/paint that is amazing, wonderful, awful. To work with it? or leave it as it emerged with the raw edge of meaning.

If I work on it, I can easily destroy the liveliness and the inventiveness. At least on the computer, I can make a copy to work on. Then I can come back to this as it was, not risk losing it for ever. The risk though is good for me. Makes for bolder work.

Regroup, look closely at what emerged. I wanted to paint a metaphorical image of empathy, using the metaphors I have become so familiar with. What emerged was the bare narrative talk, the agonies, etched into my memory, as happened with Pat's words, "Now that's all lost", that suddenly floated to the top of my mind, in the sea, one summer holiday.

If it was a painting, I would scratch into it, layer it with water, and see what happens . . .

IMAGES OF EMPATHY (2)

---

empathy in the moment as connecting with the Other

seated on a sofa, not making eye contact, only word contact

letting words talk, sculpting what matters, carefully so the other can see and feel something of what you felt. Placing the lumps of clay where they seem to be needed. Gradually making a shape in the space between you, using your hands to mould the shape, to smooth the words that do not quite fit.

sculpture after sculpture. Each one constructed so carefully, then put away. And the next time, a new sculpture will be made into shapes that become ever more familiar but always slightly different. Does he see what I am sculpting here? Does she recognise this shape to know it as I do?

Sometimes harsh, distorted, painful shapes that hurl their meaning at the viewer.

Two shapes in the space between, and effort, effort to read the hardening clay, desire to take it and learn from its sculpting; its being from its coming into being.

In time the shape of the Other's sculpting becomes more comfortable and familiar. You welcome the chance to be in the creative space where you can mould what happens; the wet clay in your hands is power; you are the sculptor here, while it lasts.

Commentary on *Images of Empathy* (2)

This time what emerged was a metaphor for the conciliation talk—not theirs, as I intended, but mine. Only the first line of the earlier version was used. As if the layer of water washed away most of the earlier marks. It seems that reconstructing conciliation from their metaphors would be more like making a collage from old birthday cards and pictures torn from magazines. Quite enjoyable but without the edge of creativity. An odd word or phrase can be ripped out and added to these paintings, like the cubists did.

Now to work with the first two images to produce a more finished version . . .

IMAGES OF EMPATHY (3)

Understanding the Other through this connection and through listening, really hearing—experiencing—the stories, feeling with the story
teller, living the events again through their telling: of the places, the
noises, the human sounds of screaming and silence, the rattles of fear
and the clanging of prison doors, the freedom of the streets and the
closing down of the streets confining of personal space, of places to
be free to think.

The walking, walking, walking down city streets to forget and to
remember. Walking on to ferries, into strange rooms, meeting sad
people, lost people, finding people who understand.

Walking, on and on, in the hope of finding something or someone
that will unravel the mess.

The physical presence of the Other, the silences, the coffins, and the
memories crowding empty rooms, forcing themselves between you,
filling the space, urging you on.

Flickering of human feelings across the table, sorrow, remorse,
hurt—do you see them or imagine them? act on them anyway, act as
if and it may come to be.

Empathy in the moment as a connecting with the Other.

Seated on a sofa, not making eye contact, only word contact.

Letting words talk, sculpting what matters, carefully so the other can
see and feel something of what you felt. Placing the lumps of clay
where they seem to be needed by what is taking shape. Gradually
making a shape in the space between you, using your hands to mould
the shape, to smooth the words that do not quite fit.

Sculpture after sculpture. Each one constructed so carefully, then put
away. And the next time, a new sculpture will be made into shapes that
become ever more familiar but always slightly different. Does he see what
I am sculpting here? Does she recognise this shape to know it as I do?

Sometimes harsh, distorted, painful shapes that hurl their meaning
at the viewer, created through tears that, blinding, send more urgent

(continued)

power to the scraping, pushing, squeezing fingers. Then you do not care if the Other is there or not. The Other feels your movements, is scraped, pushed, squeezed.

Two shapes in the space between, and effort, effort to read the hardening clay, desire to take the other shape and learn from its sculpting; its being from its coming into being. Fingers retaining memories from each shaping, and each reading.

In time the shape of the Other's sculpting becomes more comfortable and familiar. You know how the hands will shape the clay, how the figure is built up, its proportions and angles can be predicted. Each time a new part is added, and echoes of earlier versions are pressed into slightly different shapes.

You welcome the chance to be in the creative space where you can mould what happens; the wet clay in your hands is power; you are the sculptor here, while it lasts.

Empathy with the Other as fellow sculptor—known now from watching them at work, known through the habits of moulding and shaping, known through the characteristic ways that shapes emerge from the shapeless. Watched now with understanding, and with the poignancy of knowing the felt emotion of another human being.

Commentary on *Images of Empathy (3)*

This time I work deliberately. I think about effect. I like my image of the conciliation process as a sculpting. It captures my theory of language use and prompts an image of Giacometti sculpting a head I have on a postcard. What are the shapes between them? It feels like they should be heads, or figures—metonymies, I suppose, for the person and all that shaped and shapes them. When I try the substitution, it seems too specific. Who knows what they are trying to say from the words they utter? I would not risk claiming to know. After years spent with their words, I seem to 'feel what they mean'. This is the empathy required of the researcher. The sculpting image can be left partially specified—metaphors work best this way.

The two sections seem to work together more or less as they came out on the page. The movement back and forth from the sculpting process, the conciliation talking-and-thinking, to events in the real world that started this all off, echoes the way their talk together moved in and out of the present, as past experiences were brought into the talk, talked about, reflected on and left. Another piece of clay added; the shape takes shape.

And as I wrote this last paragraph, an image came to my mind: television pictures of victims being taken on stretchers from the bombed, wrecked hotel in Brighton, October 1984, covered in dust, like corpses in Pompeii, like sculptures, I realise. Who knows what images prompt our thinking from the inside, unknown to us?

I adjust words and phrases:

I write about "movement" to capture affect. I write—"the Other is moved", as knowing pun, with emotional impact metaphorised as movement. Then look back and change it to use the verbs in the previous sentence—"is scraped, pushed, squeezed"—let the reader work out that this is being moved by simulated action, enjoy the discovery, be moved themselves by attending to it.

There are bits that please me, so I try to keep them. The danger, as I know from watercolour painting, is that one move may ruin what was working well. I tentatively add an indefinite article: "a connecting". That looks good. Stop while it's still good.

I add an "of" after "flickering", thereby nominalising the verb participle—it's supposed not to be good, but it works here, to my ear.

I add to the image with a final paragraph, to capture how sitting down together time after time, talking about the same events, has an effect. How the same or similar metaphors are used in different events, and how retellings contain echoes of previous tellings. This must be an important part of the conciliation process—the growing familiarity with the Other's story. The harshest bare narratives are not repeated, just mentioned. There is some reassurance and comfort in the familiarity of tellings, much needed when simply to be there and to be open is to make oneself vulnerable.

Finally, I am satisfied with what I have crafted. There is some aesthetically pleasing writing, some depth of meaning, and, crucially, a truthfulness to the understanding I have inched towards through these years.

Appendix
Using Metaphor in Reconciliation: Implications for Mediators

Having examined how Jo Berry and Pat Magee use metaphor in their process of coming to understand each other, what implications suggest themselves for mediators of reconciliation in other contexts?

Reconciliation talk has the objective of bringing together people who have been on different sides of a conflict so that they can understand more about the other and so that, through understanding, cycles of violence and hatred can be broken. The challenge of conciliation talk is therefore to find a way for each person to move from their starting position to one that allows some validity for the other's viewpoint. Perpetrators of violence and victims come to reconciliation from very different starting points. Adjusting perspectives that are long established and rooted within membership of social or political groups is not easy. As a member of a particular group with a history and public statements about group beliefs and values, individuals risk their sense of identity and self-respect (and sometimes more) when they open up to other perspectives.

Metaphor may help with this challenge by offering alternative ways to talk about issues that move away from the established language of both groups. Metaphor may create a new, more neutral 'discourse space', in which there is safety and room to be oneself, preserving identity and dignity, while at the same time allowing a shift in perspective. In what follows, suggestions are made for how mediators might work with metaphor, based on what was found in this study.

USING METAPHORS TO FRAME KEY ISSUES

There are likely to be two or three metaphors that take a framing role, naming aspects of the issues and framing the central problems in the situation. For example, reconciliation was framed as A JOURNEY, as CONNECTING BY BUILDING A BRIDGE and as LISTENING TO THE OTHER'S STORY. Framing metaphors are fairly easy to spot because they occur in many places in talk about key issues. Mediators should be aware that framing metaphors may change and develop over time, and that some framing metaphors may offer a better chance of convergence and shared understanding across the speakers (the neutral discourse space) than others. It would be useful for mediators to identify how speakers are framing their situations, to consider which framing metaphors offer the most potential and then to encourage the talk to move into this space and converge towards shared understanding.

Having spotted framing metaphors, it will be useful to compare

- what they are used to refer to (the metaphor topics);
- how the metaphor is extended (the metaphor vehicles);
- use by individual speakers;
- whether speakers seem happy to pick up a metaphor used by the other and use it themselves;
- whether speakers challenge the use of the metaphor by the other.

It may then become clear which of the metaphors offers the most possibilities for increasing shared understanding. A metaphor has potential for supporting convergence if:

- it is flexible in offering variations but not so wide and flexible that speakers can avoid convergence;
- both speakers use it;
- speakers use it in similar ways;
- the metaphor can link into the real worlds of the speakers.

Once a possible shared framing metaphor is identified, a mediator can encourage speakers to move into the space, framing aspects of the key issues using this metaphor, e.g. through the use of questions, such as

"Did you feel that people were listening to your story?"
"Was not being heard a problem for you?"

CHANGING METAPHORS TO BE MORE HELPFUL TO RECONCILIATION

Violent and negative metaphors may reflect emotional trauma that results from physical trauma. Intuitively, it would seem that reducing the level of violence in the words used might be helpful in creating a good climate for conciliation, particularly as talk moves on. Also, mediators might usefully have a set of alternative metaphors that they could put into the talk when they summarise contributions. Non-violent metaphors are available as alternatives to violent ones, e.g. *saying no* rather than *breaking down*.

Perpetrators and their groups are likely to have conventionalised ways of talking about their activities that carry strong connotations for victims, e.g. *the struggle*. Intuitively, it would seem to be a very positive move to 'loosen up' the ownership of these metaphors by using them in more general ways.

EXPLORING NEGATIVE ALTERNATIVES TO RECONCILIATION THROUGH HYPOTHETICAL SCENARIOS

Imaginary or hypothetical scenarios seem to offer participants a way to explore alternative reactions to violence, bereavement and other difficult events. They also seem to offer an opportunity for speakers to agree on the evaluation of other possibilities. Participants may 'activate' these scenarios by talking about other people, or more personally by describing what they did and did not choose to do.

Mediators could use either technique to suggest hypothetical scenarios, both positive and negative, to talk through. The use of metaphor can be encouraged through questions such as "How would it have felt if you had . . . ?" or "If you were that person, what would you feel/do?"

The metaphors that participants use in talking about these scenarios will show their attitudes towards the alternative responses. By exploring alternatives, participants may come to see reconciliation as a better, or only, way forward.

PRESENTING THE HUMAN CONSEQUENCES OF VIOLENCE

Using the words of other people, including children, affected by violence seems to be a potentially useful strategy, as it can present perpetrators with a very direct understanding of the consequences of their actions. Even a short stretch of such talk seems likely to have an impact, which may reveal itself later.

Metaphor is important in accounts of traumatic events because it can distance speakers from the immediacy of the painful memory. If talk becomes too direct for too long, mediators can use metaphor in their prompts and questions to push talk back into a more comfortable zone.

THE POETICS OF PLACE: CONNECTING EMOTIONS, EVENTS AND PLACES

Visual images of places connected to the conflict may be useful to evoke memories of events. Listening for how speakers connect metaphors into the real world, e.g. mention of physical actions like walking connected to JOURNEY metaphors, may be revealing. These are likely to be very powerful images and actions for individuals that mediators can explore and perhaps use as symbolic actions; e.g. a shared walk might carry meaning far beyond its physical activity.

ADOPTING AND ADAPTING METAPHORS

By listening out for how one speaker responds to the metaphors of the other, mediators can get insights as to the level of understanding being built in the various topics of the talk. In particular, it may be helpful to note

- when a metaphor is adopted across speakers;
- when a metaphor is adopted but also adjusted or challenged—this will offer clues as to how the speakers' perceptions differ;
- when one speaker 'allows' the other to appropriate a particularly emotive or personal metaphor to refer to their own feelings or experiences.

Listening for how speakers extend or elaborate their own or others' metaphors will help understand the details of different perspectives.

The potential for extending and shifting metaphors is available for mediators to use in intervening in talk:

- to explore ideas in more detail by extending and elaborating a metaphorical scenario;
- to encourage the sharing of metaphors;
- to explicitly encourage the challenging of metaphors.

Notes

NOTES TO CHAPTER 2

1. See Preface.
2. By emphasising the affective, I do not necessarily separate it from the cognitive, but insist on its importance.
3. 'Discourse' is here defined as social interaction that involves language, and includes mental processes that relate to ongoing talk (in a similar way to its use in Fairclough, 1989, and in critical discourse analysis approaches that derive from this work, e.g. Koller, 2008). The approach is compatible with the strand of discursive psychology that accepts the relevance of social psychology alongside a commitment to working with language in use and discourse as social action (Wetherell, 2007).
4. The purpose of a theoretical framework for an empirical investigation is to provide a consistent way of thinking about the research problem. It should include labels for and workable definitions of key ideas, as was done in the previous chapter for the construct of empathy, and in this chapter will be done for metaphor in discourse. A framework also needs to include explanatory theory, i.e. ways of explaining the relations between key ideas. In this case, explanatory theory includes descriptions and explanations of what is happening when people use metaphor in talk and how a metaphor used in talk can relate to a person's thinking. A framework needs to include a clear distinction between what is assumed and what is to be found out; for example, in this study the nature of 'conciliation' and 'connecting processes' is not assumed but to be discovered, while the importance of considering the dynamics of talk and metaphor is assumed.
5. The term 'discourse event' is used to refer to a period of continuous discourse activity with a clear beginning and end, and usually with a specific goal or focus, such as a lecture, an interview or a conversation. Human constraints, physical and attentional, seem to produce discourse events with comfortable lengths of around an hour or so. Discourse event is used rather than 'speech event' to emphasise the social interaction involved rather than the individual performances. Within discourse events, there may be shorter episodes of interaction that are clearly bounded in terms of topic, i.e. what is talked about, and/or in terms of discourse action, i.e. what participants achieve with the talk. Within, and between, episodes, discourse activity can usually be divided into smaller segments of discourse action, where something specific is attempted or achieved. Extract 2.1, for example, is an episode in the discourse event of the first conversation of the dataset. There are two segments of discourse action: from 87 to 104 Jo tells Pat about her perspective and motivation for meeting him as it seemed at the time of the bombing;

from 106 to 109, she reflects on experiencing that perspective then and connecting to their current meeting. Processes that contribute to conciliation and empathy may be found at the scale of the event, of the episode and of the segment.

6. Pat reports the deliberate care that he takes when addressing Jo in the seminar transcript.

7. Systematic metaphors are different from the cognitive 'discourse metaphors' of Zinken, Hellsten and Nerlich (2008). Systematic metaphors are connected metaphorical instances of discourse activity collected together in temporal sequence.

8. Being 'shared' does not, in a complexity perspective, mean that each speaker somehow has an identical version. Rather, it is to suggest that, dialogically, there is sufficient commonality in each individual person's use of the metaphor for no obvious problems in interpretation to arise when it is used in talking together.

9. The phase space landscape of a complex dynamic system is a multi-dimensional graph on which each point is a possible phase of the system (imagine figure 2.2 not flat and two dimensional but in multiple dimensions). The actual phases of the system are then successive points on the landscape, creating a 'trajectory' or path across the landscape.

NOTES TO CHAPTER 3

1. The first line of each extract also indicates which conversation it is taken from. For example, 2–124 indicates the data is from the second conversation, starting at intonation unit 124.

2. In cognitive metaphor theory, the vehicle term would refer to a concept in the 'source domain', and the metaphor topic would be called 'target'.

3. As would have been the case in the 'classical' theory of metaphor, where metaphor was required to be active and striking (e.g. Black, 1979).

4. On the basis that the *thing* morpheme in *nothing* has, as indicated by pronunciation, become so tightly incorporated that it can be considered metaphorical only etymologically.

5. Native speaker knowledge can be checked, supplemented or replaced by use of an up to date large corpus, or a dictionary based on such a corpus.

6. In this principle, the method is similar to that of conversation analysis, but permits use of knowledge of the context beyond the data.

7. Soft assembly is a (metaphorical) term from complex dynamic systems theory, where it refers to selection and adaptation of resources in the moment and to achieve a goal, e.g. as a child reaches out and grasps a toy (Thelen and Smith, 1994).

8. The implications of this are profound, including the untenable separation of system and use that underpins much of linguistics, including cognitive linguistics (e.g. Steen, 2007).

9. In homage to Gaston Bachelard's *The Poetics of Space* (1964), a fascinating volume that considers houses in terms of metaphors and embodiment, drawing on folk tales, poetry and psychology to explore the richness of symbolised interior spaces. Findings across my empirical metaphor studies urge a similar exploration of exterior landscapes and their multiple connections to meaning making.

10. A systematic metaphor is quite a different theoretical entity from a conceptual metaphor. It is specific to the discourse event from which the grouping has emerged and is warranted by discourse evidence. In conceptual metaphor

theory, metaphors in language use are seen as instantiations of a pre-existing, theoretically founded, conceptual metaphor.

11. *ITALIC SMALL CAPITALS* are used for labels of emergent groupings.

12. This grouping process illustrates what was meant earlier in saying that the discourse dynamic approach, while distinct from conceptual metaphor theory, is 'inspired and informed' by it. Conceptual metaphor theory is just one hypothesis to explain systematic connections between metaphors that appear in use. Lakoff and Johnson (1980) used examples from their intuited discourse data to construct conceptual metaphor theory in the first place, so it is not surprising to find groupings in discourse that resemble conceptual metaphors. However, conceptual metaphor theory requires an assumption of a generalised mapping or conceptual metaphor that is then expressed in language, and would thence assume that the examples in table 3.1 represent expressions of the 'EVENT STRUCTURE' conceptual metaphor, and in particular of the mappings: STATES ARE LOCATIONS; CHANGE IS MOVEMENT (Lakoff, 1993). The discourse dynamics approach does not assume that the metaphorically used words and phrases are necessarily expressions of a larger conceptual metaphor or that each discourse participant has a full range of conceptual metaphors available as they talk. On the contrary, it is considered to be of relevance and interest to discover which metaphors participants actually use in a discourse event.

13. Or metonymy, see chapter 6.

NOTES TO CHAPTER 4

1. http://www.glencree.ie/index.htm.

2. The conventionalised metaphor UNDERSTANDING IS SEEING in the English language makes frequent use of a rather similar perceptual metaphor, in which the perception (*seeing*, *hearing*) stands for deeper processes of understanding. Conceptual metaphor theory holds that these both derive from a larger or more general metaphor, IDEAS ARE PERCEPTIONS (Lakoff, Evenson and Schwarz, 1991). It is also suggested that some languages and cultures, and specifically semitic languages such as Arabic and Hebrew, have an alternative conventionalised and cultural metaphor UNDERSTANDING IS HEARING, that connects to expressions such as *I hear what you say*. However, this metaphor does not seem adequate to include all of the meaning that Jo expresses or implies through the metaphor.

3. The collocates of a word are the words that are regularly used in its close neighbourhood; e.g. *listening* was a common collocate of *story* in the data. Examining the frequent collocates of a word can show patterns of use across groups of speakers or types of discourse activity. The number of different collocates indicates the range of its adaptability.

NOTES TO CHAPTER 5

1. Metaphor density can be calculated as the number of metaphors per 1000 words of transcribed talk or text (Cameron, 2003). The density in clusters should be several times higher than the overall metaphor density; in a recent project, overall density was around 20, and to be included as a cluster, an episode needed a density of over 100.

2. There was no mediator present when Jo and Pat talked together in their conversations. This left the discourse management in their hands, so that topics

would continue until one or the other changed the topic by asking a question or speaking of something else.
3. The term 'narrative' is used to refer to an account of a specific event or series of events in the past.

NOTES TO CHAPTER 7

1. Girdwood Barracks and Castlereagh were buildings used by the army, police and special branch in Belfast during the years of conflict. A Saracen is an armoured personnel carrier used by the British army on the streets of Northern Ireland. The RUC (Royal Ulster Constabulary) was the name of the police force in Northern Ireland, changed in 2001.
2. The phrase *like treating cattle* has the form of a simile but is also metaphorical because *treating cattle* has a meaning distinct from its contextual meaning of dealing with those held on suspicion by the British army.

NOTES TO CHAPTER 9

1. 'Word' is a literal translation from the Russian слово. However, this term is also used metonymically to refer to 'speaking' or to something very like 'talking-and-thinking' in the idiom *к слову пришлось*, which means the same as 'it sprang to mind', but literally translates as *to words it came.*
2. Jo and Pat meet as individuals, not as representatives of social groups. In other contexts, such as the recent Australian government apology to child migrants, healing practices may operate at group level (as well as individually).

NOTES TO CHAPTER 10

1. March 2010.
2. The systematic metaphors emerged, it should again be noted, for the analyst and not necessarily for the participants.
3. In complex systems terms, Self and Other work as a coupled system where the activity of individual systems affects the emergent joint system.
4. For a complex dynamics approach, the term 'unit' is unsuitable and also annoyingly difficult to replace. It is unsuitable because it suggests an object or separable quantity, quite incompatible with the idea that all is dynamics and in flux; flow cannot be separated into units. What we need is a way to describe flow on a smaller level, perhaps in a fractal sense. This remains a problem to be addressed.

Bibliography

Arbib, M. (2002). The mirror system, imitation and the evolution of language. In C. Nehaniv & K. Dautenhahn (Eds.), *Imitation in Animals and Artifacts* (pp. 229–280). Cambridge, MA: MIT Press.

Bachelard, G. (1964). *The Poetics of Space* (M. Jolas, Trans.). Boston: Beacon Press.

Bakhtin, M. (1981). *The Dialogic Imagination: Four Essays*. Austin: University of Texas Press.

Barr, D. (2004). Establishing conventional communication systems: Is common knowledge necessary? *Cognitive Science, 28,* 937–962.

Barsalou, L. W. (2008). Grounded cognition. *Annual Review of Psychology, 59,* 617–645.

Black, M. (1979). More about metaphor. In A.Ortony (Ed.), *Metaphor and Thought* (pp. 19–41). New York: Cambridge University Press.

Brennan, S., & Clark, H. (1996). Conceptual pacts and lexical choices in conversation. *Journal of Experimental Psychology: Learning, Memory, and Cognition, 22*(6), 1482–1493.

Burke, K. (1945). *A Grammar of Motives*. New York: Prentice Hall.

Cameron, L. (1999a). Identifying and describing metaphor in spoken discourse data. In L. Cameron & G. Low (Eds.), *Researching and Applying Metaphor* (pp. 105–132). Cambridge: Cambridge University Press.

Cameron, L. (1999b). Operationalising metaphor for applied linguistic research. In L. Cameron & G. Low (Eds.), *Researching and Applying Metaphor* (pp. 3–28). Cambridge: Cambridge University Press.

Cameron, L. (2003). *Metaphor in Educational Discourse*. London: Continuum.

Cameron, L. (2007a). Confrontation or complementarity: Metaphor in language use and cognitive metaphor theory. *Annual Review of Cognitive Linguistics, 5,* 107–135.

Cameron, L. (2007b). Patterns of metaphor use in reconciliation talk. *Discourse and Society, 18*(2), 197–222.

Cameron, L. (2008). Metaphor shifting in the dynamics of talk. In M. S. Zanotto, L. Cameron & M. Cavalcanti (Eds.), *Confronting Metaphor in Use* (pp. 45–62). Amsterdam: John Benjamins.

Cameron, L. (2010). The discourse dynamics framework for metaphor. In L. Cameron & R. Maslen (Eds.), *Metaphor analysis: Research practice in applied linguistics, social sciences and the humanities.* (pp. 77–94). London: Equinox.

Cameron, L. (In press). Metaphor in physical-and-speech action expressions. In A. Deignan, L. Cameron, G. Low & Z. Todd (Eds.), *Researching and Applying Metaphor in the Real World*. Amsterdam: John Benjamin.

Cameron, L., & Deignan, A. (2006). The emergence of metaphor in discourse. *Applied Linguistics, 27*(4), 671–690.

Cameron, L., Maslen, R., & Low, G. (2010). Finding systematicity in metaphor use. In L. Cameron & R. Maslen (Eds.), *Metaphor Analysis: Research Practice in Applied Linguistics, Social Sciences and the Humanities* (pp. 116–146). London: Equinox.

Cameron, L., Maslen, R., Todd, Z., Maule, J., Stratton, P., & Stanley, N. (2009). The discourse dynamics approach to metaphor and metaphor-led discourse analysis. *Metaphor & Symbol, 24*(2), 63–89.

Cameron, L., & Stelma, J. (2004). Metaphor clusters in discourse. *Journal of Applied Linguistics, 1*(2), 7–36.

Chafe, W. (1994). *Discourse, consciousness and time.* Chicago: University of Chicago Press.

Cienki, A. (2010). Multimodal metaphor analysis. In L. Cameron and G. Low (Eds.), *Metaphor Analysis: A Guide to Research Practice in Applied Linguistics, Social Sciences and the Humanities* (pp. 195–214). London: Equinox.

Cienki, A., & Müller, C. (Eds.). (2008). *Metaphor and Gesture.* Amsterdam: John Benjamins.

Corts, D., & Meyers, K. (2002). Conceptual clusters in figurative language production. *Journal of Psycholinguistic Research, 31*(4), 391–408.

Corts, D., & Pollio, H. (1999). Spontaneous production of figurative language and gesture in college lectures. *Metaphor and Symbol, 14*(1), 81–100.

Damasio, A. (1994). *Descartes' Error: Emotion, Reason, and the Human Brain.* New York: Putnam.

Damasio, A. (1999). *The feeling of what happens.* London: Vintage Books.

Damasio, A. (2003). *Looking for Spinoza: Joy, sorrow and the feeling brain.* New York: Harcourt.

Deignan, A. (2005). *Metaphor and Corpus Linguistics.* Amsterdam: John Benjamins.

Du Bois, J., Schuetze-Coburn, S., Cumming, S., & Paolino, D. (1993). Outline of discourse transcription. In J. Edwards & M. Lampert (Eds.), *Talking Data: Transcription and Coding in Discourse Research* (pp. 45–90). Hillsdale, NJ: Lawrence Erlbaum Associates.

Fairclough, N. (1989). *Language and Power.* London: Longman.

Galinsky, A. D., Maddux, W. W., Gilin, D., & White, J. B. (2008). Why it pays to get inside the head of your opponent: The differential effects of perspective taking and empathy in negotiations. *Psychological Science, 19*(4), 378–381.

Gallese, V. (2003). The roots of empathy: The shared manifold hypothesis and the neural bases of intersubjectivity. *Psychopathology, 36*, 171–180.

Gallese, V. (2005). Being like me. In S. Hurley & N. Chater (Eds.), *Perspectives on Imitation: From Neuroscience to Social Science* (Vol. 1, pp. 101–118). Cambridge, MA: MIT Press.

Gibbs, R. W. (1994). *The Poetics of Mind: Figurative Thought, Language and Understanding.* Cambridge: Cambridge University Press.

Gibbs, R. W. (2006a). *Embodiment and Cognitive Science.* New York: Cambridge University Press.

Gibbs, R. W. (2006b). Metaphor interpretation as embodied simulation. *Mind & Language, 21*(3), 434–458.

Gibbs, R. W., & Cameron, L. (2008). The social-cognitive dynamics of metaphor performance. *Journal of Cognitive Systems Research, 9*(1–2), 64–75.

Goatly, A. (1997). *The Language of Metaphors.* London: Routledge.

Grady, J. (1999). A typology of motivation for conceptual metaphor: Correlation vs. resemblance. In R. W. Gibbs & G. Steen (Eds.), *Metaphor in Cognitive Linguistics* (pp. 101–124). Amsterdam: John Benjamins.

Halpern, J., & Weinstein, H. M. (2004). Rehumanizing the Other: Empathy and Reconciliation. *Human Rights Quarterly, 26*, 561–583.

Iacoboni, M. (2005). Understanding others: Imitation, language, empathy. In S. Hurley & N. Chater (Eds.), *Perspectives on Imitation: From Mirror Neurons to Memes* (Vol. 2, pp. 77–100). Cambridge, MA: MIT Press.

Khalil, E. (2002). Similarity versus familiarity: When empathy becomes selfish. *Behavioral and Brain Sciences*, *25*(1), 41.

Kimmel, M. (2010). Why we mix metaphors (and mix them well): Discourse coherence, conceptual metaphor, and beyond. *Journal of Pragmatics*, *42*(1), 97–115.

Kirmayer, L. (2004). The cultural diversity of healing: Meaning, metaphor and mechanism. *British Medical Bulletin*, *69*, 33–48.

Koller, V. (2003). Metaphor clusters, metaphor chains: Analyzing the multifunctionality of metaphor in text. *Metaphorik* (5), 115–134.

Koller, V. (2008). Brothers in arms: Contradictory metaphors in contemporary m,arketing discourse. In M. Zanotto, L. Cameron & M. Cavalcanti (Eds.), *Confronting Metaphor in Use: An Applied Linguistic Approach* (pp. 103–126). Amsterdam: John Benjamins.

Labov, W., & Waletzsky, J. (1967). Narrative analysis: Oral versions of personal experience. In J. Helm (Ed.), *Essays on the Verbal and Visual Arts: Proceeedings of the 1966 Annual Spring Meeting of the American Ethnological Society* (pp. 12–44). Seattle: University of Washington Press.

Lakoff, G. (1993). The contemporary theory of metaphor. In A. Ortony (Ed.), *Metaphor and Thought* (2nd ed., pp. 202–251). New York: Cambridge University Press.

Lakoff, G. (2008). The neural theory of metaphor. In R. W. Gibbs (Ed.), *The Cambridge Handbook of Metaphor and Thought* (pp. 17–38). Cambridge Cambridge University Press.

Lakoff, G., Evenson, J., & Schwarz, A. (1991). The Master Metaphor List (2nd ed.). Available from araw.mede.uic.edu/~alansz/metaphor/METAPHORLIST.pdf

Lakoff, G., & Johnson, M. (1980). *Metaphors We Live By*. Chicago: University of Chicago Press.

Lakoff, G., & Johnson, M. (1999). *Philosophy in the Flesh*. New York: Cambridge University Press.

Lamm, C., Batson, C. D., & Decety, J. (2007). The neural substrate of human empathy: Effects of perspectives-taking and cognitive appraisal. *Journal of Cognitive Neuroscience*, *19*(1), 42–58.

Lamm, C., Meltzoff, A. N., & Decety, J. (2009). How do we empathise with someone who is not like us? A functional magnetic resonance imaging study. *Journal of Cognitive Neuroscience*, *22*(2). 362–76.

Larsen-Freeman, D., & Cameron, L. (2008). *Complex Systems and Applied Linguistics*. Oxford: Oxford University Press.

Lincoln, Y., & Guba, E. (1985). *Naturalistic Inquiry*. Beverly Hills, CA: Sage.

Lipps, T. (1903). Einfühlung, innere Nachahmung und Organempfindung. *Archiv für die gesamte Psychologie*, *1*, 465–519.

Louw, W. (1993). Irony in the text or insincerity in the writer? In M. Baker, G. Francis, E. Tognini-Bonelli & Sinclair (Eds.), *Text and technology: Essays in honour of John Sinclair* (pp. 157–176). Amsterdam: John Benjamins.

Low, G. (1997). *A celebration of squid sandwiches: Figurative language and the management of (non-core) academic text*. Unpublished report: University of York.

Markova, I., Linell, P., Grossen, M., & Orvig, A. S. (2007). *Dialogue in Focus Groups*. London: Equinox.

McGilchrist, I. (2009). *The Master and His Emissary*. New Haven, CT: Yale University Press.

McNeill, D. (1992). *Hand and Mind: What Gestures Reveal About Thought*. Chicago: University of Chicago Press.

Merleau-Ponty, M. (1962). *Phemonology of Perception* (C. Smith, Trans.). London: Routledge and Kegan Paul.

Morson, G. S., & Emerson, C. (1990). *Mikhail Bakhtin: Creation of a Prosaics.* Stanford, CA: Stanford University Press.

Oberschall, A. (2000). The manipulation of ethnicity: From ethnic cooperation to violence and war in Yugoslavia. *Ethnic and Racial Studies, 23*(6), 982–1001.

Pedersen, R. (2008). Empathy: A wolf in sheep's clothing? *Medicine, Health Care and Philosophy, 11,* 325–335.

Poland, W. S. (2007). The limits of empathy. *American Imago, 64*(1), 87–93.

Pomerantz, A. (1986). Extreme case formulations: A way of legitimizing claims. *Journal of Human Studies 9*(2–3), 219–229.

Ponterotto, D. (2003). The cohesive role of cognitive metaphor in discourse and conversation. In A. Barcelona (Ed.), *Metaphor and Metonymy at the Crossroads* (pp. 283–298). Berlin: Mouton de Gruyter.

Pope John Paul II. (1994). Tertio Millennio Adveniente. *Apostolic Letter.* Retrieved 10 April 2010 from http://www.vatican.va/holy_father/john_paul_ii/apost_letters/documents/hf_jp-ii_apl_10111994_tertio-millennio-adveniente_en.html

pragglejaz group. (2007). MIP: A method for identifying metaphorically-used words in discourse. *Metaphor and Symbol, 22*(1), 1–40.

Preston, S., & de Waal, F. (2002). Empathy: Its ultimate and proximate bases. *Behavioral and Brain Sciences, 25,* 1–72.

Ritchie, D. (2006). *Context and Connection in Metaphor.* Basingstoke, UK: Palgrave Macmillan.

Ritchie, D. (2010). Between mind and language: A journey worth taking. In L. Cameron & R. Maslen (Eds.), *Metaphor Analysis: Research Practice in Applied Linguistics, Social Sciences and the Humanities.* London: Equinox.

Slobin, D. (1996) From "Thought and Language" to "Thinking and Speaking". In J. Gumperz and S. Levinson (Eds.), *Rethinking Linguistic Relativity* (pp. 70–96). New York: Cambridge University Press.

Spreng, R. N., McKinnon, M., & Mar, R. (2009). The Toronto empathy questionnaire: Scale development and initial validation of a factor-analytic solution to multiple empathy measures. *Journal of Personality Assessment, 91*(1), 62–71.

Steen, G. (1992). *Metaphor in Literary Reception.* Doctoral Dissertation. Vrije Universiteit, Amsterdam.

Steen, G. (2007). *Finding Metaphor in Grammar and Usage.* Amsterdam: John Benjamins.

Stelma, J., & Cameron, L. (2007). Intonation units in research on spoken interaction. *Text and Talk, 27*(3), 361–393.

Sweetser, E. (1990). *From Etymology to Pragmatics: Metaphorical and Cultural Aspects of Semantic Structure.* Cambridge: Cambridge University Press.

Tajfel, H. (1981). *Human Groups and Social Categories.* Cambridge: Cambridge University Press.

Thelen, E., & Smith, L. (1994). *A Dynamic Systems Approach to the Development of Cognition and Action.* Cambridge, MA: MIT Press.

Valentino, R. S. (2005). The oxymoron of empathic criticism. *Poroi, 4*(1), 5. Retrieved [10 April 2010] from http://inpress.lic.uiowa.edu/poroi/papers/valentino050301.html

van Langenhove, L., and Harré, R. (Eds.). (1999). *Positioning Theory.* Oxford: Blackwell.

Vygotsky, L. (1962) *Thought and Language.* Cambridge, MA: MIT Press.

Wertsch, J. (1998). *Mind as Action.* New York: Oxford University Press.

Wetherell, M. (2007). A step too far: Discursive psychology, linguistic ethnography and questions of identity. *Journal of Sociolinguistics, 11*(5), 661–681.

Wynn, R., & Wynn, M. (2006). Empathy as an interactionally achieved phenomenon in psychotherapy: Characteristics of some conversational resources. *Journal of Pragmatics, 38*, 1385–1397.

Xu, X., Zuo, X., Wang, X., & Han, S. (2009). Do you feel my pain? Racial group membership modulates empathic neural responses. *Journal of Neuroscience, 29*(26), 8525–8529.

Zinken, J., Hellsten, I., & Nerlich, B. (2008). Discourse metaphors. In R. Dirven, R. Frank, T. Ziemke & E. Bernardez (Eds.), *Body, Language, and Mind: Sociocultural Situatedness* (Vol. 2, pp. 363–385). Berlin: Mouton de Gruyter.

Index